The Longest Trek
My Tour of the Galaxy

The Longest Trek
My Tour of the Galaxy

By Grace Lee Whitney
With Jim Denney

Foreward by Leonard Nimoy

Quill
Driver
Books

Fresno, California

Second Edition — 2007

Published by Quill Driver Books
An Imprint of Linden Publishing
2006 S. Mary St., Fresno, California 93721
(559) 233-6633 / (800) 345-4447
QuillDriverBooks.com

Quill Driver Books and Colophon are trademarks of
Linden Publishing, Inc.

To order a copy of this book
please call 1-800-345-4447

ISBN 1-884956-03-3 • 978-1884956-03-4
Ltd. Ed. 1-884956-05-X • 978-1884956-05-8

Printed in the United States of America

Quill Driver BooksProject Cadre:
Donna Parker Mettee
Jane Mettee
Stephen Blake Mettee
Cindy Wathen
Linda Kay Weber

Library of Congress Cataloging-in-Publication Data

Whitney, Grace Lee, 1930–
    The longest trek : my tour of the galaxy / by Grace Lee Whitney
with Jim Denney.
        p.   cm.
    Includes bibliographical references.
    ISBN 1–884956–03–3 (trade paperpack)
    ISBN 1-884956–05–x (limited edition hardcover)
    1. Whitney, Grace Lee, 1930–   . 2. Actors– –United States–
–Biography. I. Denney, Jim, 1953–   . II. Title.
PN2287.W4583A3   1998
791.45'028'092
[B]– –DC21   98–12679
                                                                                    CIP

To my sons,
who loved me through this story;

To my *Star Trek* friends,
Leonard, Harlan, Bill, George,
Jimmy, DeForest, and Nichelle,
who were all such a part of this story;

To my fans,
who demanded this story;

And to my brothers and sisters in recovery,
who enabled me to survive it,
by the grace of God.

Contents

· · · · · · · · · · ·

Foreword

· · · · · · · · · · · ·

I call her Amazing Grace. She rejects that name and denies that she is amazing, but I insist, because she *is*.

There have been countless books written about *Star Trek*—many, perhaps too many, by those who were actively involved. I've done two myself. But until now (and I admit I haven't read each and every one of them), I would place a large bet that no one has written as personal, moving, and powerful a one as Grace has written.

If you think this is simply another book of *Star Trek* anecdotes and inside jokes, take a deep breath and plunge in. This is a *Star Trek* book which will transform people's lives. It will give insight into a human condition and guidance to many in need.

It is a blessing to all of us that she has put this life of hers to such generous use.

My thanks to Grace—always amazing.

Leonard Nimoy

"Grace, are You Sitting Down?"

Star Trek was my world, my Higher Power. I gave up my marriage for *Star Trek*. I had grown up not knowing who I was, who my birth parents were, or where I came from. But when I stepped aboard the Starship *Enterprise*, I truly felt I was *home*.

Over the years, I had played a hundred roles in different films and TV series. I was a working actress. I would play my part for a few days' filming on "The Untouchables" or "Bewitched" or "The Outer Limits," working with some of the biggest stars and best directors in Hollywood—but when those few days were over, it was on to the next part, the next show, the next studio.

Finally, in the summer of 1966, on Stage 9 at Desilu Studios, I was home. I belonged. In Yeoman Janice Rand, I had a character of my own to explore and develop, week after week. I was part of something wonderful and exciting, something called *Star Trek*.

I had no idea how soon it would all be ripped away from me.

Friday, August 26, 1966.

We were just a little over halfway through shooting the episode entitled "Miri." To this day—in spite of what happened to me that Friday night—this episode remains one of my favorite *Treks*. It's a sentimental favorite for me because my sons appear among the children in the episode, as well as Bill Shatner's daughters Lizabeth and Melanie.

In the story, Captain Kirk (William Shatner), Mr. Spock (Leonard Nimoy), Dr. McCoy (DeForest Kelly), and my character, Yeoman Janice Rand, are transported down to an Earthlike planet where the entire adult population has been destroyed by a man-made virus. Only children are left alive—but the virus has slowed the aging process in the children. These children are, in fact, hundreds of years old—but once they reach puberty, they suddenly develop horrible symptoms of the virus: skin splotches, rapid aging, homicidal madness and death. Once we are beamed down to the planet, Kirk, Spock, McCoy and I became infected too. We can't return to the ship without infecting everyone aboard. Trapped on the planet, racing against time, we have to find a cure before we, too, go mad and die.

One of the weekly traditions during the filming of the original *Star Trek* series was the Friday night wrap party. Actually, these parties were more like "TGIF" parties than wrap parties, because they were held on the set in Stage 9 at the end of shooting every Friday, whether we had wrapped an episode or not. The cast, crew, studio execs and occasionally a network exec or two would gather to have a few drinks, laugh, tell stories and generally shed the pressures of the week.

At around 7 p.m., the production came to a halt and the big hanger doors were opened, flooding the sound stage with the fading summer sunlight. Any cast members still in costume headed for the dressing rooms to change. A wet bar was wheeled out near the dressing rooms, laden with bottles of liquor, a big bowl of ice cubes, salted nuts, chips, veggies, dip and shrimp on ice, all catered by the studio commissary.

The party was in full swing when I stepped out and made my way to the ladies room. A few minutes later, as I was walking back toward the party, I heard a male voice call, "Grace Lee! Wait up!"

I turned. It was The Executive. He was smiling and his face was a little flushed. He'd had a few drinks, just as I had.

I returned his smile. "You want to walk me back to the party?" I asked.

He waved his hand dismissively. "The party's breaking up. I wanted to talk to you. I have some ideas for changes we could make in the show—changes that would affect you. I'd like to get your thoughts on those ideas before the next production meeting."

"Oh?" I was intrigued. "What kind of changes?"

"I think Yeoman Janice Rand has been under-utilized. The character has been developing some interesting possibilities in the past few episodes. I have some ideas— Why don't we find a place to sit down and talk about it?"

"Well..." I hesitated for the briefest moment, a thrill of excitement at the thought that The Executive wanted to talk to me about my character. I was always looking for ways to advance my career, to enlarge my part and get more lines. He had reached the very thing that made me tick: my *ambition*. "Where would you like to talk?" I asked.

"How about the E building? We can find an empty office over there."

I'd had a few drinks. My inhibitions were down and my judgment was impaired. "Fine," I said. "Let's go."

The sun was down, but it was still light outside as we walked out of the hangerlike sound stage. We crossed the driveway from the Gower Avenue entrance of Desilu Studios, and entered the office building. I don't remember exactly what we said as we walked—small talk, I think, about the show. We had nearly finished shooting the first dozen episodes of *Star Trek*, and the premiere broadcast was less than two weeks away. The excitement among the cast, creators and crew of the show was growing as our first airdate neared. We believed we had a hit on our hands, and the suspense of waiting for the audience response was exciting—and a little nerve-wracking.

The building was unlocked and we walked right in. The Executive put his arm on mine as we made our way down the darkened corridor. There were lights on in some of the offices, but the building was quiet, empty and mostly dark. There was no one in the building but The Executive, me, and possibly a janitor somewhere. The Executive opened a door, flipped on a light, and ushered me in. He indicated a chair for me. I was alone with him, but I didn't care. We were one big happy family on *Star Trek,* and I trusted him.

In this scene from "Miri," I've been tied up by the children—and I'm waiting for Captain Kirk to rescue me. I was so much into the role, I found it hard to separate fantasy and reality. It was a genuinely scary experience, being tied up, trapped and victimized.

There was a stereo in the room. I settled into the chair he offered me, and he put on some soft music. The office had a private wet bar. He went and poured a couple of drinks, not bothering to ask if I wanted one. He knew I did. He handed me a glass, then sat down behind the desk.

We talked. And we laughed. And we drank.

He told me about upcoming scripts, and suggested story angles that could bring out a stronger relationship between Yeoman Rand and Captain Kirk. He put himself in Kirk's place, saying, "Now I'm the Captain and you're the Yeoman. What would Rand say to Kirk in this situation? Put yourself into the role. Pour your heart out to me." And we did some very sexy role-playing—purely across the desk, about 10 feet apart. In my mind, we were simply improvising with the characters to explore the Kirk-Rand relationship for story possibilities. In his mind, I later realized, it was all part of a carefully laid strategy.

"You know," he said after we'd been talking a while, "the thing that is so fascinating about Janice Rand is her repressed desire—her hunger for sex."

"Not sex," I said. "Love. She loves the Captain."

"Same thing," said The Executive. "She wants the Captain so badly, but she represses it. She doesn't admit it—not even to herself. We all know what she *really* wants—but *she* herself doesn't know. She denies it. Janice Rand can't face her own desires, her own sexuality."

"Absolutely," I agreed. "That's the key to the character."

"And you're just like Janice Rand."

"I'm— What? What did you say?" I was vaguely aware that our discussion had just turned a sharp corner. But the buzz in my brain prevented me from grasping where The Executive was steering the conversation.

"You're hungry inside," he said, "just like Janice Rand. Hungry, needy, full of desire. But you repress it. You bottle it up. That's not healthy, Grace."

There were no alarms going off, no warning bells. I just laughed, settled back, and smugly replied, "I'm not bottling up *anything*. If there is anyone who is completely uninhibited, it's me."

"Oh?" he said lightly. "Well, good, then. Let's see how uninhibited you are. Undress for me."

"What?!" I burst out laughing. "You're kidding!"

The Executive rose and came around the desk, towering over me. "I'm not kidding, Grace. We both know what we want—if we're willing to be honest with each other. I'm being honest with you right now. I want you. I want to see you as you are, underneath...all of that." With a gesture, he indicated my clothes, from my neck to my feet. "I want you to undress for me," he repeated.

Then he unbuckled his belt and unbuttoned his shirt. Suddenly, I knew he was completely serious. This man had a lot of power over my future, and he expected me to come across. If I didn't— At that moment, I had a sinking feeling of horror, a sense of impending doom. I needed to get out of this situation somehow—but how? My head was too muzzy to think clearly. I glanced over my shoulder, toward the door, then started to get out of the chair. "I can't undress for you," I said. "Don't ask me to do that."

"Why can't you?" He took a few steps closer, positioning himself between me and the office door. His voice was smooth, he was smiling, his manner was still charming—but there was an unmistakable air of threat in the way he blocked my path to the door. "It's not as if you're married anymore," he said.

"I'm not divorced yet, only separated. I can't—"

"What's the big deal? You just said you're 'completely uninhibited.' So prove it."

"I won't do that," I said. "I'm with someone else now, and I'm true to him. I wouldn't cheat on him."

When I said this, he suddenly became enraged. It was a Jekyll-to-Hyde transformation—and it scared me to death. "You'd sleep with someone else," he bellowed, "but not with me? Is that what you're telling me? Do you have any idea what you're saying to me?"

Frightened, I desperately groped for some word to bring him down from his rage. I mentioned the name of the woman he was involved with. "You love her, don't you?" I asked. "And she loves you. We can't do this behind her back!"

"She doesn't care," he shrugged defensively, guiltily, unconvincingly. "She knows I'm with other women. She understands." He was still moving toward me as I tried to back away from him. I only succeeded in backing myself into an adjoining room—a meeting room with a sofa, a few chairs, and a table. The only way out of it was the doorway I had just come through—and The Executive blocked my path. He followed me into the meeting room, closed the door, and locked it with a key.

He continued undressing himself. "Now," he said, "you're not going anywhere. So take off your clothes."

I shook my head. "No," I insisted. "I won't do that."

We argued about it for what seemed a long time—maybe 20 minutes or more. The whole time, he stood there in front of me, exposed, saying he wanted to examine me as if he was a doctor. He made it clear that I wasn't going anywhere until he got what he wanted. He had the power to destroy my career and we both knew it.

I had been chased around the office by producers, directors and executives before. I had been chased by some of the biggest names in Hollywood—but no one ever caught me if I didn't want to be caught. I wanted parts, I wanted to work, and I figured if I could turn these guys on, I could advance my career. It was always a delicate balancing act—being a turn-on and a tease without getting cornered and having to put out.

This was different. This time I was trapped in a locked room, alone with this man in a building where I could yell all I wanted—and no one would hear me. I don't remember if he undressed me or if I undressed myself. Either way, I had no choice in the matter.

I had known this man for a couple years, and had never known him to be violent. A womanizer, yes, but not a monster. This night was different. This night, he was drunk. We both were. Not so drunk that we didn't know what was happening, not so drunk that we wouldn't remember it all later. But he was clearly drunk enough that his personality was altered from that of The Executive I had known all these months. He was angry with me—and, I think, angry with himself. His carefully plotted "seduction" wasn't going the way he had planned, and he was growing impatient and frustrated.

He made me get up on the table in the meeting room and dance for him. He told me to tease him and flirt with him. He yelled at me and threw things at me. He sat down on the sofa, watching me—but he didn't seem to be enjoying it. He just got angrier and angrier—and that made me all the more scared. I didn't know what he might do to me. I never would have imagined he was capable of such a thing, even drunk. How could I know what *else* he might be capable of?

I tried to do what he wanted me to, so I could get it over with. I knew, deep down inside, that I was finished on *Star Trek*. At that moment, however, I didn't care about that. Nothing else mattered—not my tarnished virtue, not my career, not my role on *Star Trek*. The only thing that mattered was getting out of that room alive.

But he wouldn't let me get down off the table. He wasn't getting aroused—and that made him even more menacing. "Come on!" he demanded. "You're supposed to be the sexpot! Make me want you! Come on!" I didn't know why he couldn't get aroused—I tried. I really tried. Was it that he'd had too much to drink? Or that I had argued too long with him, and he was just too angry to get aroused? Or that he'd had too many women and he just couldn't get it up anymore? Or—

Or was it *me*? Was there something wrong with me? After getting up on that table and dancing for him, was I just …disappointing to him?

"Please," I begged. "Let me down. Let me out of here. Please."

He groaned in disgust. "All right!" he said fiercely. "Get down!"

I got down off the table.

"But," he added, leaning back on the sofa, "we're not done yet. When we're done, you can go. Now…come here."

He wanted me to go down on him. I pleaded. I protested. But in the end, I did what he told me to do.

It was very dark as I got into my car. It was probably a couple hours or so since I had left Stage 9 with The Executive and walked with him to the office. The whole time I spent with him had seemed like an eternity. Once it was over, I must have been in shock, because I have very little recollection of how I got my clothes and shoes back on, or how I made my way out of the office building.

I started my car and drove off the Desilu lot—but I didn't go home. I was too upset, and I needed to talk to someone.

Among the cast of *Star Trek*, my best friend was Leonard Nimoy. Unlike the cold, logical Vulcan he played on the show, Leonard is a very warm and empathetic listener and a good friend. I had talked to him from time to time about problems I was going through during the summer of 1966, such as the breakup of my marriage and the struggle to be a good single mother to my two boys. He had also been my acting coach during the first weeks of shooting *Star Trek,* helping me to get in touch with Janice Rand, so that I could play her more believably. Shaken and scared, the first person I thought to confide in was Leonard.

When he answered his door, Leonard found a disheveled, terrified, incoherent mess on the doorstep. It was at least ten o'clock at night, maybe later, and I'm sure I was the last thing he expected to see on his porch at that time of night. "Grace!" he said, looking stunned. "What happened? I mean, come in, come in! What's wrong?"

I went in and sat down in his living room and poured out the whole story to him. Poor Leonard! I'm sure that large parts of my story made no sense to him at all—but he sat there and listened while I dumped all my pain and fear in a big, jumbled pile on the floor. I don't remember crying—I think I was still too much in shock to cry. I just sat there, feeling numb inside, while the story spilled out of me. Leonard was very kind, a wonderful listener—but he was also completely dumbfounded by what I told him. He didn't know what to say. How could anyone know what to say in such a situation?

"Grace, if I'd only known," he said helplessly. "I had no idea that you were— I mean, I didn't see you leave, and when I noticed you were gone, I just thought you had left the party early."

"How could you have known?" I responded. "I didn't know myself what was happening until it was too late. I just want to put this behind me somehow. Lock it away and forget about it. The thing is, Leonard, I don't even know exactly what happened to me. I know I was violated—but was I raped? I don't think you can call it rape. In fact, it would have been easier on me if he *had* raped me. Because then it would have been over within a few minutes. Instead, he was furious with me. And it never seemed to end, and it just got scarier and scarier—I thought he was going to kill me!"

Nowadays, of course, it's commonly understood that when a man forces a woman into an act of oral sex, it's a crime, a sexual assault. Back then, however, I really didn't know what to call this traumatic violation I had just been through. I blamed The Executive for what he did to me—but I also blamed myself. I felt stupid for allowing myself to get lured into such a situation: "Come over to my office, sweetheart, and let's talk about your career—I've got big plans for you, little lady!" My gosh, it was the oldest trick in the book, and I fell for it.

I'm not sure how long I stayed and talked to Leonard—probably a couple hours. But by the time he had listened to my whole story, it was after midnight and I had calmed down a lot. He was very worried about me and offered to drive me home or follow me in his car, but I told him I'd be all right.

So I went home to Sherman Oaks. The house was dark and quiet when I arrived. The housekeeper and my two little boys were in bed. I checked on the boys, then went to the kitchen and poured myself a drink, maybe two. Then I went to bed.

I had a lot more to drink that weekend.

Monday morning, August 29, 1966.

I went back to the studio. We had two more days of "Miri" to shoot, and I was sick to my stomach with fear and worry as I drove onto the Desilu lot and parked my car in my accustomed space. What would I do when *he* came in? What would I say to him? How would I react?

And what would he say to me?

My nausea increased as I entered Stage 9 and went to the makeup room. There were two reclining barber chairs in the room. Leonard Nimoy was in one of them as makeup supervisor Fred Phillips worked on him. His pointed Vulcan ears had already been fitted and his high Vulcan eyebrows applied. Fred was touching up Leonard's yellow pallor. I sat down in the chair next to Leonard, so that hairdresser Virginia Darcy could attach Yeoman Janice Rand's trademark beehive wig to my head.

As Virginia worked on my hair, Fred Phillips looked over at me and seemed to groan a silent "Oh, no!" He saw he had quite a reconstruction job to do on me as soon as he was through with Leonard. My face was swollen and distorted from a weekend of too much crying and too much drinking. I know I looked sick, not only from anxiety but from being hung over.

Virginia had just finished my hair and Fred had not yet started on my face when the door to the makeup room opened. I looked out of the corner of my eye—and my heart jumped in my throat and stuck there. It was *him*—The Executive. If Fred or Virginia noticed the burning flush rise to my cheeks, they didn't say anything.

The Executive came over to me, took something from the pocket of his coat, and held it out to me, cradling it in both hands. "This is something I made for you," he said, "and I'd like you to have it." I looked at it. It was a polished gray stone, like you might find in a river bed, but smooth and shiny as glass. It was not large—you could place it in your palm and close your fingers around it.

I put my hand out and he placed the stone in it. I looked up at him and eyed him very closely, checking him out. He seemed harmless—but something felt very wrong. The most awful feeling swept over me, a replay of a feeling I had experienced in the office that night: a sense of impending doom. A little hoarsely, I whispered, "Thank you," but there was no gratitude in my voice.

The Executive smiled a nervous little smile—then walked out of the room.

I turned and looked at Leonard's profile. He was still lying flat in the makeup chair, looking straight at the ceiling, keeping his face still as Fred finished applying his makeup. I waited until Fred was done, then I said to Leonard, "You heard?"

"I heard," he said. "What did he give you?"

I got up and held out the stone for Leonard to see.

He laughed—an ironic, humorless laugh. "The son of a bitch!" he said. "It should have been a diamond."

I went through the rest of that day with a sinking feeling that I had shot myself in the foot—no, in both feet. Getting ahead in Hollyweird is often a matter of knowing who holds the power, then finding a way to get close to that power, and even in bed with that power. I had refused to get in bed with the power. It might have been a morally defensible choice—but it was tactically stupid, in terms of my career. Inwardly, I kicked myself for not playing along, because in the end I was just as violated and exploited by this man as if I had—yet I had no career advancement to show for it. *Bad move, Whitney*, I thought. *You've done it to yourself again.*

The Executive's gift didn't make me feel better. It felt like the thud of the first shoe dropping. Deep inside, I knew there had to be another shoe coming.

On one level, perhaps, the stone was an apology, an attempt to make amends for the violation—but it was never accompanied by the words, "I'm sorry, please forgive me." In fact, the incident was never mentioned between The Executive and me again.

The shock waves of that incident, however, were far from over. I didn't realize it then, but those shock waves would continue reverberating in my life for a long time to come.

In fact, the worst shock of all was just a few days away.

❖ ❖ ❖

The next day, Tuesday the 30th of August, we wrapped the final day of shooting on "Miri." Then began a two-week hiatus for Labor Day before we were to begin shooting the next episode, "The Conscience of the King."

Just a couple days into that hiatus—I think it may have been Thursday, September 1—I was in the kitchen of my Sherman Oaks home. I was alone, fixing lunch for my two boys (they were playing outside or in some other part of the house). The phone rang. It was Alex Brewis, my agent. "Grace," he said, "are you sitting down?"

"No. Why?"

He said, "You'd better sit down."

So I did.

"Grace," he continued, "you've been written out of the show."

I heard him plainly, but the words refused to make sense to me. I couldn't think of anything to say in response.

"Grace, do you understand what I just said?"

"I don't know," I said. "What does that mean—'written out'?"

"It means," Alex explained slowly and deliberately, almost as if he was talking to a child, "that they've taken the character of Janice Rand out of the show. They're not going to replace you. Your character will no longer appear in the show. You've been written out."

"But why?"

"Well," Alex explained, "I'm told it's a creative decision. The producers feel the romantic relationship between Kirk and Rand is becoming too obvious, and it limits the story possibilities. Apparently, they think Captain Kirk needs to be free to have affairs with other women on all these different planets. If the relationship between Kirk and Rand is too intense, it looks like he's two-timing Janice Rand. The viewers will get mad at Kirk and tune out. At least, that's what they tell me."

The explanation tasted bitter in my mouth. I couldn't help noticing that the reasoning behind it was completely the opposite of what The Executive had said to me the previous Friday night—about how the Kirk-Rand relationship could be strengthened, and about all the wonderful story possibilities that would result from expanding my role.

Feeling physically sick inside, I asked, "Does this mean I'm through?"

"You have a contract for thirteen episodes. You have one more episode to shoot. You can finish out your contract, and then you'll be through."

And then you'll be through. It sounded so final. Like the ultimate rejection. Or like death.

That night, I went to a concert at UCLA. I can't remember who was performing or even what kind of music it was—I just remember that a lot of cast members from the show had tickets for this concert, and we all were going together. I was still in shock from the news my agent had given me, and I hadn't told anyone about it. I remember walking up to the imposing double doors of the theater and seeing Jimmy

Doohan—Engineering Officer Montgomery Scott of the Starship *Enterprise*—standing outside. He saw me and smiled. "Grace," he said, "how are you?"

"Well, Jimmy," I said, "I don't know. I think I'm still in shock."

His brow furrowed. "In shock? About what?" he asked.

"I got a call this afternoon from my agent," I replied. "He said I've been written out of the show."

His mouth fell open. "Written out! You?! Are they crazy? How can they write *you* out?"

Jimmy's shock was understandable. I was one of the first actors signed to do *Star Trek*, and I had signed as a lead, not a featured player. The pre-production publicity shots for *Star Trek* showed three characters—Captain Kirk, Mr. Spock, and Yeoman Janice Rand. In the closing credits, my name was on the same card with DeForest Kelly (Dr. McCoy). Creator Gene Roddenberry's original vision of the show's chemistry was built around a nucleus of four characters—Kirk, Spock, McCoy, and Rand—much as "Gunsmoke" was built around the nucleus of Marshal Dillon, Doc, Chester, and Miss Kitty. That's exactly how Gene explained it to me from the very beginning. So for me to be dropped from the show was a major shake-up—a sudden disruption of the chemical balance of the show.

Jimmy Doohan had a very sympathetic ear for my plight. After appearing in the second pilot,* "Where No Man Has Gone Before," Jimmy found out in early 1966 that the show had been picked up by NBC. *Great!* he thought. *Steady employment at last!* Three or four days later, his hopes were dashed when he received a note from Gene Roddenberry, informing him, "We don't think we need an engineer in the series." Jimmy instantly called his agent, who went flying into Gene's office at warp factor ten, and got Jimmy Doohan back on board.

Star Trek made its network debut the following week, on Thursday, September 8, 1966. I watched the show in the living room of my good friend Virginia Darcy, the hairdresser on the show. The episode NBC chose for the unveiling was "The Man Trap," the fourth regular-season episode we had filmed (the episodes were not aired in the same order in which they were shot).

In the show's maiden voyage, a landing party from the *Enterprise* contacts a space archaeologist and his wife at the ancient ruins they are excavating on a supposedly lifeless planet. When members of the landing party are found dead with red,

---

* Star Trek is probably the only TV show in history to have produced *two* pilot episodes; NBC found the first pilot, "The Cage," to be promising, but was not convinced to buy the show until after viewing the second pilot.

Perhaps when I told Jimmy what had happened to me that afternoon, he wondered if I was just the first casualty in a growing struggle to rein in the costs of this budget-embattled show. Having already been told once before that he was expendable, Jimmy may well have wondered if Mr. Scott was next in line to be phasered into oblivion. In fact, he said to me, "My gosh, if it can happen to you, it can happen to anybody!"

ring-shaped splotches on their bodies, Kirk demands answers from the couple—Professor Robert Crater (Alfred Ryder) and his wife Nancy (Jeanne Bal). Years before, Dr. McCoy had nearly married Nancy, and he still carries a torch for her. In the end, it turns out that the real Nancy Crater is long dead. What *appears* to be Nancy Crater is actually a hideous alien creature which can assume the guise of human beings—and which survives by suctioning the salt out of its victims, leaving the red, ring-shaped marks. Ultimately, Dr. McCoy must ignore what his senses tell him and kill the creature which has taken the form of the woman he once loved.

In the course of the story, I'm stalked by the "salt vampire" in the form of an *Enterprise* crewman, and I have a fun, comedic interlude with Sulu (George Takei) and an alien, woman-grabbing plant named Beauregard. When we filmed the episode, I absolutely loved it.

But when I sat on Virginia Darcy's living room sofa, watching the finished episode, I hated it. I was just sick throughout the entire broadcast—not because the show was bad, but because it was *good*. I knew *Star Trek* would be something special. I was convinced it would be a hit. And now that I was no longer part of it, I wanted *Star Trek* to fall flat on its face. Not a very admirable attitude, I admit—but that's the kind of pain I was in.

As part of NBC's publicity blitz for its new space series, I had given lots of interviews and posed for lots of photos. The media loved me. I was scheduled to do a number of talk shows, including "The Tonight Show" with Johnny Carson. Suddenly it was all canceled. No more interviews, no more photos, no more talk shows. It was as if I had suddenly become poison—no one wanted to talk to me anymore. The sense of rejection was shattering.

One of the most painful aspects of that entire nightmare was having to come back to the studio for one last appearance on the show. The episode was "The Conscience of the King," about a space-traveling troupe of Shakespearean actors led by a man running from his past as the notorious mass murderer, Kodos the Executioner. In the course of the episode, Captain Kirk becomes romantically involved with Lenore, the daughter of Kodos.

Sometime during the week of Monday, September 12, I came in for my final early morning call. When I drove onto the Desilu lot and parked my car, I was shocked to see that they had already painted over my name on the parking space. I walked into Stage 9 and reported to makeup, where Fred Phillips applied my hair and makeup one last time. Then I went out to the set of the *Enterprise* bridge and waited to be called.

In that episode, I appear in one scene. It begins with a flirty exchange between the Captain and Lenore (Barbara Anderson). Then Lenore steps to the turboshaft (or elevator), the doors whoosh open and I step out. I look Lenore up and down as she enters the lift. She is alluringly outfitted in what appears to be a short mink coat and nothing else. I give her a jealous appraisal, as if thinking, *Hmph! Is this the woman the Captain loves now? Is this the woman who's replacing me?* Then I step over to one of the bridge consoles and turn my back to the camera. My entire appearance in the episode lasts about six seconds—no lines.

Then I'm history.

On Thursday of that week, the second episode of *Star Trek* aired, "Charlie X"—an episode in which Charlie, a orphaned human teenager raised from infancy by aliens, becomes infatuated with Yeoman Janice Rand. It was a beautiful episode—gentle and sensitive in its treatment of a troubled, confused adolescent with godlike powers. I didn't want to watch it, but I couldn't stay away. It was even better than "The Man Trap." It killed me inside because the show was so great, and I was not a part of it anymore.

So I drank even more. I ran away from everything. I hid from everything. The pain was so intense, I wanted to check out. I wanted to die, so I tried to drink myself to death.

One time, shortly after I was written out, a friend left a case of booze with me while he went on vacation. A week later he came back for his case of booze—and it was gone. I drank it all! I drank it because I had to kill the pain and once I started drinking, I couldn't stop. If I had to drink myself to death in order to kill the pain, fine, I would do it. I drank so much and felt so suicidal, I often wonder how I managed to survive. Maybe I was just too chicken to kill myself (I admit it—I'm a wimp).

But I'd like to believe that I really stayed alive for my children. If it wasn't for them, I think I would have gone ahead and killed myself. My two boys were all I had to hang on to, and I couldn't bear the thought of them going through life without a mother.

My poor kids. What I did to them! I did the best I could in my own alcoholic way, but it didn't work. Nothing worked. I had sabotaged my marriage. I had thrown out the boys' father—because that's what alcoholics do. We throw people out of our lives. We become isolated. We throw this one out and go on to the next one. Every good alcoholic woman has to find the next one to "fix it," to make her feel whole.

I had thought that *Star Trek* was going to make me rich and famous, so I hadn't even bothered to ask for alimony in the divorce settlement. When I called my ex-husband and told him I had been written out of the show, he said, "Good. I'm glad you're out on your ass!"

The one person who really reached out to me after I was written out of *Star Trek* was Leonard Nimoy. He was the only one who really knew how much I was hurting. No one but Leonard knew what had happened to me that horrible Friday night, after the wrap party.

Leonard called me one Saturday and asked if I needed to talk. He was very worried that I might kill myself. So he picked me up in his car and we drove up to Santa Barbara. We spent a couple hours walking on the beach. That day, as he had always been, Leonard was a good listener. I certainly couldn't have been easy to listen to—I was so full of fury, resentment and suicidal feelings that I know I was miserable to be around. I literally didn't care if I lived or died. I told him I wanted to kill myself, but he reminded me that I had to live for my two boys. He said he knew I was going through incredible pain, but he promised I would get through it if I didn't give up.

I had the stone with me—the polished stone that The Executive had given me in the makeup room. As Leonard and I walked, I took the stone from my pocket and bounced it in my hand, thinking black thoughts about The Executive. "He never even said he was sorry, Leonard," I reflected bitterly, my eyes stinging. "He never even acknowledged what he did to me. He just gave me this lousy stone. That's how cheaply he bought me off! A worthless stone and a phone call to my agent—and I'm gone as if I never existed."

A dark rage came over me like a wave of emotional nausea. On a sudden impulse, I threw the stone as far as I could. It splashed into the rolling surf of the Pacific Ocean and disappeared.

We walked a little further down the beach. At one point, Leonard paused, bent down, and picked up something from the sand. He held it out to me, and I saw it was a stone, slightly larger than the one I had just thrown away. It was black, very smooth and shiny, and naturally polished by the ocean. It was beautiful. "Here," he said, handing it to me, "let me give you a new stone."

I kept that stone in my garden for many years, and often thought of Leonard's kindness to me that day.

Over the next few weeks, *Star Trek* attracted millions of loyal viewers. It wasn't a top-rated show by the Nielsen standards, but *Star Trek* fans were fanatical, adoring and vocal. Something happened to me that had rarely happened before: I got fan mail—lots and lots of fan mail. I didn't want to look at it, because it was fan mail for someone who no longer existed. I was popular, the fans loved me, and I was already gone from the show.

I withdrew from my friends at *Star Trek*. I even withdrew from Leonard, who had been so kind to me. His character, Mr. Spock, was rapidly becoming one of the most popular aspects of the entire series—and (though I'm ashamed to admit it) I was jealous of his success. Envy ate me up alive.

Though I didn't know it at the time, I had a disease within me—a disease called alcoholism. For most of my life up to that time, it was a manageable disease. I might get loaded from time to time—but only on weekends or at parties where it was socially acceptable. I was never impaired on the job. I was a professional. Only when I lost my role on *Star Trek* did my alcoholism finally kick me over the edge. I couldn't stand the pain of that loss. I needed a constant anesthetic, and my anesthetic of choice was alcohol.

I sat home by myself while my kids went back to school, while my friends went back to work on their successful TV show. Bill Shatner, Leonard Nimoy, DeForest Kelly, Nichelle Nichols, Jimmy Doohan, George Takei, Majel Barrett—all of them were working where I used to work, on the show I loved. And me? I was home drinking. Or going to bars and drinking. Or waiting for people to call and drinking. Or feeling sorry for myself and drinking.

I had lost my television family, my place of belonging. I had lost my favorite role among all the roles I had performed. I had suffered a financial loss, a career loss, an emotional loss.

And I blamed The Executive for all my pain.

A number of years ago, I was offered a considerable sum of money by a major New York publisher to write a book and tell this story—*if* I would publicly name the man who did this to me. I refused to do that. It wasn't because I was so noble and wanted to protect him. The fact is, there were two reasons I refused to name him: One, I am a recovering alcoholic, and in order to keep my sobriety, I must take a continual, day-by-day moral inventory of myself, and I must make amends to all persons I have harmed—even those who have hurt me. I must not harm others. So I refused to hurt this man or his reputation. And two, I was afraid of him and what he might do to me.

Today, The Executive can no longer hurt me—but I still refuse to name him. This book is my story, not his. Naturally, I can't tell my story without disclosing some of my interactions with other people—but I'm not going to tell anyone else's story or damage anyone else's reputation. Ask me about my life and my story, and I'll be happy to share it all with you. Ask me the identity of The Executive, I will not answer you. So please respect my wishes. Don't ask.

I'm not whitewashing what that man did to me. It was a horrible act, and I believe it was a planned, premeditated act. He's 100 percent responsible for what he did.

But I'm also 100 percent responsible for putting myself in a position where that could happen to me. I had been drinking. No, I wasn't falling-down drunk, but I was certainly impaired—and that made me vulnerable. I have learned that once I take a drink, I lose control over what happens to me. A lot of women need to learn what I found out the hard way: There are predatory men out there. As women, we need to keep our guard up and our wits about us, because the predators take time to plan it all out before we are even aware of them. They steer us away from the crowd, maneuver us into the secluded room, lock the door and spring the trap—and we still think we're having fun, that we are in control. We laugh, we joke, we have another drink—and we don't even know that we have already been conquered.

The moment we take responsibility for our choices, our actions, our drinking, and the things we do while we are impaired, that's the moment we take control of our lives. As women, we all too often accept the stereotype of ourselves as helpless little things who are always being pushed around by the big, mean, powerful men. The fact is, we have power and we can make choices. We can keep ourselves out of the clutches of predatory men by simply choosing not to make ourselves chemically stupid by soaking our brains in alcohol or other drugs.

What if I hadn't been drinking that night? The Executive would have asked me to sneak off to an empty office, just the two of us—and I would have probably said, "Sorry, I can't do that tonight, I have to get home to my boys. Why don't we get together sometime next week—say, over lunch?" If I had been sober, I wouldn't have gone with him alone at night. I allowed this incident in my life because I liked to party, my inhibitions were down, and I was not attentive to the signs.

And look at what it cost me.

A few years ago, Bill Shatner called me about a book he was working on with a writer named Chris Kreski. Bill interviewed me by phone for over an hour. About a year later, I received a copy of Bill's book, *Star Trek Memories*, which he had very nicely autographed to me. I opened the book—and was shocked by what I read about myself in that book. Understand, Bill is a friend, and I truly believe he tried to do my story justice. However, Bill's version of my life is riddled with glaring inaccuracies. Just one example: Bill says I claim to have experienced *two* sexual assaults while I was in the *Star Trek* cast.* No, there was only one incident—the incident I've described. It occurred just a few days before I was informed that Janice Rand had been written out of the series.

Because those events happened just a few days apart—the Friday night sexual assault and the call informing me that I had been written out of the show—there has always been a clear cause-and-effect linkage in my mind. I have always believed that The Executive had me removed from *Star Trek* because he didn't want to be reminded of what he did to me that night. In other words, I was sacrificed on the altar of one man's lust and guilt.

This is what I believe—but is it really true? Or is there some other explanation? Because I never received any official explanation, there was always that faint glimmer of doubt in my mind—the nagging suspicion that maybe I was jettisoned from *Star Trek* for some other, unknown reason. In the mid-1970s, Susan Sackett (Gene Roddenberry's gal Friday), wrote a book called *Letters to Star Trek*. On the back cover she listed the 10 questions about the show most frequently asked by *Star Trek* fans. The No. 3 question on the list: "Whatever happened to Grace Lee Whitney?" It's a question that even Grace Lee Whitney has wanted answered.

A number of conflicting theories have been advanced in various *Trek*-oriented books and magazines to explain why I was let go from the series, yet no single, definitive, once-and-for-all answer was ever put forward. No internal memo ever surfaced that said, "The producers of *Star Trek* have decided to toss Yeoman Janice Rand out the nearest airlock because..." But in the course of writing this book, after researching the events of those years and talking to people who were there, I think I've solved the mystery. And that's one of the things I'll be talking about in this book.

Reading Bill Shatner's version of my story in *Star Trek Memories* was very instructive to me: I learned that it's virtually impossible, even with the best of intentions, to tell another person's story and do it justice. I know Bill meant well, but the story he told about me in that book is not really my story. I don't blame him for getting some of the details and chronology wrong. In fact, I'm sure I told him things in our phone interview that gave him the wrong impression or that were easily misinterpreted. The point is that when we try to tell another person's story, errors, misunderstanding, and

---

*After *Star Trek Memories* appeared, I received phone calls from several men who used to work in one capacity or another on the *Star Trek* series. Not one of the men who called me was The Executive who actually committed the assault, yet each of these men asked the same question: "Were you talking about *me* in Shatner's book?" I thought it was the strangest thing that a man with a clean conscience would ask me such a question. So I answered, "What do you mean, was I talking about you? Was it you?" And each of them hastily said, "No, it wasn't me—I just wanted to make sure you didn't mean me." And I said, "Well, if it wasn't you, then I wasn't talking about you."

our own filtering creeps in. So in this book, I am being careful to tell only my story—no one else's. All I am attempting to do is to tell you what it was like, what happened, and what it's like now.

At times, life has been incredibly painful. But there were other times when life was unbelievably exciting. And what is life like now? Fabulous! Absolutely fabulous! My trip through the galaxy has been an incredible roller-coaster ride, from the deepest pits of despair and hopelessness to the very heart of love at the center of the universe. Along this wild up-and-down journey, I've been amazingly privileged to see and touch the Infinite. I want to tell you about the incredible things I've witnessed and the amazing discoveries I've made.

After you've read my story in my own words, feel free to believe or disbelieve—that's entirely up to you. But believe it or not, I assure you that everything I am about to tell you is exactly as I remember it.

This is my story. This is my trek.

"Who am I?"

. . . .

*S*tar Trek was just a TV show, right? It was a job. Actors find jobs and lose jobs, then move on and find something else. Losing a part in a TV show isn't the end of the world—or at least it wouldn't be for most people. So why was this loss so devastating for me? It has to do with who and what I am. And who am I?

My name is Mary Ann C., and I'm an alcoholic.

Mary Ann is the name my birth mother gave me when I was born. It was my adoptive mother who named me Grace.

For years before I came along, my adoptive parents had tried to have a baby, but my mother miscarried five times. She stayed in bed throughout each of those pregnancies, bleeding into the sheets, trying to save the baby—each time without success. With one pregnancy, she stayed in bed for six months, but she lost the baby anyway. So the Whitneys decided to adopt. When my mother brought me home and finally had a baby to hold in her arms, she gave me the name Grace because she believed it was God's grace that brought me into her life.

That was in 1930, when attitudes toward adoption were much different than today. Back then, many people considered it shameful not to be able to bear children, so adoption was also sometimes considered shameful. That's how it was for my mother. In her mind, her inability to conceive and bring a child to term was deeply embarrassing, so I was adopted in secret. But, of course, it could not remain a secret very long.

When my mother brought me home for the first time, the entire neighborhood knew that she had never been pregnant and that she suddenly had a baby. Everyone knew that the little Whitney girl down the street was illegitimate. As I grew up, some of the other mothers on the block didn't let their children play with me because of the stigma of my adoption. To them, I was illegitimate, a bastard, a "bad seed." I didn't understand this. It seemed everyone was in on my secret except me.

Even so, I enjoyed my early childhood. We went to church every Sunday, and we often went camping—there are 11,000 lakes in the state of Michigan, and we tried to visit as many of them as possible. Both of my parents loved me—though my mother actually loved me *too* much, with a smothering kind of love. I was a very spoiled child, an only child, and I was given everything, I was indulged and protected from all consequences of my actions, and—although my parents intended the best for me—I was emotionally and morally crippled by their overprotection.

One of my earliest memories as a toddler was that my mother often put me in a kind of halter with a leash. Though I was only 2 or 3 at the time, I remember it vividly, as if it was a torture device. Nowadays, of course, with so many child abductions, you

I was 4 months old when this photo was taken on August 1, 1930. As you can see, even at that tender age I was already working on my Yeoman Rand beehive!

This picture was taken in 1937, when I was 7. In those days, itinerant photographers went door to door with their ponies and cameras, snapping children's pictures for a few dollars. This picture was taken by our home in Detroit.

can buy similar "child leash" devices in most department stores, but when I was a child, it just wasn't done. I saw dogs on leashes, but not other children, so I felt it was humiliating. I didn't understand that my mother was scared to death of losing me. She had waited all her life to have a child, and she was taking no chances of anything happening to me.

As a child, I thought my father was aloof and uncaring, but later I came to realize he was really just quiet. He did not have a demonstrative, outgoing, affectionate personality—and I misinterpreted that as coldness and lack of love. It's a truism among alcoholics that we drink because we got no love at all or because we were smothered with love. In a sense, I drank for both reasons—because I was smothered with love by my mother and doubted the love of my father. My mother loved me so much it made me sick—and I didn't realize how much my father loved me until decades later in life.

Until I learned I was adopted, I grew up thinking I was the most special person on the face of the earth. That's what made the news of the adoption impossible for me to understand.

I was only 7 years old. My mother—the only mother I had ever known—came to me and said, "Grace, come here and sit with me. I want to talk to you."

She sat down in a rocking chair in the living room and lifted me onto her lap. I remember it as if it were yesterday. I can feel her arms wrapped around me and hear the softness of her voice—practically a whisper—as she began to tell me a story. "When you were a little baby," she said, "Dad and I chose you to be our very own. I didn't give birth to you. Another woman was your birth mother. She was not able to keep you and raise you. She gave you to a woman named Dr. Snow, and asked her to find a good home for you. Dr. Snow knew we wanted to have a baby, so she asked us if we would adopt you. We had to go through all kinds of tests and answer all kinds of questions in order to be qualified to take you home with us. We adopted you as our own child, and you've been with us ever since you were a few months old. So, you see, we chose you as our own. You are a chosen child."

I looked at my mother with disbelief. I knew she had tried to make this story sound like a good and wonderful thing—but I felt that the bottom had dropped out of my entire world. I said, "You mean ...you're not my mother?"

"No," she said, "I'm not."

"Then, who are you?"

"I'm your adopted mother."

"Well, where is my mother?"

"I don't know where she lives now. I just know she had to give you up for adoption because you didn't have a father."

"Well, where is my father?"

"Honey, we don't know."

In those few moments, my safe, secure world vanished like a vapor. Suddenly, I didn't know who I was. I didn't know who my parents were. I didn't feel I belonged anywhere or to anyone. I felt I had been set adrift in the dark.

Three decades later, I would go through another shattering experience, and it would be like déja vu. Just as my mother had once instructed me to sit with her, I would pick up my phone and hear my agent say, "Grace, are you sitting down?" And once again I would receive the shocking news that my family—my *Star Trek* family—was not my family anymore. I would learn that I suddenly had no place to belong to—I was adrift in the dark once more. I have a very clear recollection of experiencing the same horrible feeling of emptiness and lostness, both when I learned I was adopted and when I learned I was being written out of *Star Trek*—the very same feeling.

From the moment I sat in that rocking chair and heard the story of my early life, and for years afterwards, until I was in my fifties, I felt massive resentment against the woman who gave me life, the woman who gave me away. I couldn't understand how my birth mother could do that. Worst of all, I suspected that it meant there was

This picture of me in my confirmation dress was taken when I was 10 years old—just one year before I took up smoking and three years before my first drink.

something terribly wrong with me. If I was not defective somehow, if I were truly worth anything and deserving of a mother's love, how could my birth mother do that?

The more I thought about it, the more terrible the whole situation became. My mother had called me a "chosen child." Sure—but *why* was I chosen? Because my adoptive parents could not bear a child of their own, that's why! I was Plan B, I was the alternate choice, I was flying standby. I didn't want to be the second choice, I wanted to be the first choice. In my 7-year-old mind, being second choice was worse than not being chosen at all. And if my adoptive mother had been able to bring a child to term, I *wouldn't* have been chosen, period!

My mother tried to tell me in a loving, gentle way. She tried to make sure I felt loved and chosen. None of that mattered to me. Every positive word she said, I rewrote as a negative. It's one of the things we alcoholics do, turning ice cream into caca, and it starts long before we take our first drink.

It was around that same time that I learned there is no Santa Claus. I began to feel that everything I had ever trusted and believed in was a myth. I didn't know what was real or what was unreal. My parents weren't my parents. Santa Claus was a lie. What's next? Immediately, I thought of all the things I had learned in Sunday school about God, about Jesus. *So it's all a myth*, I concluded. And that's why, at a very early age, I ceased to believe in God.

My mother once told me that when I was 9 years old, my father stood at the door of our home and watched me playing in the yard with a few friends. "I wonder what's wrong with her?" he said.

He knew, just by looking at the way I interacted with the other kids, that there was something not right with me. I was bossy and controlling. I demanded that the other kids pay attention to me and do what I say. He didn't understand what made me like that—but he was on to the fact that there was something wrong with me.

He didn't know it, but he was observing the symptoms of my disease. He was on to my alcoholic tendencies. The abuse of alcohol is just a symptom of a much deeper disorder—a disorder that recovering alcoholics call "self-will-run-riot." That was me, even at age 9: consumed with self-will, a bossy, bratty, demanding, attention-seeking child. Even though I wouldn't take my first drink until I was 13, all the makings of an alcoholic were already in place inside me.

It doesn't matter what we are addicted to—alcohol, heroin, cocaine, Valium, tobacco, food, sex—these are just the outward symptoms. The real disease is self-will-run-riot. And self-will-run-riot is really a form of self-centered *fear*—fear you won't get something you want, or that you'll lose something you have. I was full of that fear when I was a child—and it is never far from me today. It has taken me 60-some-odd years to get in touch with that fear, to recognize it, to realize that it's self-centered fear that makes me tick. I've had it all my life.

My father saw it in me that day when he looked out the front door and said, "I wonder what's wrong with her?"

I underwent a lot of changes when I was around 13 or 14 years old. The pain of wondering why my birth mother gave me up began to grow more and more acute. It was also around that time that I first became sexually active—and I began drinking. I got my driver's license at 14, the legal age in Michigan at that time, and began to drive my parents' car.

One day I was driving on Grand River Avenue in Detroit—a big, wide street with a median strip down the middle. I had been drinking, and I was out driving the car by myself. Ahead of me, an older man was standing on the median strip—and just as I was approaching, he fell in the road, right in front of my car. I didn't even have time to hit the brakes. I felt the car bounce as it ran over him. I looked back, but I didn't stop, didn't even slow down. I just knew I had killed the man.

I went home and hid in the house. I was certain the police would come knocking on my door any moment—but they never did. I was never caught, and I never told anyone at the time. I suppose there's a chance the man survived—but in my mind, I was convinced I had just killed a man. And I probably did.

That was just the beginning of my drunk driving career. When I was 15, I was stopped for drunk driving in Canada (I talked my way out of getting cited). Years later

I got into an accident on Santa Monica Boulevard in Hollywood. No one was seriously hurt—and again I was not cited because I had an alcoholic's ability to lie convincingly, and the officer bought my story that I only had one drink.

When I was 14, I went on a search for my birth mother, and my adoptive mother went with me. We went to the house in Ann Arbor where Dr. Snow had lived. She had moved, and we weren't able to locate her. I later made up a story that I told various people: "I walked in the doctor's house," I would tell them, "and the doctor looked at me with amazement and said, 'You look just like your natural mother!'" That was the fantasy I built—a fantasy that there was someone in the world I was physically, emotionally connected to, someone I looked like. I fantasized about my birth mother most of my life.

For years, I stuffed all my feelings of disappointment over not being able to find my birth mother. Eventually, I located her—but that was *50 years* after my initial search. Worse yet, I didn't find her until two years after she died. I couldn't believe it that, after half a century, I missed her by only two years! I couldn't believe God would let such a thing happen, and I was angry and disappointed with him. It's one of the things I don't understand about God.

My birth mother's name was Irene, and she had named me Mary Ann. She was a buyer in a Grand Rapids department store, and got involved with a traveling salesman who called on the store. Her grandfather—my biological great-grandfather—was a bootlegger, a Russian immigrant who died when he was only 40 years old from an overdose of his own bathtub gin. (Incidentally, gin was my drink of choice as well—does the disease of alcoholism run in the genes or what?)

When I located my birth family, no one would agree to meet with me or acknowledge me except one cousin and her husband. She had me autograph a photo for her children, and I felt wonderfully accepted by them. She and I keep in touch to this day. The rest of the family, however, didn't want to hear anything about me. I was in my sixties, I had found my birth family—and I felt rejected all over again.

My mother's best friend was a woman named Edith, a friend from the Methodist church we went to. I remember many weekends while I was between 7 and 12 or so, we'd load up the tent, hitch up the trailer, and go camping with Edith and her family. The men would fish while my mother and Edith would cook and swim and take care of the kids. My best friend was Edith's daughter, Barbara. She taught me how to smoke, how to drink—all that "grown-up" stuff.

When I was entering adolescence, Edith got my mother involved in going to seances. "I know a really gifted medium," Edith said. "She can help you get in touch with all your stillborn children. I just know they're waiting to talk to you from the other side."

So my mother went to these seances. When she came home, I asked her, "Why did you go to a seance? What do you do there?"

"I go," she explained, "and talk to my *real* children. My children who were still-born are there in heaven, and they talk to me through the medium."

My real children. Those words stabbed at me. Wasn't I real? But no, of course I wasn't. I wasn't my mother's *real* child, and she wasn't my *real* mother. That's why she drilled into me that I was never to tell anyone I was adopted—because being adopted meant I was not my mother's daughter. The real circumstances of my birth were a shameful secret.

One day when I was 13 or 14, my mother came home and showed me five little clear stones, like rough jewels in various colors. "These are from my real children," she said. "They gave me these stones from heaven."

My mother really believed those stones came from heaven, from her five "real" children, the ones that had died in my mother's five miscarriages. She wanted to believe, so she believed.

I looked at the stones that supposedly came from her dead children and I asked, "If the children in heaven are your real children, then who am I?"

"Well, you're my child too," she replied, "but these stones are from my *real* children—the children who came from inside me. You didn't, you came from another mother."

I showed all the signs of an addiction-prone personality at an early age. I was a compulsive overeater, and very chubby as a preadolescent. I started smoking at 11, and I started drinking when I was 13. I drank Southern Comfort to get rid of the voices in my head that told me, *You're no good! Your mother gave you up because you're not good enough. This woman has other children, real children, in heaven. You don't belong here. You're not a real child—you're a misfit!**

When that first splash of Southern Comfort hit the back of my throat and started going down, I couldn't imagine ever living without it again. It fixed me. It filled all the holes where the wind was blowing through and causing me so much pain. As soon as that first drink hit bottom, the pain stopped—and that's all I cared about.

I started drinking and I couldn't stop. And for years it was a real mystery to me why I did that, because I grew up in a very strict Methodist home. My mother was

---

*Recovering alcoholics have a term for those inner voices. We call it "the Committee." Until I got into recovery, I didn't know that other people had these voices. Now I know that all alcoholics have these voices—and perhaps all human beings, period. Most people just don't get in touch with those voices and learn to recognize them until they get into recovery.

The Committee makes you feel bad about yourself and tells you to do what you don't want to do. The Committee condemns and harasses many alcoholics to the point of despair. For some, the Committee is practically an audible voice that says, "Turn here," and causes you to have an accident, or, "Take off your clothes," and causes you to embarrass yourself. Most alcoholics have the Committee buzzing inside their heads nonstop—which is why it's sometimes called "head noise."

I once spoke at a meeting and saw a plaque on the wall that read, "God so loved the world that he did not send a Committee." I love that statement so much, I now quote it often when I speak in recovery groups. In recovery, we learn to listen to the voice of God instead of the voices of the Committee.

actually president of the local chapter of the Women's Christian Temperance Movement. She was a Bible thumper from way back. From the time I was 3, she used to take me to meetings where they sang hymns and preached about how terrible alcohol is, and how women need to close all the bars and get their men out of those sinful taverns. Every year on my birthday, she would tie a white ribbon on my wrist in the name of Jesus, which was supposed to help keep me away from alcohol. We had no alcohol in the house. No one in my family drank. It just didn't make sense that, given my environment, I would turn out to be an alcoholic.

Decades later, after I located my biological parents, I discovered that my genetic history included alcoholism. Suddenly it made sense. This disease I have is transmitted in the genes. Finally, I could understand where my cravings came from, and I became firmly convinced that the predisposition to alcoholism is passed on through the genes. That doesn't mean I'm not responsible for my own behavior, or for taking that first drink and every drink that followed. I am 100 percent responsible for my self-induced illness, and for my sobriety. But it helps me to understand what makes me want to drink.

I started smoking at 11, sneaking my father's cigarettes (alcoholics love to sneak—the sneakier the behavior, the more fun it is). I began drinking at age 13, in total opposition to my upbringing. In a rigidly teetotaler home, I was sneaking a drink every chance I got. Only when I understood the *ism*, the dis-ease of alcoholism, did I understand why I began drinking, and why I couldn't stop drinking. Understanding the ism of alcoholism also helped me to understand why, at age 13, I gave away my virginity.

David was my first love. He was 14, a year older than me, and he lived across the street. David didn't have a father, so he was the man in his house and he had his own car—a gorgeous stick-shift Ford roadster. I was crazy about him, and wanted to possess him in every way possible, including sexually.

I met David through my baby-sitter, who was related to him. The baby-sitter was 18 or 19 at the time, and (I later learned) a lesbian. My mother was so overprotective that she felt I couldn't be left alone at age 13, so she hired this girl to stay with me. While we were alone together, the baby-sitter would teach me how to dance. She would hold me very close and touch me in an intimate way. She knew exactly what she was doing. Even though I didn't understand what was happening, and even though she never actually seduced me, I experienced a sexual awakening in the way she held me, talked to me and touched me.

The baby-sitter introduced me to David, and I quickly fell crazy in love with him. This was shortly after my failed search to find my birth mother. In fact, I switched my codependence from trying to find my mother to obsessing over David. I practically smothered him with my possessiveness and my dependence on him. Recovering alcoholics often say that alcoholics don't have relationships, we take hostages. That's what I did to David. Out of my self-centered, self-willed fear of losing David, I tried to control him, I tried to possess him, I tried to merge with him. It was a completely obsessive relationship—and David was as obsessed with me as I was with him. I wasn't even having my period yet, and we were totally, wildly, sexually involved with each other.

Even before I became involved with David, I was fascinated with sex. I played doctor with the little boys when I was in kindergarten. In fact, I had to be removed from one kindergarten and sent to another school because I wouldn't leave the boys alone. I didn't really understand what this fascination with boys was all about, however, until I was 9 years old. That's when a girlfriend of mine told me all about sex—how a man's anatomy connects with a woman's anatomy, and what happens when they have sex.

My parents raised me to be pure. They took me to Sunday school where I learned about Jesus. My mother gave me my first Bible at the age of 5, and I still have it today. I loved Jesus. I loved to hear the stories about him, though I couldn't relate to him in a personal way. I didn't see how his teachings had anything to do with my everyday life. Once I became obsessed with boys, I had no room in my heart for God.

At that time, the only god in my life was David.

I gave him my virginity in a cabin in northern Michigan. My parents and his had gone on vacation together. They put us in the same room in bunk beds—and that's where we gave ourselves to each other for the first time. It's hard to imagine parents being so naive that they would actually put a teenage boy and a teenage girl in the same room, in bunk beds, and think nothing would happen—but that's what they did. I remember it vividly. Afterwards, I said, "David, I'm yours forever. I've given this part of myself to you, and now I belong to you." Even at 13, I was very dramatic.

He was my first love, and I was his first. It was a real Romeo and Juliet thing, and we clung to each other constantly. Decades later, when I went back to Detroit for my class reunion at Cooley High School, nobody could really remember anything about me except that I was always with David. He ran track at Cooley High, and I was always out at the track, admiring him as he ran. He had earned many letters in sports, and I wore his sweater.

Our love lasted several years, until I was 16. That's when I discovered that David had been seeing another girl. In fact, he had gotten her pregnant. Her name was Margaret, and she lived a few blocks away. When I found out David had betrayed me, I exploded. I absolutely would not forgive him. He came to my door and begged me to take him back, but I wouldn't see him. My mother came to me and said, "Grace, don't do this to yourself. David is so heartbroken, you have to take him back."

I *wanted* to take David back. I wanted to forgive him. I *loved* him. But being the alcoholic personality I am, I couldn't do something so healthy as to forgive the boy I loved. No, I turned my back on him. It hurt me more than anything I've ever done, but that's the way alcoholics think. There's an expression to describe this kind of thinking: *I'll show you! I'll get me!* In other words, I'll hurt myself, even destroy myself, in order to get back at you. I'll burn my own house down just to get back at you. It's a sick, twisted way of thinking—but then, alcoholism is a sick, twisted way of living. Alcoholics sabotage everything of value in their lives.

David tried so hard to win my forgiveness. He came back to me and said, "If you won't forgive me, I'll have to marry Margaret for the sake of the baby. But if you'll take me back, I won't marry her. I promise I'll be true to you." But I wouldn't have him back. I cursed him. I screamed at him, "You went to bed with her, and now she's having your baby, and I will never, ever forgive you!" My relationship with David was the one thing I valued above all else at that time in my life—but my resentment was so intense that I deliberately destroyed it. *I'll show you! I'll get me!*

My love for David reminds me of the pathos in the Natalie Wood-Warren Beattie film *Splendor in the Grass*. Their life together is just one disappointment after another, and though they clearly belong together, they drive each other away. In the end, they are left standing there, looking at each other, thinking, *I can't believe our lives took these turns and we let each other go. How did we miss each other like this?* That's the way it was with David and me. He drove me away with his betrayal, and I drove him away with my bitterness and unwillingness to forgive. I ached over that loss, and for many years I drank over it too.

David married Margaret, and they had a boy named John. David and I went our separate ways and lived our separate lives—but there is a tragic postscript to the story.

Almost two decades later, when I was living in California and working in television—this was about 1964 or '65—I was at home with my two babies. My doorbell rang, and I answered it—and nearly fainted. There on my doorstep was David, looking exactly as he looked when we were dating. I knew it was impossible, because I was in my thirties and here was David, looking like he was still in high school. Then he spoke and said, "Hello—are you Grace Lee Whitney? I'm John. You knew my father, David."

Of course it was John—the boy David had fathered with Margaret. I invited John in and we talked. I'm not sure why John came to see me—perhaps he just happened to be in L.A., and his dad had suggested that he look me up. I asked John how his father was doing.

"Great, great," said John. "He's one of the top salesmen with Pontiac, doing real well. You know, everybody back in Detroit talks about you. They talk about how you and Dad used to go together, and how you came out to California and became a movie star."

"Well, I'm not a movie star."

"Okay," said John. "An actress, then."

We chatted for about an hour or so, then John left. I watched him as he got in his car and drove off. I couldn't get over it. He looked so much like David.

I think it was about a year or two later that I got a call from David's sister, Ruth. She told me that David's son, John, had been killed in a shooting in Chicago. I was stunned and devastated. I could scarcely imagine the pain that David must have been going through. I tried to reach David by phone, but without success.

Years later, after I was sober, I went back to Detroit for a high school reunion. I was hoping to see David there, but he didn't come. I haven't seen him since. I don't know if David is alive or dead—but to this day, I think of him often.

After my teenage love affair with David broke up, I got involved with one of his friends just to spite him. I would go to Freddie's for the night. In one room, Freddie's mother was sleeping with her boyfriend; in another bedroom, Freddie's younger sister was sleeping with her boyfriend; in another bedroom, Freddie and I slept together. This family was not exactly "Father Knows Best!" I was 16 or 17 at the time, and I didn't set out to get pregnant, but Freddie was not careful, like David had always been with me.

When I got pregnant, Freddie's mother's boyfriend said, "I know how to fix that." And he performed the "coathanger abortion" on me—not with a literal coathanger, but with a long piece of steel which he used to get the process going. Of course, there was no anesthetic available but gin, so it hurt a lot. Then he gave me ergotrate, which causes contractions and bleeding.

After the bleeding and contractions started, Freddie took me to a jazz concert at the Michigan Theater on Woodward in Detroit. I stood in the back of the theater, watching Sarah Vaughn performing on stage. It was the same theater where, many times before, I had seen Nat King Cole, Frank Sinatra and other stars. This night, however, I didn't enjoy the concert. Standing there, I bled so heavily the blood ran down my legs and into my shoes. I was so scared, I thought I was going to die. Finally I told Freddie, "I have to go home. I'm too covered with blood."

I went home and the baby passed out of me in shreds. It looked like long pieces of raw liver.

❖ ❖ ❖

I grew up hungry for attention and applause. I was a constant performer in school—singing and dancing in the gym, playing the lead in school plays. I loved putting on makeup and wearing beautiful costumes. I learned to read music playing the song flute in elementary school—and that's how I got on the radio.

At 13, I auditioned and won a spot as a singer with the Don Large Chorus, which was an auxiliary of Fred Waring's music organization. Waring was a business-savvy bandleader who adapted chorus music to the jazz and swing music of the 1920s, '30s and '40s. He was one of the first to see the enormous potential of the new technologies of radio and phonograph records, and he had several groups like the Don Large Chorus that developed and fed talent into his main performing group, The Pennsylvanians. (He was also the marketing genius behind the Waring blender.)

The Don Large Chorus consisted of an adult group and a youth chorus. Every Saturday, the young people's group performed live on WJR radio in Detroit. That was my first taste of professional show biz—and I loved every moment of it. I was called upon to sing *a capella* with nothing but a belltone to give me the pitch, because I learned to read notes while studying piano for eight years.

In 1997, I went to Detroit for a *Star Trek* convention and was interviewed for an article in the *Detroit Free Press*. It turns out that the daughter of Don Large still lives in

Detroit. She saw the article, in which I mentioned singing in her father's chorus. She contacted me through the newspaper and my agent, and told me, "My father would be so proud of you. He talked about you often. He thought you were going to be a star—not as an actress, but as a singer."

Performing was something I wanted to do, not something I was pushed into. I pursued my love of music right through high school, singing in the Del Delbridge Band. My mother didn't try to encourage me or discourage me from a singing career. She was a singer herself, and had a lovely voice. She sang in church and appeared in a production of Gilbert and Sullivan's *HMS Pinafore*. She thought it was wonderful that I loved to sing, and was very proud of all my endeavors.

Singing and performing meant more to me than simply providing entertainment for people and receiving their applause. Once I learned I was not my parents' biological child, I became desperate to find out who and what I was. I didn't feel I belonged in my parents home, so I was desperate to find my own place in the world. Performing gave me a chance to get away from myself, out of myself, to become someone else— and I liked that. I thought, *I'll show them! I'll be rich and famous! I'll be somebody! I'll show my birth mother that she was wrong to reject me!*

I also loved going to the movies and seeing these perfect people with their idealized, romanticized lives projected larger than life on the silver screen. I fantasized about seeing myself up there, about recreating my own identity in a succession of romantic, idealized roles in the movies. I saw the movie screen as a wonderful place to escape to, and I saw real life as something dirty, something to escape from.

In my late teens, I left home and went to Saugatuck, Michigan, southwest of Grand Rapids. There I started singing with a band in a bar called The Dock, near Lake Michigan. It was a place with sawdust on the floor, and it catered to a yacht-set clientele—guys in dungarees and tee-shirts, but with plenty of spending money. I was underage, so I had to sign a note that I wouldn't drink on the job. Later, when I found out that the drinking age in Illinois was 18, I left Michigan and went to Chicago. That's where I had my first legal drink.

Moving away from home was the best thing I ever did. Throughout my childhood and adolescence, I was afflicted with horrible migraine headaches. I would vomit, see spots, and writhe in pain for hours. The moment I moved out of the house, I stopped having headaches. I realized later that the headaches must have been caused by my mother's smothering love. She often said that without me, she would die. I had a constant pushme-pullyou going on inside—my mother's smothering affection continually conflicted with a sense that I was a misfit, living in a place where I didn't belong. I stuffed so many feelings when I lived at home, and constantly felt pressure, pressure, pressure. I didn't want to hurt my mother, but I couldn't stand living there any longer.

Leaving home, I felt emancipated—free to reinvent myself, to construct my own identity and reality. I changed my name from Grace Elaine Whitney (the name my mother gave me) to Lee Whitney. I was embarrassed by the name "Grace" because it sounded too square and Christian to me. I wanted to be hip, slick, and cool. "Lee" sounded cool to me.

I got my own apartment near a bar called Augustino's at Bellvue and Rush Street. I sang, I became a model, I entered the Miss Chicago contest (and won second place).

I felt my life had finally begun.

In Chicago, I was immersed in the world of jazz and blues. I loved hanging out in the bars with gangsters and other lowlifes. To me, all that sleaze and the smell of the bars was the height of glamour. I'd dance and flirt and drink—and that was my idea of a good time. I remember I used to fall down stairs a lot, but I never got hurt. Drunks rarely get hurt falling downstairs. They're too relaxed and rubber-jointed to get hurt.

I started singing at a place called the Prevue, singing "Pretty-Eyed Baby" with Danny Casella's trio. Danny's trio was the relief act when the main act, the Buddy Rich Band, was taking a break. That was one of the nicer nightspots in town. After a few weeks at the Prevue, I got a job opening shows at the Band Box, a "padded toilet" at the corner of Randolph and State Street. The place is a parking lot now, but for all its sleazy charm, it used to be a great little club. The Prevue and the Band Box were like night and day. While the Prevue was filled with lights and I sang up on the stage, the Band Box was dark, and I stood right on the dance floor when I sang—I felt like I was in a hole. The Prevue was up, the Band Box was down. I performed for a few weeks at one place, then the other, back and forth.

The Band Box was in the cellar, and there was a bar called The Brass Rail upstairs. In the Band Box, which seated maybe 150 or 200 people, there were B girls sitting around with their skirts hiked up to *here* and cleavage down to *there*. They'd sit in these little chairs with a mini bar around them, and the guys would come up and play cards with the girls and buy them drinks and spend a lot of money.

And me? I was a green kid wearing bobby sox with my high-heeled shoes, taking it all in with my youthful fascination. With my new, sophisticated-sounding stage name, Lee Whitney, I was trying desperately to fit in with all these grown-ups. I felt like such a child—and I was.

That was in 1948 or '49, and I was running around like crazy, going to modeling jobs during the day and singing on stage at night as the warm-up for the big acts. I started making my own gowns in those days to wear on the bandstand, and I continued making my own gowns until I gave up nightclub singing in 1981. Throughout the '50s and '60s, even during *Star Trek* and beyond, I carried on my singing career right alongside my acting career. Many of the gowns I made to wear on the bandstand I also wore in front of the camera when I did guest shots on TV shows.

The biggest act I opened for at the Band Box was Billie Holliday—the legendary "Lady Day" whose tragic story was told in the movie *Lady Sings the Blues*. Billie was a heroin addict. She'd be shaking uncontrollably when the guys with the junk came in out of the alley to deliver it to her. She looked like she was dying, she needed a fix so bad. Sometimes I guarded the door to the john while they came in with the bag, tied her off, and shot her up. Then she'd relax.

This picture of me with my parents was taken by the Detroit News *for a "local girl makes good" story on me which the newspaper ran near the beginning of my stage career.*

Billie would go right back on stage after that. The band would give her the intro, and she didn't even know what the song was. I'd stand in the back of the room behind the spotlight, and she'd ask, "What song is this, Lee?" And I'd say, "Them There Eyes" or "Body and Soul" or "Good Morning, Heartache" or "God Bless the Child." And she'd sing it with so much passion and pain, it would make you cry.

I know this sounds like a contradiction, but Billie was a very spiritual person. She really loved Jesus and talked about him all the time. She was a very loving woman, but she was sick, strung out and addicted. Heroin was something she did against her own will, and she knew it. It was killing her, but she had to do it. Once something like heroin or alcohol gets you, you're caught, and it's unbelievably hard to get free. Addiction is insidious beyond belief.

At the time, however, I thought all the drug use and alcoholism I saw was glamorous. I never tried heroin, because I was drinking gin, and that's all I needed. All the musicians were stoned on pot, but I didn't use pot then. I was an alcoholic, pure and simple.

Billie moved on, playing in club after club for the next 10 years. I was living in Hollywood when I heard that Lady Day had died in Metropolitan Hospital in New York. She was under arrest for possession of heroin. The heroin took her over slowly, day by day, year by year, until it finally killed her.

Billie's tenor player was Lester Young, one of the greatest saxophonists in jazz history. I didn't have a clue how great that man was, or that he had played for years with the great Count Basie. I was watching and listening to some of the greatest jazz and blues performers ever—Buddy Rich, Charlie Parker, Anita O'Day, Gene Krupa—and I didn't even know it. I loved their music and I enjoyed it often—but now I look back and realize that I was surrounded by legends, absolute legends, and didn't even know it.

Danny Casella, the band leader I started with at the Prevue, was crazy about me and kept trying to get me to go to Las Vegas with him to sing in the clubs out there. I kept telling him, "I don't want to sing in bars all my life. I want to sing on the stage. I want New York, Broadway, the theater—not a nightclub in Vegas."

"Look," he said, "I'm buying 40 acres in Vegas. I'll buy some land for you if you'll come out to Vegas with me."

"Thanks," I said, "but no thanks."

The 40 acres he bought was right on the Strip. It was cheap, empty land back then. Now it's chockablock with neon casinos. Before long, those 40 acres made Danny Casella a millionaire—while I was still making 120 bucks a week as a singer. For years afterward, Danny sent me notes saying, "See what you missed?"

I toured for a while with Red Ingle's band. Red had worked with Spike Jones before going out on his own, and his act was heavily influenced by Spike's noisy, fast-paced, zany comedy style. Red had a big hit single that went to Number 1 on the charts—a country-western satire called "Temptation" (if you've ever seen "Hee-Haw," you get the general idea of this song). He hired me to sing "Temptation" on his road tour, because it was written completely out of meter, and I was the only singer he could find who could sing out of meter without getting lost.

I later formed my own group in Chicago, Lee Whitney and Her Trio, and we went on the road, performing in bars and clubs. The group consisted of piano, string bass, drums, and me at the microphone.

Some hoodlums in Pittsburgh heard me sing at a club, and they signed me to a contract that gave them the right to manage my career. They bought me train fare to New York and paid for a hotel room so that I could audition for a part in a new play by

In both the Broadway stage production (above) and the movie version (right) of Top Banana, I was "Miss Holland," the twin-propeller job next to Phil Silvers.

George Abbott, the great Broadway writer-director-producer (*Damn Yankees, Pal Joey, A Funny Thing Happened on the Way to the Forum, The Pajama Game*, and *Fiorello!*). Abbott frowned at me throughout the audition, and when I was done, he said, "My advice to you is to go home, get married, and have kids. In short, Miss Whitney, you have no talent." I felt like a turd.

When I went back to Pittsburgh and told my managers what Abbott said, they tore up my contract. But I was determined not to let one discouragement stop me. Two years later, I came back and auditioned once more for the high and mighty George Abbott. I was scared to death he would recognize me from the previous audition, but he didn't. My chutzpah got me the part in his new burlesque revival, *Top Banana*, where I got to work alongside stars like Phil Silvers, Jack Albertson, Joey Faye, Herbie Faye and Rose Marie (remember her as Sally on "The Dick Van Dyke Show"?). We later came out to California and shot a movie version of *Top Banana* at ZIV Studios. The critics panned it, but the public loved it, and I got a lot of fan mail because of that movie.

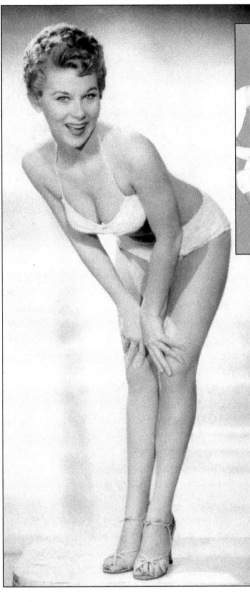

The cheesecake shot (left) was taken of me when I was on "The Edgar Bergen-Charlie McCarthy" show. I loved live radio and working with Bergen and McCarthy (above). I remember being at the CBS studio while Edgar was preparing to do a show. He had another dummy on his knee, Mortimer Snerd, and was carrying on a conversation with it, getting into character. Just then, Edgar's 8-year-old daughter, Candice, walked up and Bergen introduced us. Today, of course, that little girl is TV's "Murphy Brown."

Phil Silvers was one of the greatest comedic performers of all time, and it was fascinating to watch him prepare for a performance. As he waited for the curtain to rise, he would pace furiously, back and forth, back and forth, for at least 15 or 20 minutes. He was getting up a big head of steam, building up energy and momentum so that when he came out on stage, he would *burst* onto the stage with blazing energy. That was the secret to the vibrant performances he gave. I never saw another actor prepare himself to go on the way Phil Silvers did.

After the last show, Phil would be so exhausted, he had to go straight home to bed. Often, between shows, Phil and I would go out for coffee or a bite to eat. Sometimes there'd be other cast members with us, and other times it was just Phil and me. Though he was a bundle of energy onstage, offstage Phil was quiet, lonely, and often depressed. In private moments, this brilliant, funny man with the impeccable timing struck me as a totally tragic figure. He didn't seem to have many close friends, his wife was leaving him, and he carried the burden of a very demanding role in a big Broadway musical. After all, he was not just the star of *Top Banana*—he *was* the top banana. The weight of the world was all on his shoulders, and when he wasn't performing, he carried it around like an anchor.

Phil's sidekick in *Top Banana* was Jack Albertson. Jack had quite a career in films and TV (he was the curmudgeonly garage-owner in the Freddie Prinze sitcom "Chico and the Man"). He was the first person in my entire life to tell me I was an alcoholic. When I came into the theater in the morning to understudy, he'd tell me, "Lee, you *smell* like an alcoholic."

"I can't be an alcoholic—I'm too young!" I replied. "I'm only twenty-one." I thought it was absurd that he thought I smelled like an alcoholic. I didn't drink in the morning, and he couldn't possibly smell booze on my breath from the night before, could he? But I've since learned that alcoholics don't metabolize alcohol properly, and they do smell like alcohol even the following day. Jack Albertson was right about me.

While we were doing *Top Banana* on Broadway, I noticed that the drummer in the orchestra pit looked just like Gene Krupa—dark-haired and handsome. I was attracted by his smile, his looks, his playing. He totally knocked me out. And as he watched me on the stage from the orchestra pit, night after night, he decided I was a knockout, too. I had great legs, a great figure, and I was scantily dressed as Miss Holland. I had windmill-like propellers on my boobs, and I would come up next to Phil Silvers and he would spin my propellors—then suddenly stop them. When Phil stopped the windmills, I would make a sudden jerk and the drummer would hit a rimshot from the orchestra pit. That always got a big laugh. There were rimshots and visual gags all through *Top Banana*.

I fell in love with the drummer—his name was Steve—and we started sharing hotel rooms in New York and on the road. He was a Sfardic Syrian Jew, which was very intriguing to me. Even before I met Steve, I had been leaning toward converting to Judaism. When I was 17, I heard the Jews described as "the chosen people," and I thought, *Wouldn't it be wonderful to be chosen by God!* I felt I was not truly chosen as an adopted child, I was *second* choice. If my mother had been able to conceive and bear a child, I never would have been chosen. So I began investigating Judaism. When I met Steve, it seemed like a natural match: I would convert and become Jewish and I would marry a nice Jewish boy, we would be in show business together, and wouldn't it be a wonderful life!

I was also attracted to Steve because he didn't drink. I drank all the time, but Steve was an abstainer. I thought, *Maybe if I marry him, I'll stop drinking. I'll be a good girl.* I saw myself as bad, but I really wanted to be good. I thought a nice Jewish boy would help me to be a good Jewish girl.

❖ ❖ ❖

Steve and I moved to Hollywood when he was offered a job as Betty Hutton's drummer. Later, we both got jobs working on "The Edger Bergen and Charlie McCarthy Show" on CBS Radio, which was broadcast live from the CBS studios on Sunset and Gower a door or two away from the Palladium. Steve became the drummer with the Ray Noble Orchestra, which was featured on "Bergen and McCarthy," and I did the singing commercials as Miss Chicken of the Sea. I sang the jingle—"Miss Chicken of the Sea is on the la-a-a-a-a-bel"—and I had lots of pictures taken in a mermaid costume. Those pictures became the prototype for the mermaid who still appears on the tuna can today.

Steve and I got an apartment a block south of Sunset Boulevard, and I would often walk our beautiful Dalmatian along the boulevard, and guys would drive slowly alongside me and look. Sometimes they'd call out a smutty proposition, sometimes they'd just leer and drive by. I got used to it, and figured, "Hey, that's just Hollywood." One time a black car pulled up and stopped. A man got out and introduced himself. "I'm Walter Mayhew," he said, "and I work for Mr. Howard Hughes. Mr. Hughes would like to meet you."

Well, everyone knew who Howard Hughes was—a record-setting aviator, a business tycoon, a movie producer, a man whose name had been romantically linked with Katherine Hepburn, Ginger Rogers, Bette Davis, Marilyn Monroe, Lana Turner, Rita Hayworth, Ava Gardner, Linda Darnell, Jean Peters, Gene Tierney, Yvonne DeCarlo, Kathryn Grayson, and on and on and on! "Why would Howard Hughes want to meet me?" I asked, absolutely dumbfounded. "He doesn't even know me!"

"Oh, he knows you, all right," said Mayhew. And he proceeded to outline the offer Mr. Hughes was making me: a contract with RKO Studios, movie roles, free acting and singing lessons, an oceanside cabana to live in, and a generous weekly allowance. All I had to do was leave the man I was shacked up with (a drummer making $30 a week) and become the concubine of Howard Hughes (a billionaire industrialist with incredible clout in Hollywood), and it would all be mine.

I turned it down. I was in love with Steve. Of course, I would later regret choosing love over a billionaire's money—but only until the facts started coming out about how totally *weird* Howard Hughes really was.

It turns out that the playboy industrialist maintained an entire harem—and I would have just been one of the girls. He was also suffering from syphilitic dementia, one of the reasons he had an obsessive-compulsive fanaticism about washing himself and avoiding germs. Long before he died in 1976 of kidney failure, weighing only 93 pounds, with his teeth rattling in their sockets, he apparently had developed a slippery grip on reality.

By the 1950s, Hughes had a system for finding and procuring women for his enjoyment. He'd find girls in magazines or movies, and he'd simply tell his staff, "Find her for me." His private security force investigated the women, approached them, made an offer, and procured them. They would be put up in an apartment, hotel, or beach house owned by the Hughes corporation. Sometimes, when a girl wanted to get away from Mr. Hughes, she couldn't. He and his security force wouldn't let her leave until *he* was ready for her to leave. His security agents maintained very thorough background and surveillance files on all the women Hughes was interested in. That's why Hughes already knew so much about me the day Mayhew stopped me on the street.

I was approached and propositioned several times by Howard Hughes' pimps over a period of about a year. But I always said no.

It was around this time that Universal Studios offered to sign me as a contract player. They told me they were going to build my image as a blond comedic actress.

Here I am as the Chicken of the Sea mermaid— stuffed into a suit with a fishtail at the bottom and no legs! Even though "Bergen and McCarthy" was radio, we did the show on a stage before a large studio audience, so the visual part of the show was still important. It was important that the mermaid who sang the tuna jingle look the part. Because I couldn't walk in that costume, stagehands had to pick me up and carry me out onstage. I would sing the commercial, then they'd pick me up and carry me off again as I waved my wand to the audience.

"You'll be the next Judy Holliday," they said, referring to the popular star of *Born Yesterday* and *The Solid Gold Cadillac*. Being under contract meant you practically lived at the studio and became studio property. You had to be seen with other actors they paired you with for the sake of the studio publicity mill. That was all fine with me, as long as it led toward stardom.

I auditioned for a part in Phil Silvers' television show, "Sergeant Bilko," and the producers liked what they saw. Steve and I were living together at the time, but not married. So I went home to Steve and told him that Universal wanted to put me under contract. I was thrilled, I was ecstatic—and I thought he would be too. I was wrong.

"Baby," he said, "you've got a choice to make. You can have a career—or you can have me. What'll it be?"

Until that moment, I had never truly understood his attitude toward women, toward me, toward my career. I had seen him as this very cool, with-it musician, with a jazzman's relaxed attitude toward life. But I suddenly discovered that a lot of his thinking came straight from the old country, where a man was expected to keep his wife barefoot, pregnant, and on all fours, scrubbing the linoleum. That wasn't the Jewish side of him talking, but the Arab side.

Stupid me. I loved the guy. I chose Steve over my career. I told Universal thanks, but no thanks.

It killed me inside to say that. I didn't want to stay home and scrub floors for my husband. I wanted to perform, I wanted to be a star, and it was the only thing I ever wanted from the time I was very young. It was my dream to be up there, on the screen, and I was completely torn between my ambition for stardom and my love for this man. I chose the man and let the career go, and I never forgave him for that. But in reality, I never forgave myself for that—because it was truly my own choice.

That was the beginning of my resentment toward Steve. But I stuffed those feelings because I really did love him, and I wanted to be a good Jewish wife for him.

In California, I began training for my conversion to Judaism. I went to *schul*, I never missed a class, I read all the books on Jewish history and tradition, and I renounced my Christian upbringing. I took a Hebrew name, Ruth (which I added to my list of AKAs—Mary Ann, Grace Elaine Whitney, Lee Whitney, and so on). The rabbi told my husband he was getting a real winner, and that I was going to be a good Jewish girl—and the rabbi was right. Becoming Jewish was not a casual formality I went through just so I could marry a Jewish man. I converted with all my heart, and have not considered myself a Gentile since. Even after a series of spiritual awakenings, I remain Jewish to the bone.

One of the rites I underwent as part of my conversion to Judaism was the *mikvah*, a ritual bathing and cleansing ceremony. The *mikvah* is actually the first form of baptism ever performed, and Orthodox Jewish women are expected to undergo this ritual cleansing after every menstrual period, before marital relations can be resumed.

As is the custom, I had several handmaidens helping me prepare for the *mikvah*. They removed all my nail polish, washed my hair, and scrubbed my skin with a loofa to symbolically remove all the sin and contamination from me. Then they had me step into a pool of water, about four feet deep. I was in the pool with the rabbi's daughter, who was also undergoing the *mikvah*, and we are both totally nude. Meanwhile, the rabbi was standing at the edge of the pool with his back to us, reading the Scripture. There's a whole ritual associated with the Scripture reading, in which the

In 1953, I auditioned for a TV Guide *cover photo, along with Angie Dickenson and a number of other actresses. It was a bathing suit shot, and they only picked actresses with one-piece suits (I only owned bikinis). The girls who got the job would appear on the cover with Jimmy Durante and Groucho Marx. Though I didn't get the modeling job, I was a big hit with Jimmy and Groucho, who insisted on having their picture taken with me. Later that year, I appeared on Groucho's quiz show, "You Bet Your Life."*

rabbi holds the book out before him and stands with his feet together, *dovening**— rocking back and forth—as he reads.

I looked at the rabbi, and I was shocked to see that he kept peeking over his shoulder at us as he was reading. Here were his daughter and I, naked in the water, and he was looking at us while he was reading the Scripture! I put my head under the water, as the ritual requires, but the rabbi's daughter wouldn't do it. She was afraid of the water. But I knew we couldn't get out of the pool until she had completed the *mikvah*. I kept saying, "Dunk your head under!" but she kept shaking her head no. "Here," I said, "do it like this." And I went under to show her how it's done, but she still wouldn't dunk.

Finally I just got so mad at her! I was getting cold, the rabbi was peeking at me, and I wanted out of that water. So I said, "Listen, sister, I want to get out of here, so you're going to dunk!" And I took her head and I pushed it way down under the water. As she came up sputtering, I looked up at the rabbi, and I saw a big smile on his face. He was delighted that I had dunked her. He went right back to reading the Scripture and he never peeked again. Then I realized that he wasn't peeking at me—he just wanted to make sure his daughter went all the way under the water. Once I dunked her, he was happy.

At last, I was really Jewish. Now we could get married. Only one problem: Steve wouldn't marry me. He was happy just shacking up. We lived that way for three years— and I was miserable. I wanted to be legit.

---

* *Doven* is pronounced "dah-ven." When I converted to Judaism, I learned to *doven* as I prayed, and to this day I *doven* when I say the Lord's Prayer.

Finally, I went to counseling and asked the therapist what I could do to get Steve to marry me. She said, "As long as the two of you are shacking up, he gets everything he wants with no obligation, no commitment. He's not going to marry you as long as you keep giving him something for nothing. You've got to give him an ultimatum."

So I went home and told Steve, "Either you marry me or I'm leaving."

It didn't take long. In 1953, we were married by a justice of the peace in Santa Monica. His family wouldn't hear of Steve having only a civil ceremony, so we went back to New York to have a big Jewish wedding. His family thought I was a movie star, even though at that time I had never even been on a movie set. The wedding was a huge production. Because we had so many friends in the music business, we had a lavish orchestra. They played a jazz tune, "Lullaby of Birdland," sweet and slow, as I came down the aisle. I wore a gown I had made myself out of blue-beaded taffeta. I sewed all the beads on myself.

I didn't invite my parents to the wedding. In fact, I didn't even tell them I was getting married. I figured, *I'm Jewish now. I don't want my Christian parents at my Jewish wedding.*

My mother and father found out about my marriage in about the worst way imaginable—by watching television. I was a contestant on the Groucho Marx quiz show, "You Bet Your Life."* My parents didn't even know I was going to be on the show. They just happened to tune in and there I was. Groucho's sidekick and announcer, George Fenneman, brought me out and introduced me, "Groucho, meet Lee Whitney." And while I was chatting with Groucho, I mentioned the fact that I had just gotten married.

I was so self-centered at that time, I didn't even think of how my parents would feel if they heard about my marriage that way, but I know now that it absolutely crushed them. I cheated my dad out of walking his only daughter down the aisle. It broke his heart, and my mother's too, but I never got in touch with their pain until years later, when I got sober.

The day after my wedding in 1953, I started rehearsals for another George Abbott musical on Broadway, *The Pajama Game*, choreographed by Bob Fosse. I understudied

---

*You may remember how "You Bet Your Life" worked. At the beginning of each show, before the contestants came out, a duck would come down from the ceiling with the secret word written on a card. Then, as the contestants came out on stage, Groucho would tell them, "Say the secret word and win a hundred dollars." He would sit behind his desk, puff on his cigar, and chat with the contestants. If a contestant happened to say the secret word, a trumpet fanfare would sound and the duck would come down with the money. The producer slipped the secret word to me before the show, so I won a bunch of money.

I became pregnant soon after our wedding, but during the road trip for *The Pajama Game*, I miscarried. I was in the Ford Hospital in Detroit, and my mother and dad were with me when I lost the baby.

the role of Babe, played by one of my idols, Janis Paige. She taught me a lot about acting, as did the actress who took over the role in the touring company, Fran Warren.

I was really happy. I was finally legit with Steve. I had this wonderful job on Broadway. Later, Steve and I toured with the national company. We did *The Pajama Game* for three or four years, saved $12,000, and in 1956, put it all down on a $21,500 house in Sherman Oaks, California.

I continued to tour with *The Pajama Game*—and I got pregnant again. Several times with that pregnancy, I developed severe bleeding and had to be rushed to the hospital. For weeks, I wondered if I was going to have this child or not. One night, I was walking across the stage during a performance in Toledo when the baby suddenly kicked—and boy, did I feel it! I looked down and I could see his foot pushing a little bulge in the belly of my costume, a tight one-piece bathing suit. After that performance, I went back home and laid down on the bed, just hugging my belly and experiencing the joy of knowing my baby was alive and kicking inside me. A woman who had miscarried several times once told me that after you feel that first kick, you know the child's going to be okay.

Once I felt my baby kicking, I immediately quit the production and went home to L.A. I didn't want to take any chances of hurting this child. He was born in 1957 and we named him Scott. Holding him in my arms for the first time was the most incredible experience. He was the first blood relative I ever knew. Finally, I was biologically connected to another human being, my firstborn son.

After Scott was born, I had another miscarriage. That got me started on a health food kick. I was bound and determined that my next baby would be healthy, and sure enough, my secondborn, Jonathan, came out like a bull, the most healthy child you ever saw in your life.

My parents moved from Detroit to L.A. the same year Scott was born. They wanted to be close to their only daughter and their first grandchild. As my kids were growing up, we would spend Christmas with my parents, then observe Chanukah at our own house. So my kids grew up experiencing both Gentile-Christian traditions and Jewish traditions.

I spent the next few years on the stage in both New York and L.A. On Broadway, I worked with Lotte Lenya, understudying the role of Lucy Brown in the outrageous, subversive Bertold Brecht-Kurt Weill musical, *Three Penny Opera*, which introduced the song "Mack the Knife." Lotte trained me for the L.A. premiere, which I opened. She told me she was thrilled with my interpretation of "The Barber Song." It was a marvelously energetic production, and I got to work with stars like Joel Grey, Tige Andrews and Estelle Parsons—and I got terrific reviews. Of all the roles I've ever played, my favorite was Lucy Brown in *Three Penny Opera*.

I went back to New York and understudied in *Gentlemen Prefer Blondes*, but never went on the stage in that show. While I was waiting in the wings, my agent called and said, "Lee, get back to L.A. I got you an audition for a new TV series called 'Peter Gunn.'" So I flew back to L.A. I just knew I was going to be a TV star, maybe even a movie star.

But like they say, life is what happens to you when you're making other plans.

Going Hollywood

I n 1957, I came to Hollywood to audition for Blake Edwards' TV crimestopper show, "Peter Gunn." Sexy hunk Craig Stevens was cast in the role of Gunn, the cool, jazz-loving private eye. I was angling for the female lead, Gunn's blond assistant, Edie Hart. That role went to Lola Albright, and she deserved it—she brought a sophisticated Lauren Bacall-like quality to the part. Even though I had been on the stage in New York and on tour, most of my experience was understudy experience. I would have given anything for that part, and it hurt me terribly not to get it, but I was just too young and green.

After the audition, I was talking with one of the guys in the crew, telling him how disappointed I was that I didn't get the part. He said, "Well, Billy Wilder is casting a wonderful movie across the street. It's called *Some Like It Hot*. Why don't you see if you can get a part in that?"

"Thanks!" I said, and I whirled around and hustled myself to Goldwyn Studios across the street. I talked my way past the front gate, and found the stage where Billy Wilder was holding auditions. When I walked in, I saw Billy standing in front of a big platform, like a bandstand. On the platform were three rows of girls—the all-girl band that would perform behind Marilyn Monroe in the now-classic picture. My heart sank. I was too late—Billy had already cast the whole band.

But just as I was about to turn and walk out, I saw a familiar face—Matty Melnick, Billy Wilder's musical director. Our paths had crossed numerous times over the past few years because I was a singer with a number of bands, and Matty was in the music business. Matty motioned me over and took me to meet the director. "Billy," he said, "I think this young lady ought to be in the picture."

Billy looked at me appraisingly and smiled. "All right," he said. "Put her up in the trumpet section. Let's see how she looks with the other girls."

So Matty found a place for me up on the bandstand with the other girls. Billy looked me over and approved. "But," he said to me, "we already have enough girls without you, Miss Whitney. You will be on hand as a backup. If one of the other girls can't go on, you'll be in the picture. If not, well—" He spread his hands in a gesture that meant, *I'm not promising anything.*

I left the studio feeling I had not been very successful—I had washed out in my "Peter Gunn" audition, and on *Some Like It Hot*, I was second choice again. But the next day, the phone rang, and I got the news that another girl had backed out.

I couldn't believe it! I got the part! I was going to be in a movie—a *big* movie, directed by Hollywood legend Billy Wilder.

Sweet Sue's band from Some Like It Hot. *I'm in the back, the second trumpet player from the left.*

Some Like It Hot is Billy's spoof-tribute to gangster films, with generous dollops of gender-reversal and sex comedy. The story opens with a pair of unemployed musicians (Tony Curtis and Jack Lemmon) who accidentally witness the St. Valentine's Day Massacre in 1929 Chicago. Chased by the mob, they escape by dressing as women and joining Sweet Sue's All-Girl Band, which is taking the train to a hotel gig in Florida. Both Tony and Jack fall head over garter-belts for the band's singer, Sugar Kane (Marilyn Monroe).

The plot thickens as Tony and Jack discover that Sugar is out to snare Florida millionaire Osgood E. Fielding III (Joe E. Brown) into marriage. Changing disguises, Tony does a Cary Grant impression and poses as the playboy heir to the Shell Oil fortune. He tries to woo Sugar without her finding out that he is also the "girl" in the band she knows as "Josephine." The ultimate plot complication comes, however, when Jack and Tony discover that the mob—the same killers who have been trying to track them down—have arrived at the Florida hotel for a gangland convention. It's an incredibly fast-paced, funny movie, full of amazingly inventive plot twists and turns.

Billy named my character in the picture "Rosella," after his secretary. Before we began shooting, the hairdresser dyed my hair slightly darker than my natural platinum shade. They did this to all the girls in the band because Marilyn would not allow anyone else in the picture to be as blond as she. We were to look good—but not *too* good, and certainly not as good as the star.

We spent four days crowded into this upper berth, shooting a scene for Some Like It Hot. *Jack Lemmon is in the center of the picture, and none of us girls could keep our hands off him! Marilyn is second from the right, and I'm in the foreground on the far left.*

We spent five months shooting at the Goldwyn studio, then we moved to the location site at the Del Coronado, a beachfront hotel in San Diego that looked very Floridian. When we checked into the hotel before filming, I couldn't believe where we were—it was the most beautiful place I had ever seen. On top of that, it was my first appearance in a movie—and I was thrilled to be a part of a big production with actors and filmmakers I admired so much.

The entire experience was like one big party. The Goldwyn studio had great parties every Friday and sometimes at lunch. Then, on location, we partied at the Del Coronado. The Del was a great hotel for parties, and there was music and dancing and laughter going on all the time. Jack Lemmon, Tony Curtis and the girls in the band were always in the hotel bar after shooting, sitting back, laughing and telling stories. Jack was so young and funny, and all of us were very smitten with his wit and his jaunty good looks. He is a great jazz pianist, and when he was not learning lines or in front of the camera, you could usually find him at the piano in the bar. And Tony's wife, actress Janet Leigh, would often be there at the parties with him—she was pregnant at the time with their daughter, Jamie Lee.

The exteriors on the train were shot at Metro, using a train sitting on rails on the lot (for example, that's where Marilyn Monroe did her sizzling song-and-dance, "Running Wild"). The interior shots on the train, such as the upper berth scene, were shot on a stage at Goldwyn. It took four days to shoot the scene with Jack Lemmon (in drag), me, and the other girls in the band all crowded into one upper berth. It was a hysterically funny scene. During the last day of the shoot, where we all tumble out of the berth and onto the floor of the sleeping car, Billy brought a big platter of martinis onto the set and passed them out to the girls. I'm not sure if he wanted to lubricate our performances, or simply make us rubber-limbed during the fall so we wouldn't hurt ourselves. In any case, Billy got the scene the way he wanted and no one got hurt.

Watching that movie being made at Goldwyn and Metro was a real education for me. I "audited" the whole experience like a student auditing a class. I watched what everybody did—the actors, director, choreographer, cinematographer, cameramen, sound men, boom operators, grips, everyone. I talked to people, I kept my eyes and ears open, I was on the set every moment. A lot of the learning experience was fun, too—luxuriating in the beautiful surroundings, the beach, the yacht, the beautiful clothes; watching Jack and Tony walking around in women's clothing; being continually awed by the on-screen chemistry between Tony and Marilyn—and watching the chemistry dissolve into off-screen loathing as soon as Billy yelled "Cut!" Tony later said that his love scenes with Marilyn were "like kissing Hitler."

One thing I'll always remember about Jack Lemmon is the magic. Before doing a scene, Jack would become very introverted, and he'd withdraw deeply into his character. You didn't dare talk to him or do anything around him that might disturb his concentration. Once the director and the set were ready for him, Jack would be ready, too—and you'd know he was ready because his face would suddenly break into a tremendous grin, and he'd say, "Magic time!" And *bam!* He'd be in character, just like that. It was fascinating to watch Jack Lemmon psyche himself up for a part—and to see the magical transformation in him when he announced it was "magic time!"

Marilyn Monroe had a reputation for being difficult, and there were definitely times she drove Billy Wilder nuts. She could be demanding and pouty, and she was chronically late to the set. She was not happy that Billy chose to shoot the film in black and white—a creative decision to keep Jack and Tony from looking too garish in women's makeup and lipstick. I watched how Billy, in an effort to avoid a confrontation with his temperamental star, looked for creative ways to get her best performances on film. When she had trouble with lines, Billy would write them on pieces of paper and tape them to chairs or walls or inside dresser drawers to prompt her as she moved through the scene.

That's not to say Marilyn was incompetent—I was absolutely in awe of her. She was like a big, soft, creamy marshmallow, with clouds of gorgeous blond hair and a voice like mist on roses. The dizzy blond act was just that, an act. She was very smart and very talented, and possessed an unmatched, totally natural capacity for blending sexiness with comedic ability. You really see it in the songs she did in *Some Like It Hot*—"I'm Through with Love" (which, like the title theme, "Stairway to the Stars," was written by Matty Melnick), "I Wanna Be Loved By You," and "Running Wild."

Jack Cole was the choreographer on the film—Jack is one of my favorite people. I watched him choreograph Marilyn in those wonderful songs, and the way he did it was amazing. He would stand in front of Marilyn, out of camera range, and they would start the music, and he would do the dance routine. As he danced, she would watch him and mirror all his movements. He would even do all the facial expressions, the eyes, the lips, every shake of the tushie, every affectation and gesture of her face and body. In effect, Jack Cole did his impression of Marilyn Monroe, and Marilyn mimicked his impression—so that she was doing her impression of Jack's impression of her! So a lot of what they got on film is Marilyn—but in a real way, a lot of it is also Jack Cole.

Marilyn drank on the set—not to the point of getting drunk, but just to get loose. She was high-strung, and felt she couldn't feel relaxed enough to perform without a drink. At the time, I didn't realize how much emotional pain she carried around with her all the time, but now that I'm sober, it's obvious to me. After all, she was so much like me in many ways—I feel that we're sisters in our shared disease. I believe that Marilyn was probably an alcoholic, just like me.

Born in 1926, Marilyn grew up without a father. Not until she was 16 years old, when she went to get a marriage license, did she discover that she was born illegitimate. No wonder she spent her entire life hungering for the love and acceptance of men. Marilyn's early memories include visiting her mother in a mental institution. Marilyn lived in various foster homes and an orphanage, and suffered sexual abuse as a child. She went through years of being signed, then rejected and released, by various movie studios, including Fox and Columbia. She was married and divorced several times, and attempted suicide several times. Like me, she experienced a great deal of rejection and soul-searching over who she was, where she came from, and where she really belonged. She even converted to Judaism to marry playwright Arthur Miller, just as I did when I married Steve.

Near the end of *Some Like It Hot*, there is a scene where Marilyn, as Sugar Kane, stands on the boat dock and gives "Josephine" (Tony Curtis) a goodbye kiss. That kiss causes her to realize that "Josephine" is actually the man she loves. In the next instant, Tony and Jack (both in drag) take off running down the boat dock and jump into the speedboat of millionaire Osgood (Joe E. Brown), still running from the mob. Marilyn chases after them because she doesn't want to lose the man she loves. It's a funny scene, and one of the most crucial scenes in the movie—but it was a catastrophic scene for poor Marilyn.

At the time she was shooting the movie, Marilyn Monroe was pregnant (she was about two years into her marriage to Arthur Miller). Billy Wilder had her do endless retakes, running down the dock in spike heels after Tony Curtis. She tried to tell Billy that she couldn't do any more takes, but in the end, she did them. And it was soon after that, while the movie was still being shot, that she went into the hospital and had a miscarriage. She desperately wanted that baby, and she lost it. I really believe that the baby was Marilyn's last hope of finding someone to love, someone who would love her with a simple, childlike love.

Her marriage only lasted two or three years after that. When Arthur Miller left her, he said he couldn't live with her anymore because she was so self-obsessed, so demanding. When she was around him, he couldn't work, he practically couldn't breathe. I know what he meant, because I did the same thing to the men in my life. That's what alcoholics do. We don't have relationships, we take hostages. We're so involved with ourselves, so needy and demanding of attention, that no one can live with us.

She lost her baby in 1958, lost her marriage to Arthur Miller in 1961, had a nervous breakdown and went into a psychiatric hospital that same year. Then in 1962 she started filming a movie called (prophetically) *Something's Got to Give*. She was so incapable of functioning, due to alcohol and depression, that she was fired by the studio in July. The very next month, August 1962, she was found dead of an overdose of barbiturates and alcohol.

That was the end of the *real* Marilyn Monroe and the beginning of the myth. Most people would rather hear about the myth than the reality. I don't claim to know the real Marilyn Monroe anymore than anyone else does. But I do think I have some acquaintance with her day-to-day reality—the reality of being a pain-wracked, alcoholic woman, hungry for attention, desperate for a place of belonging, desperate for love. There's nothing glamorous or attractive about the way she lived and died. It was the most sickening, tragic waste anyone can imagine.

There has probably been a score or more books published about her life and death, each new book more sensational and off-the-mark than the one before. There have been speculations that she was murdered to keep her quiet because of her affairs with John and Bobby Kennedy. But I think the obvious explanation is the true one: Marilyn was in the grip of this disease that I know so well, and she died because she couldn't stand living with it any longer—not just the drinking, but the depression, the insecurity, the hunger for love, the self-pity, the bitterness, the enormous hole in her gut with the wind blowing through. She was my sister in the disease, and there was nothing I could have done to help her, because I was just as deep in my disease as she was in hers.

I made many good friends while filming *Some Like It Hot*. I still see Jack Lemmon and Tony Curtis from time to time.

One time, a couple years after *Some Like It Hot*, I ran into Tony Curtis and he told me that he and Janet had just bought a house in Malibu, right on the beach, for $30,000. He told me that Steve and I should buy there too. I told him that Steve and I could never afford such an expensive house. Shows you what kind of crystal ball I had. One of those $30,000 houses would sell today for several million.

One of my best friends from the movie was Marian Collier, another girl from Sweet Sue's band. She was also my roommate at the Del. Marian was married at the time to Dave Barber, Peggy Lee's former husband and accompanist. She later married E. Jack Neumann, one of the biggest names in the television industry, and the creator of many top shows. Marian is the one who brings all the girls from the band together at the Marilyn Monroe events, such as the big *Some Like It Hot* reunion parties or the issuing of the Marilyn Monroe stamp. She makes sure that all of us girls from Sweet Sue's All-Girl Band keep in touch and get together now and then. I love her dearly.

I also was close to Helen Perry, a tall, blond model who was the bass player in Sweet Sue's band—and the fact is, she could really play the bass. Helen matured gracefully over the years, and still models to this day. Another good friend from the band was Joan Fields, who was a former Miss New York. She and I sometimes got together, and my two boys would go swimming with her three daughters.

Another close friend of mine in the band was Beverly Wills, the daughter of actress Joan Davis (Joan starred with Jim Backus in an early '50s TV sitcom, "I Married Joan"). Beverly and I had a lot of fun together during *Some Like It Hot*—but after a few weeks of shooting, we knew our scenes were almost finished and our fun was about to come to an end. All the other girls in the band, like Marian, were looking forward to the end of filming—they wanted to get home to their families as soon as possible. But Beverly and I, the true alcoholics in the group, wanted to keep the party going right to the bitter end.

I felt a big twinge of guilt, of course, leaving my baby at home while I went to San Diego to shoot a movie (my second baby would be born the following year). I loved my baby, but I hated the domestic role—the diapers and housework and drudgery. I craved excitement and glamour.

While I felt guilty about leaving my son at home, I was fearful about going home to my Syrian Jewish husband. Steve had never wanted me to work in *Some Like It Hot*—though he didn't seem to mind depositing my paycheck in his bank account. I sought the role in part as an act of rebellion against him for his always wanting to keep me barefoot and chained to the bedpost. I'm not saying the problems in my marriage were all Steve's fault. I wanted to be married, but without any boundaries. I wanted the security of marriage without any of the responsibilities. My thinking was that of a self-centered, immature adolescent: "Why do I have to be home at night? Why can't I go out and play?"

After Billy Wilder finished shooting all the scenes involving Sweet Sue's All-Girl Band, he put all us girls on a bus and sent us back to L.A. No more Del Coronado, no more parties, no more fun. As Beverly and I were on the bus headed back, we talked it over and decided we weren't going home. We yelled at the bus driver, "Stop the bus! Stop the bus!" The brakes squealed and the bus ground to a halt. The driver was really annoyed with us. We didn't care. We made the driver get out and take our suitcases off the bus, then we stood there at the side of the road, waving and laughing as the rest of the girls roared off for L.A. We were about 10 miles north of San Diego, in the middle of nowhere, but we just thought it was a lark.

We hitched a ride back to the Del Coronado. I had struck up a pretty good friendship with Billy Wilder, and he never seemed to disapprove of our antics. When he saw Beverly and me walk back into the Del, he was glad to see us.

"Billy!" I called, rushing up to him. "We just couldn't bear to go back home. Could you put us up here at the Del a little while longer?"

"I can't get you a room here," he said, "but why don't you girls check into the motel across the street? You can stay there cheap—then you can come here and eat with the crew for free."

"Billy," I said, "you're terrific!"

So that's what we did for the next few days. Pretty soon, however, the wanderlust got to us, so Beverly and I decided to go down to Mexico and check out the action. I found out that Beverly was a championship ping-pong player—an absolute champ at the game. "You know," she said, "over in Tijuana, there are lots of bars with ping-pong tables and guys with money in their pockets. What do you say we go down there and get some of that money? I'll win the games, you collect our winnings, it'll be fun!"

So we went to Mexico. I would charm and cajole the men into laying down bets against Beverly, and she would play these guys and win every time. I don't know what we would have had to do if she lost. Fortunately, she never lost—she was sensational! We were down there for three or four days, and we never lacked money or booze. We did a lot of drinking in Tijuana—mostly Black Russians—then we took the bus back to the Del.

We were like two teenagers on the loose. We were escaping from our family responsibilities, and from our guilt over abandoning our families. We ran around as if we were single, with no cares, no diapers, no laundry, no one to answer to. We were out of control, and the more out of control we got, the more fun we had. But deep down, we both knew a day of reckoning was coming. When you drink, there's no guilt, no remorse, no sense of responsibility. Only when the drinking stops do you start to feel sorry and anxious about the things you've been doing. So Beverly and I tried to keep drinking to ward off those bad feelings.

There was a part of me that was very moral, that knew I was doing wrong even while I was out having fun. I drank to deaden the morality and self-hate. When I was drinking and having fun, I did immoral things and I hated myself for it. That was the way I lived my life.

Fact is, that's the way all alcoholics live. You wake up in the morning, and you remember what you did the night before, and the guilt sets in. Or you wake up in the motel room and you think, *My gosh, what am I doing here? Why aren't I home? I don't even remember how I got here!* And you just feel awful. You feel you are a terrible, bad person. And then you reach for another drink to make those feelings go away.

When we finally had enough fun and partying, Beverly and I both went home to L.A., sneaked back into our houses, weathered the inevitable storms with our husbands, and resumed our wifely, motherly duties. Beverly and I remained close friends after the picture, and I often visited with her. After my second son was born, I would take my boys over to play with her boys. We talked about all the fun we had in Tijuana, and we planned to do it again sometime. We never got the chance.

One morning, my phone rang. It was Matty Melnick. "Grace," he said, "Beverly Wills is dead."

I couldn't believe it. "What happened?" I asked.

"Apparently she'd been drinking and smoking," Matty said. "I guess she fell asleep, and the cigarette started a fire. She and her two kids were burned to death."

I cultivated a friendship with Billy Wilder—not only because he could put me in more films, introduce me to people, and help my career (all of which he did), but because I liked and admired him. I knew I could learn a lot from the man who had been involved with such screen classics as *Ball of Fire, Hold Back the Dawn, The Lost Weekend, Sunset Boulevard, Double Indemnity* and *The Seven Year Itch*. I followed him around and asked if I could watch him direct, and he was always very gracious and obliging. I was serious about my career, and I wanted to become Billy's understudy. Not only was this my first time in a movie, it was the first time I ever saw a movie being made. I was fascinated. I sat in the wings, I sat behind the camera, I sat behind Billy's chair. I was always hanging around the set, trying to soak up every drop of filmmaking knowledge I could absorb.

For years afterward, Billy was a generous friend to me, and he opened many doors for my career. I learned a lot from him about cinema, music, the arts—he was a great mentor and teacher.

One of my fondest memories of my friendship with Billy came during the filming of *Some Like It Hot*. Billy and his co-writer, I.A.L. "Izzy" Diamond, were continually working on the script after each day's shooting, trying to polish it up and make it a little better. Late afternoon, the day before the closing scene was to be shot, Billy's secretary, Rosella, let me into his studio office. Billy and Izzy were both in the office— Izzy sitting in his big, high-backed executive chair, chain-smoking, while Billy paced back and forth, also puffing away. The air was dense and blue with smoke. Billy looked up at me, his brow furrowed, as I walked into the office, and in his thick German-Jewish accent, he said, "Lee, you have to sit here a moment. We are in total concentration."

So I sat down and listened while Izzy and Billy alternated between contemplative silence and intense but amicable arguing back and forth. They were just not satisfied with the ending in the shooting script, but they couldn't come up with anything better. They needed a big laugh-line with which to close the picture.

In the final scene, as Marilyn, Tony, Jack and Joe E. Brown (as the millionaire Osgood) make their getaway in Osgood's speedboat, Jack (posing as "Daphne") tries to figure some way out of having to marry this love-sick millionaire who thinks "Daphne" is a woman. Izzy had a line he liked, which he had planned to use elsewhere in the picture, but Billy wasn't sure if the line had enough zing for a big finish. As they continued arguing back and forth, even Izzy was having his doubts. Finally, they decided that they were just too tired and too close to the matter to think objectively, so Izzy said, "Billy, I just don't know if the line works or not. Even if it's only so-so, Joe E. Brown's delivery will save it."

"I guess so," said Billy, shrugging wearily. "Maybe we can think of something better on the set."

So they kept the line that Izzy wrote, and that line—just three words long— became one of the most famous taglines in movie history. The speedboat scene was actually shot on a Goldwyn soundstage with a rear-screen projection image of the ocean in the background. Here's how the scene played out:

> "DAPHNE"
> (Jack Lemmon in drag, speaking falsetto)
> Osgood, I'm gonna level with you.
> We can't get married at all.
>
> OSGOOD
> (Joe E. Brown)
> Why not?
>
> "DAPHNE"
> Well, in the first place, I'm not a natural blond.
>
> OSGOOD
> Doesn't matter.
>
> "DAPHNE"
> I smoke. I smoke all the time.
>
> OSGOOD
> I don't care.
>
> "DAPHNE"
> Well, I have a terrible past. For three years now,
> I've been living with a saxophone player.
>
> OSGOOD
> I forgive you.
>
> "DAPHNE"
> I can never have children.
>
> OSGOOD
> We can adopt some.
>
> "DAPHNE"
> (rips off his wig, lowers his voice,
> revealing that he is a man)
> You don't understand, Osgood! I'm a man!
>
> OSGOOD
> (completely unperturbed)
> Well, nobody's perfect.

It was the perfect ending to a perfectly funny movie—and I feel so privileged to have been there while Billy and Izzy hammered out the ending to a brilliant screen treasure. *Some Like It Hot* was nominated for six Oscars, including best director, best actor (for Jack Lemmon—though he was edged out by Charleton Heston in *Ben-Hur*), and best screenplay. Jack Lemmon, Tony Curtis, Marilyn Monroe—everyone in that movie turned in career performances, and I was lucky to see it and be a part of it.

I'll never forget the wrap party for *Some Like It Hot*. Matty Melnick, the musical director, asked me to get up and sing his song, "Goody Goody," while Jack Lemmon played piano with a live band. Everyone was at the wrap party except Marilyn—she was deliberately *un*invited because she had been so difficult. Making that picture had been one of the most enjoyable experiences of my life—but at the end of the wrap party, I knew it was finally, truly over. It was time to go home and be a housewife again.

I had small parts in a number of films in the late '50s, early '60s—often without credit. I was in Frank Capra's *Pocketful of Miracles* with Bette Davis and Ann-Margret (her first film), and in *The Naked and the Dead* with Cliff Robertson and Raymond Massey. I was very career-conscious, and whenever the director asked if anyone wanted a line, I never hesitated, I was right there. I had a small part in *Critic's Choice*, and I remember the advice one of the actresses in that film gave me. She was an alcoholic, and she told me, "If you wear a little pill hat and white gloves, you can drink all you want and no one will ever think you're a lush." That was the Jackie Kennedy era, the white gloves and pill hat era. The woman who gave me that advice eventually died of alcoholism.

During that time, I also appeared on a lot of TV shows—probably 80 to 100 shows in all. I did a stint as a Vanna-type adornment to a popular daytime show called "Queen for a Day," hosted by Jack Bailey. It wasn't exactly a game show, although there were prizes given out. My job was to escort the contestants out on stage, and these women would tell their stories. The woman with the most pitiful story would score highest on the applause meter, wear a crown and a robe, get a bunch of prizes, and be "Queen" for a day.

I did a lot of comedy in those days too—mostly gag comedy on live TV, three cameras and a live audience, working with stars like Red Skelton, Jimmy Durante and Ernie Kovacs. I was usually the showgirl, the sexy secretary, the dizzy blond—a lot of early TV comedy was little more than a revival of burlesque.

When I mention live TV, a lot of people ask, "Well, weren't you petrified? What if you made a mistake, forgot your lines, fell into a camera? Isn't it scary when you know you can't do a retake?" But I didn't find it scary. I *loved* it! To me, there was nothing more exciting than live TV. I'm a stage performer, I started out in musical comedy—*Three Penny Opera, Gentlemen Prefer Blondes, Pajama Game, Top Banana*. I loved going out in front of an audience and showing what I could do. Live TV just meant that instead of a theater full of people, I was reaching *millions*, coast to coast!

There's nothing more exciting to me than to jump on stage and turn on a live audience. Many other shows I did, however, were shot in a studio without an audience. But even when it's three cameras and no audience, you can tell when you are turning on the people who handle the cameras and lights, the hands and gaffers, the director and the other actors. When you sing or perform a comedy sketch, you can tell when it's working and people are loving you. All that wonderful electricity flows back to you, and it's a beautiful, warm feeling. I love that.

To this day, I love to experience that feeling when I'm on stage at *Trek* conventions or doing TV interviews. It's a tremendous high, it's an adrenaline rush. For many performers, it's the only time they truly feel they are alive.

You don't get that same feeling on a closed set, where they shoot your performance in disjointed little bits and pieces. That's how shows like *Star Trek* are made, and it's a much more mechanical process. It's fun, but the electricity, the excitement of live TV isn't there. You're still performing, still creating a character—but you are also much more aware of the mechanics of where you have to stand, where you have to look, hitting your marks, looking out for your key lights (the lights that put the sparkle in your eyes). On a closed set, there is a lot of boredom during setups. When you're called to do your scene, you really have to reach for ways to put spontaneity and energy into your performance. A closed set is terribly restrictive compared with live TV—but when you do a good take, you get applause from the crew. And *that's* a tough audience. If the crew thinks you did a good job, you know the audience out in TV land is going to love you.

Maybe this sounds conceited, but it's true: They used to call me "One-Take Whitney." People in the business knew that if we had done our job and rehearsed the scene, and if the cameras, lights, and sound equipment were working right, then I would come through in a single take. The hectic scheduling of television doesn't always give you a chance to do your best work. When it's late in the day, everyone just wants to go home. Usually, it's your last shot, your big scene—and for some reason, they always save the close-ups till last, when you look your worst. But when you really pull it off, when everything clicks and you give one hell of a performance in the very first take, it's a great feeling to hear, "Cut! Perfect! That's a wrap!" And everybody applauds you because you let them go home 10 minutes early.

I appeared in some wonderful shows. I worked with Eddie Bracken, Mike Rhodes, and Dorothy Provine on "The Roaring Twenties," a fabulous show with beautiful old cars, period sets, gangsters and speakeasies. Because there was a writers' strike at the time, there were no new scripts being written. The producers were recycling old scripts and passing them from show to show. They took the storyline from an old "Dragnet" or whatever, changed the names of the characters and some of the other details, then shot it as an episode of "The Roaring Twenties."

I did two (or was it three?) episodes of "The Untouchables" with Robert Stack as G-Man Elliot Ness—probably the best cops-and-robbers show ever made. I was a gun moll, the girlfriend of gangster Dutch Schultz (played by Lawrence Dobkin, who would later direct the *Star Trek* episode, "Charlie X"). I was very impressed with Bob Stack—a complete professional. A lot of actors—the ones with the inflated egos—

will leave the set if they're not on camera. Not Bob Stack. He would stay and read the off-camera line. That's important, because even though he's not in the shot, even though that line could just as well be read by a script girl or the director, it helps you to stay in character and give a more convincing performance if you are really interacting with the other performer.

Equally caring and professional was Leslie Nielson, the star of "Michael Shayne." I worked with Leslie Nielsen back when nobody knew how funny he is—and Star Trek's Mr. Scott, Jimmy Doohan, actually used to room with Leslie in those days.

Robert Taylor showed that same level of caring and professionalism when I worked with him on the hard-boiled cop show, "The Detectives." On that show, I played a very bad girl named Susie Jackson, the moll of a gangster named Max (Antony Carbone). I help Max do away with a witness named Eckner who plans to testify against Max. The plan is to make it look like a hit-and-run accident, and to set up an alcoholic shoe salesman named Stanley (Joe Mantell) to take the fall. While Stanley is passed out drunk, Max runs Eckner down with Stanley's car—and when Stanley comes to, he can't remember a thing.

As Susie, I'm an accessory to murder, I try to bed every man in sight (including the cops who are investigating my role in Eckner's death), and I try to get a reformed alcoholic to start drinking again. Like I said, I play a very bad girl in this one.

Robert Taylor was perfect in the role of the tough, no-nonsense police captain, Matt Holbrook. In the scene where he interrogates me, I continually come on to him while he remains resolute and unswerving in his pursuit of justice:

> ME
> *(lounging in my slinky satin robe, flirting my brains out)*
> Say, you know somethin'? You're kinda cute.
>
> CAPTAIN HOLBROOK
> *(All business)*
> Why did you telephone Joseph Eckner the night
> before last at 2 o'clock in the morning?
>
> ME
> *(Rising, ignoring his question)*
> Would you like a drink?
>
> CAPTAIN HOLBROOK
> No, thank you. ...You do know Joseph Eckner.
>
> ME
> Vaguely. ...Tell you what. You busy for dinner?
> You can take me to Duffy's for a steak.
> I get kinda talkative after a good dinner....
> If you don't like crowded places, we could eat here.

CAPTAIN HOLBROOK
Some other time.

ME
Oh, you've got a date. Can't say I didn't try,
though, can you? ...You could question me some
other time, Captain. I'm available.

Ooh, was I ever available—but Captain Holbrook was made of stern stuff, strong moral fiber. Later, while under suspicion as an accessory to murder, I continued my pursuit of the police captain (Captain Holbrook, Captain Kirk—I guess I had a thing for captains!):

ME
You wanta hold me for anything?
Oops, that sounds kinda personal, doesn't it?
But you know what I mean.

CAPTAIN HOLBROOK
I know.

Minutes later, a police sergeant named Steve Nelson (Adam West) shows up to arrest me:

SGT. NELSON
(Stolid and all-business)
I have a warrant for your arrest, Miss Jackson.

ME
(Breezy and insouciant, still flirting like mad)
Oh, let's not be so formal. You don't need a warrant
for me, doll-boy. All you have to do is whistle.

Still dancing and swaying my hips, I let the sergeant escort me away (a few years later, Adam West would arrest me once again—this time in his guise as Gotham City's caped crusader, Batman). Also starring in that episode of "The Detectives" were series regulars Mark Goddard as Sgt. Chris Ballard and Tige Andrews (who I worked with in *Three Penny Opera* and who went on to guest star as a villainous Klingon on *Star Trek*).

While working with Danny Thomas on "Zane Grey Theater," I met his daughter, Marlo. She was just starting out as an actress—this was several years before her series, "That Girl"—and she paid me the ultimate compliment, telling me I was the actress she most wanted to be like. She told me I reminded her of Judy Holliday and Claire Trevor.

I played a frontier wife named Della in "Death Valley Days," one of the many TV westerns I appeared in during the 1950s.

The late '50s, early '60s were the heyday of the TV western—and I did a lot of them. I did an episode of "Death Valley Days" with Johnny Seven, as well as episodes of "Gunsmoke," "Bonanza," and "The Big Valley." I remember Barbara Stanwick, the star of "The Big Valley," as being very aloof—but then she had earned the right to be aloof. She was a bona fide movie queen, like Bette Davis or Joan Crawford. I had grown up watching her movies, and I could hardly believe I was appearing on the same screen with her. She was fabulous.

I loved working on "Bonanza," too. I was a cowgirl in that episode, and I had a terrific costume with a cinched-in waist. I don't remember much about the plot except that I was in peril. I loved doing westerns like "Bonanza," because you get to work on exterior sets with lots of dirt, you get to have your face all smeared up, you get to suffer and cry and get into all kinds of dramatic situations. Among the cast, I found Michael Landon (Little Joe) to be very kind and supportive, while Lorne Greene (Ben Cartwright) was very imperious and intimidating.

The exteriors for that episode of "Bonanza" were shot in Death Valley and it was terribly hot. On exterior shoots, they use big metallic reflectors to put as much sunlight on you as possible. I had a very hard time being exposed to so much bright sunlight, and the glare and heat from the reflectors made my eyes water. So there I was crying in a scene that didn't call for me to cry, and the director would get mad at me and yell "Stop crying!"—And then I *really* felt like crying! He finally told me, "If you're going to be an actress, you'll have to do something about that crying—maybe get some tinted contact lenses. To be in this business, you have to work outside in a lot of bright sunlight, so you'd better get used to it."

Left to right, this is me, Van Williams and Chad Everett in a scene from "Surfside Six." If Bill Shatner hadn't been cast in the role, I always thought that Van would have made a fabulous Captain Kirk. Inset: A promotional still of my friend Van and me from "Surfside Six."

I was in the pilot episode of "The Rifleman" with Chuck Connors. I appeared as a redhead (though the show was shot in black and white), and I did an Irish accent. I wanted the part so badly that I went all-out to prepare for it. I got phonograph records of Irish accents and I studied very hard so I would be convincing. Chuck was perfect in the role—so tall, strong and forceful—and he was married at that time to Camila

Devy, who later became a very close friend of mine. During the filming of the pilot, I knew the show was going to be a hit.

I did two episodes of "Bat Masterson"—and that was when my eyes were first opened to the vast difference between reality and movie fantasy. You're going to think I'm crazy, but I really did have a problem distinguishing between the two. I had grown up watching movies all my life, seeing men getting into fistfights, jumping off of balconies, tumbling down stairs, and crashing through windows, then getting up without a scratch. I had seen Bat Masterson himself—Gene Barry—take punches and gunshot wounds without even losing his dapper grin. He was so handsome, rugged and indestructible on the screen—but in real life, he wasn't so indestructible.

While on the set of "Bat Masterson," I happened to see Gene Barry walking across the set in his black cowboy costume, with his cowboy boots on—and he happened to trip. He wasn't badly injured—he had just stubbed his toe. But he immediately sat down and grabbed his foot, wincing with pain. Watching this screen legend holding his foot like a little boy with a big, bad boo-boo was like dousing all my movie fantasies with cold water. Suddenly I realized that these TV and movie cowboys were not larger than life—they were ordinary men who played a game of let's pretend in front of the cameras, and they really do get hurt. I thought, *Ohmigosh, movies are fantasy! They're not like reality at all.*

Now, most people grow up able to make that distinction without any problem. I didn't. I went to the movies and thought I was watching reality. And it wasn't just movie violence I mistook for reality—I bought into the movie fantasies of romance, glamour and the dream of living happily ever after. Later in life, when I got sober, I was able to look back and recognize how absurd and unrealistic my worldview had been. When I stopped drinking, I was finally able to see reality as it was. But Gene Barry's stubbed toe was my first little inkling that my perception of reality was all screwed up.

I remember I was working on a western the day I heard John F. Kennedy was shot. There was a radio on the set, and all of us on the cast and crew gathered around to hear the news from Dallas. The initial reports said he had been shot, but for a long time it wasn't clear if he was wounded or dead. We had a scene to shoot, so the director got us assembled in our places. In the scene, a cowboy actor and I were each on a horse. Just before the cameras were about to roll, someone came onto the set and said, "People, I've got some terrible news. The president didn't make it. He was pronounced dead at the hospital in Dallas."

It was such a shock. I just felt like crying, but I couldn't let myself. I had a scene to do.

Just then, the cowboy actor on the horse next to me said, "Serves that nigger-lover right." I gasped out loud! I couldn't believe anyone would say such a horrible thing at that moment. Everyone on the set (except the idiot on the horse) was too stunned to go on. The director said, "Let's call it a day, people." We resumed shooting the next day.

One of the most memorable westerns I appeared in was "Cimmaron Strip"— and the reason I remember the show so well is that it was there that I first met Harlan

Ellison, who would later become a dear friend. Harlan, of course, is the brilliant science fiction writer who authored such stories as "'Repent, Harlequin!' Said the Ticktockman" and "I Have No Mouth, And I Must Scream," as well as the script for the *Star Trek* episode "The City on the Edge of Forever." His script for "Cimmaron Strip" was a thrilling, suspenseful story in which I was one of three women being stalked by the legendary killer, Jack the Ripper.

Unlike most writers who turn in their script and move on to the next show, Harlan would actually come to the set and watch the production like a mother hen watching over her chicks. He's a perfectionist, and he demands that his scripts be done right. I loved watching him on the set, because he stirred things up and kept things interesting between takes. He would argue, yell, gesture like a madman—but only because he cared so much about the quality of his work. We met on that show and instantly hit it off as friends. A few years later, I would run into him again on the set of *Star Trek*—but that's another chapter.

I did two westerns with Jeffrey Hunter—the pilot for the TV series "Temple Houston" and a motion picture, *The Man from Galveston* (I played a madam, Texas Rose). Jeff portrayed Christ in the 1961 biblical epic *King of Kings*, and was Christopher Pike, the first captain of the Starship *Enterprise* in the original pilot episode of *Star Trek*. The role of captain in the series passed to Bill Shatner after Jeff turned it down. Jeff met a tragic end in 1969 when he fell down a flight of stairs and was killed.

Jeff Hunter was a close friend of Van Williams, one of the stars of the crime show, "Surfside Six." I first got to know Van through Jeff, then I later appeared in an episode of "Surfside Six" with Van, Troy Donohue and Diane McBain. Troy was a playboy detective named Sandy Winfield II, and Van was his partner, Ken Madison. They operated out of a houseboat (which the show was named after), docked near the Fountainbleu Hotel on Miami Beach. Van later starred as "The Green Hornet," and I still keep in touch with him and see him at conventions (he's as gorgeous as ever!).

Other crime dramas I did during those years included "Highway Patrol" with Broderick Crawford, "Run For Your Life" with Ben Gazzara, and "77 Sunset Strip" with Efrem Zimbalist, Jr., Roger Smith and Eddie Byrnes as the jazz-talking "Kookie" Kookson III—he parked cars at the restaurant next to the Sunset detectives' office, and was always combing his hair and saying things like, "I really dig those threads, man!" Efrem, "Kookie" Byrnes, Roger and I got to be good friends. Roger and his family would come to my house, then his two kids and my two kids would pile into his van and we'd all go to Disneyland together (this was before Roger married Ann-Margret).

I did a number of military comedies in the early '60s: "McHale's Navy," the PT boat sitcom with Ernest Borgnine and Tim Conway; "No Time For Sergeants" with Sammy Jackson, Hayden Rorke, and lovable old-timer Andy Clyde; and "Hennesey," the comedy adventures of a Navy medical officer, starring Jackie Cooper as Chick Hennesey and Abby Dalton as his wife (Ed Nelson guest-starred with me in that episode).

My favorite sitcom appearance of all was on "Bewitched" with Elizabeth Montgomery as the witch Samantha, married to mortal advertising man Darrin Stephens

Here I am as the romantic lead, a woman of substance named Texas Rose, in a scene from "The Man from Galveston." Also pictured: Preston Foster as Judge Homer Black (left) and Jeffrey Hunter (Star Trek's Captain Pike) as Timothy Higgins.

(Dick York). I was in episode 3 of this long-running (254 episodes) show—a 1964 segment called "It Shouldn't Happen to a Dog." I played Babs Livingston, the girl-friend of lecherous Rex Barker (Jack Warden), Darrin's client. When Barker makes unwanted advances on Samantha, she turns him into a dog. Elizabeth Montgomery's husband, William Asher, directed the episode.

I just loved and admired Elizabeth Montgomery. She was a wonderful actress because you never got the idea she was acting. She was so natural. At the time I did the show, she had just had a baby, and she kept the baby near the set all the time. Whenever she wasn't in front of the camera, she was by the crib, being with her child.

My favorite thing was comedy—and I wish I had done more. I think I'm a good little comedienne.

When you work in Hollywood, the temptation to give in to your lusts can be almost unbearable at times—even for a married woman who really wants to be good. There are always so many gorgeous men, and you are thrown into make-believe romantic situations with them. In order to give as convincing a performance as pos-

I played a madam, Tangerine O'Shea, in a 1964 episode of "Temple Houston," "Do Unto Others, Then Gallop."

sible, you really try to tap into your romantic, sexual feelings and bring them to the surface. So I often felt a tremendous attraction to the actors I worked with—and I often had a terrible time keeping it legit.

A lot of starlets were bedding actors, directors, producers, casting directors—but I really wanted to be true to my husband, and I was. It was only later, as I fell deeper and more full-blown into my alcoholism that my moral standards collapsed. The more I drank, the more immoral I got, because alcohol lowers your inhibitions and your opinion of yourself.

Here's Eddie "Kookie" Byrnes and me on the set of "77 Sunset Strip." The way we're both holding our backs and looking pained, we must have injured our sacros while dancing "The Twist!"

There was a casting director at Warner Brothers who tried to get me to go to bed with him. I told him I was true to my husband and never fooled around. As soon as I turned him down, I thought, *Way to go Whitney. You just made an enemy of the man who hires all the actors for the biggest studio in town.* But I was pleasantly surprised. He actually respected me for saying no. "Grace," he said, "you're not only sexy, but virtuous, too. You're beautiful on the outside and the inside." Because of that, he really liked me and wanted to see me get ahead, so he cast me in a lot of shows. I worked pretty steadily as a contract player at Warner Brothers, often appearing in two shows a week.

I have to admit that I hadn't been as virtuous in my life as this casting director thought. But he was right about this: When I wasn't drinking, I wanted to be a good girl. Though I was restless and unhappy in my marriage, I wasn't drinking heavily in the early '60s. I was taking care of my babies while pursuing an acting career, and I was living with my husband. Despite my rebellious attitude toward what I viewed as my husband's controlling behavior, I still rejected the idea of being unfaithful to him. However I felt about Steve, I saw adultery as a sin against God, against my family, and against my own sense of right and wrong. The casting director at Warners saw that in me, he liked that moral side of me, and he got me a part in a lot of shows because of that.

I had a bicycle that I rode around the Warner Brothers studio at the time, and sometimes on my breaks I would ride to the front gate and talk to the guard at the entrance. I'm not sure why I picked him to be my confidante and counselor—for some reason he just seemed like a good listener. I told him I was in a bad marriage and I resented it. "I don't understand," I complained. "Why can't I go out and date guys and have fun? Just because I'm a married woman, why do I have to go home every night? I don't even like my husband!"

"Your thinking is convoluted," he'd say. "You can't be married to one man and go out and date other men. If you want to go out on the town with other men, you have to get a divorce."

"Oh, I don't believe in divorce," I replied. And I meant it. But I was beginning to think more and more about divorce all the time.

My husband tried to discourage me from having a career. He told me, "If you're going to work, you have to pay for a nanny out of your earnings—I'm not paying for it." He said this after I had already given him all of my earnings. I'd hand it all over to him—yet he wouldn't pay any of my bills. Instead, he used that money to put himself through school. He got a degree in psychology and later began working with, of all things, alcoholics.

My husband didn't believe in buying medicine for our children. I had to go to my parents and borrow money for medicine. If the boys needed antibiotics, he just shrugged and said, "They'll get over it." It wasn't that Steve didn't love his kids—he loved them very much and tried to be a good father to them. He just figured kids could get along fine without a lot of expensive medicines.

The doctor once called him and told him, "I have to take out your son's tonsils, but before I can take them out, he has to have an antibiotic to clear up the infection. If you don't buy your son the medicine he needs, I'm going to turn you in to the authorities. Without that medicine, this boy could die." So Steve bought the medicine.

In order to make sure I had money of my own, I had to get a separate checking account—and that wasn't easy. Those were the days when a woman couldn't get a credit card unless her husband got it for her. Everything was in my husband's name, and he had complete control over me and my money—and I resented it.

I got to know a lot of fascinating people at Warner Brothers. Angie Dickenson, Troy Donohue, Suzanne Pleshette and Connie Stevens were all contract players at the studio when I was there. After work I used to go to a bar across the street from the studio, El Chiquita, and hang out with other actors—Lee Marvin, Van Williams, Troy, Chad Everett and many others.

I was in makeup with Sharon Tate a number of times, and I remember her as a very friendly, sweet girl in her early twenties. We used to gossip like schoolgirls about how cute Troy and Chad were. Like me, she was doing a lot of episodic television—shows like the "The Beverly Hillbillies" and" The Man From U.N.C.L.E." I vividly recall how shocked and horrified I was a few years later when I heard that, while pregnant, she had been tortured and murdered in the Tate-LaBianca slayings.

During the early '60s, while I was busy as an actress, I also continued with my singing career. I sang with the Desi Arnaz Orchestra at Indian Wells, near Palm Springs. Desi was the biggest womanizer you ever met. He and Lucille Ball were still married at the time, yet he was all over me. I was always fending him off because I was married and didn't want to fool around.

Desi knew I was an actress as well as a singer, and he told me that Lucy was conducting an acting class at the Desilu studio. So I took his advice and got into Lucy's class. She was a wonderful teacher. The best advice she ever gave me was, "Don't act." I said, "Huh?" She said it again: "Don't act. React. To react, you have to listen carefully to what the other actors are saying—then you react to it. That's what makes you believable." Lucy taught me a lot in that class about acting and comedic timing. She was the best teacher in the world, especially for playing comedy. After all, who had better timing than Lucille Ball?

I found out early that the acting business can be hazardous to your health. I appeared on a show with Neville Brand (I can't remember which show—I think it was "The Untouchables"). The script called for Neville to throw me over the top of a sofa, then reach behind the sofa and stab me with a knife. It sounded simple enough—but they couldn't get it right in one take. They kept telling him to throw me over the sofa again and again! The result was that I ended up in traction for a few weeks. When I got out of traction, I had to wear a neck brace for over a year.

I went to the union office to turn in a disability claim for my injury. The woman at the union office said, "Are you sure you want to turn in this claim? I mean, you can if you want—but if you do, you'll never work again. You'll be blackballed." So I decided not to turn in the claim. I just paid the medical bills out of my own pocket.

One of my next jobs was a TV pilot with Jack Kelly (of "Maverick" fame) and Senta Berger. I played the part of a ski instructor. We shot the pilot at a ski resort at Mammoth in the Sierra Nevadas. Senta ended up getting temporarily snow-blind, and I was in constant pain throughout the shoot. When it was time for me to perform, I took my neck brace off. Between takes, I put it on again. That whole experience is kind of a blur, because I was on very heavy pain medication at the time. To top it off, the pilot didn't sell.

One of the most traumatic experiences I had as an actress came while filming an episode of "Mickey Spillane," a hard-boiled private eye show in the early '60s. The show starred Darren McGavin, and the episode was directed by Boris Sagal, who went on to become a very big motion picture director. It was one of my first experiences in a lead role. The set was tense and stressful, because Darren McGavin and Boris Sagal were at odds with each other throughout the entire production. They simply could not agree on *anything*.

Here I am, strutting my stuff as Irma's friend Kiki the Cossack in Billy Wilder's Irma la Douce.

The battle between them kept escalating until I found myself caught in a tug-o-war between them over one specific scene. Darren demanded that we play it one way, Boris wanted it done his way, and both of them put enormous pressure on me. In my experience, the director was the boss, and I wanted to please him. But Darren took me aside and told me that if I did the scene Sagal's way, he would screw it up and make me look bad.

I was under such pressure from these two men that I had to run to my dressing room and cry it out. I tried to incorporate some of Darren's ideas and some of the director's, but I ended up giving a terrible performance because of the stress I was under. Boris was very displeased with me, and I knew I would never work for him again. It was one of the most horrible days of my entire career.

In 1962, I got a chance to work with Billy Wilder and Jack Lemmon again. The film: *Irma la Douce*. Originally, Billy and Izzy Diamond wrote the script around Marilyn Monroe. But in August of that year, Marilyn was found dead of a drug overdose. The role of Irma went instead to Shirley MacLaine.

Like *Some Like It Hot*, *Irma* is a comedy about sexual role-playing, disguises and mistaken identity. Jack Lemmon plays a prudish policeman who falls in love with Irma, the prostitute with a heart of gold. In order to keep Irma's love all to himself, he uses a number of disguises to prevent her from selling herself on the street. For example, he disguises himself as a pimp, so he can keep tabs on her, and as an impotent customer, "Lord X," who pays Irma to maintain a platonic relationship with him—and to stay away from other customers.

I got the part of Irma's closest friend and fellow prostitute, Kiki the Cossack. It was a beautiful, lavish production, and I remember Billy Wilder's wife, Audrey, being personally involved in all the costuming—helping with the fittings, making decisions on the precise length of the boots and skirts, and making sure the prostitutes all looked as glamorous and beautiful as showgirls. The film is an acknowledged classic, and Shirley MacLaine was wonderful in the part—but it's intriguing to imagine how the movie might have turned out if Marilyn had lived to play Irma.

During breaks in shooting *Irma la Douce*, many of us would go to the Formosa bar and have lunch or drinks with the "Rat Pack"—Dean Martin, Frank Sinatra, Sammy Davis, Jr. and Joey Bishop. While we were shooting *Irma* at the Samuel Goldwyn Studio, Sidney Poitier and Sammy were shooting *Porgy and Bess* on the next stage. I used to go to lunch with Sidney every day and sit at the table with all these incredible guys. We'd eat and drink, and Sammy would stand at the head of the table and tell the most outrageous stories. Jack Lemmon would often be there, and so would Hope Holliday, who played Lolita (the hooker with the heart-shaped glasses) in *Irma*. It was a fabulous time.

There was, however, one horrible moment for me during the filming of *Irma la Douce*. It happened while we were working on a scene where Jack Lemmon as the policeman, Nestor Patou, has arrested all of the prostitutes and put us in the paddy wagon. It's a very cute, funny scene, and all of the girls, myself included, had a lot of lines. Before we started shooting the scene, Billy Wilder came over to me and said in his thick accent, "Lee, I've invited a director friend to come over while we shoot the paddy wagon scene. He's looking for a female lead in his new TV show, and I told him he should watch you work."

"Great!" I said. "Oh, thank you, Billy! You're an angel! Who is it?"

He grinned impishly. "A very big name in television. You'll see!"

A few minutes later, Billy brought a man over. I looked at Billy's friend, and Billy's friend looked at me—and then he began yelling. "No! No! No! I will not have that woman on my set!"

Billy's jaw dropped in astonishment. He had no idea that his friend had already directed me in a TV show a few years earlier. Billy's friend, of course, was Boris Sagal—and he had never forgiven me for my poor performance in the "Mickey Spillane" episode with Darren McGavin.

But Billy didn't stop trying to help me. He introduced me to a number of directors and producers who gave me parts in movies and TV shows.

One common feature of the disease of alcoholism (which was progressing in me at that time, but not yet full-blown) is a tendency to be obsessive-compulsive. That was me all the way. I was obsessed with putting my two children in Hebrew school—the Emek Hebrew Academy in North Hollywood. While my boys were going to the Academy, I attended a PTA meeting where they announced a fund-raising drive to buy a bus to pick up the children and take them to school. They planned to raise the money over a period of two or three years. In my compulsiveness, I jumped to my feet and blurted out, "Why wait two or three years? I'll give you the money so you can buy the bus right now!"

During the early '60s, I was a working actress, but I was certainly not rich. My poor musician husband was struggling to make ends meet. I had a little over $1,500 in the bank and they needed $1,500 for the bus, so I just wrote a check from my savings and bought the bus for the school. All the way home, I tried to think of some way to tell my husband, but there was no way to break it gently. When I told him, it was like grounds for divorce. He couldn't believe I had done something so stupid and impulsive. He wanted me to go back to the school, say I made a mistake, and ask for my check back.

I said, "Don't worry, Steve! I'll give you all my residuals, and we'll replace the money in the account! But I just couldn't bear to see the kids have to wait two years for this bus. Besides, our boys will get to ride in it!" I was so excited about this good thing I had done for the school that he just didn't have the heart to make me break my promise to the school.

The next week, I went to Billy Wilder's office at the Goldwyn Studio on Formosa and Santa Monica. The producer, Walter Mirisch, was there, and so was Izzy Diamond. Billy looked at me and a big smile lit up his face. "Lee!" he said. "How are you!"

"Billy," I said, "I'm so excited! You'll never believe what I just did!"

"What?"

"I bought a bus!"

The puzzled expression on Billy's face was priceless. "A bus!" he said. "Lee, what are you going to do with a bus?"

"It's not for me!" I said. "I'm buying a school bus for the Hebrew Academy where my boys go to school."

Billy's eyebrows went up. "Oh, really? What does your husband, the drummer, think of this?"

"Oh, he fussed about it for a while," I said, "but I'm going to do it anyway. It's my fifteen-hundred dollars, and I can give it away if I want."

"I tell you what," said Billy, taking his money clip from his pocket. "I think that a bus for the Hebrew Academy is such a worthy cause that you shouldn't have all the fun of giving." And he took $500 out of his wallet and pressed the money into my hands.

"Oh, Billy, I can't—"

Mr. Mirisch interrupted me and said, "I'm with Billy." And he took out his wallet and gave me $500.

Then Izzy Diamond stood up and said, "Well, I'm not letting you two bums have all the fun. Here, Lee—" And he handed me $500, too!

"Well, gentlemen," I said, brushing at the tears that were welling up in my eyes, "I didn't come in here to pass the hat—"

"We know, we know," said Billy. "Listen, kiddo, you're a nice girl trying to do a nice thing. But you can't afford to buy that bus. Here we are, three Jewish fellas who can easily afford it. We're the ones who should be buying that bus, not you."

I just couldn't believe their generosity. It was only a few days later that a little yellow bus pulled up in front of my house for the very first time. My boys got on, and the bus pulled away. As I stood on the curb and waved goodbye, I noticed the words EMEK HEBREW ACADEMY on the side of the bus—and I began to cry. It was the greatest thrill of my life to see that little bus pick up my children and take them off to school.

In 1964, I appeared in a show that foreshadowed *Star Trek*—the acclaimed science fiction anthology series, "The Outer Limits." It was there that I first met Robert Justman. Bob was the assistant director on "Outer Limits," and he would later become associate producer on *Star Trek*, and Gene Roddenberry's right-hand man. Bob is one of the kindest men you'd ever want to meet, and he was always in my corner at *Star Trek*. He even went to bat for me when my character was written out of *Star Trek*. He wanted them to at least bring me back on a guest-starring basis in future episodes, but I was never invited back.

"The Outer Limits" episode I did, "Controlled Experiment," was written and directed by Leslie Stevens and was the only comedy-satire episode produced during the two-season run of this dramatic and scary science fiction series. Carroll O'Connor ("All In the Family's" Archie Bunker) and Barry Morse (of "The Fugitive" and "Space: 1999") play a pair of Martians who are concerned about Planet Earth's growing threat to the rest of the solar system due to humanity's tinkering with nuclear weapons. So, using a machine that can manipulate time like a VCR running a videotape (fast-forward, rewind, slow-motion, pause), these two Martians conduct a "controlled experiment" with time in an attempt to understand why earthlings kill each other.

That's where I come in. I play a blond sexpot named Carla Duveen, whose boyfriend is cheating on her in a love nest on an upper floor of a New York hotel. I wait in the hotel lobby with a gun in my purse—then, when my boyfriend steps off the elevator, I pull the gun and confront him. As he's staring at the business end of my revolver, I shout, "Bert Hamil, you're a two-faced, no-good, black-hearted two-timer!" Then I pump him full of lead.

As I'm sending my two-timing lover to his eternal reward, the two Martians are observing from behind the lobby ferns. Using their time gizmo, they run the murder backwards, forwards, slow it down, and even watch the bullet crawl through the air like a snail on a sidewalk, all in an attempt to understand why we human beings kill one another. In the process, they make a lot of amusing and even profound observations on the human condition.

Much of the show was shot using a special camera which shoots the scene at a very high speed. When it is played back at the normal 24 frames per second, the result is a very smooth slow motion effect. A speed camera is very expensive to rent, so it was only used for a couple days. While most of the murder sequences are shot with the speed camera, there is one scene where Barry Morse comes up to me just before the murder and examines the contents of my purse. I had to act as if I'm in slow motion while Barry, in the same shot, is speaking normally to Carroll O'Connor. I had to blink my eyelids, turn my head, and move my body in slow motion to simulate the fact that I was not in the same time phase as the two Martians. The result was very effective.

Bert Hamil, my two-timing lover, was played by a very funny and talented actor, Robert Fortier. Carroll and Barry were wonderful as a pair of bemused Martians struggling to understand my murderous motives. They had a Laurel and Hardy chemistry on-screen. Off-screen, between takes, you could always find them together, hunched over a chessboard, deep in thought.

"Controlled Experiment" was the sixth episode of the series, and was shot in late June of 1963 (it first aired on January 13, 1964). It's a wry and wonderfully written episode. The quality of the writing and staging of "Controlled Experiment" is all the more remarkable given that it was done in a hurry and on the cheap. Leslie Stevens wrote the bulk of the script on a flight from New York to L.A., and the show was shot using only three sets and five actors. It took a mere four days to shoot the hour-long episode (which has to be come kind of record). It cost less than $100,000 to make.

Shortly before joining the cast of *Star Trek*, I appeared in a two-part episode of the campy cult classic "Batman," shot at Twentieth Century-Fox. The two-part episode is entitled "King Tut's Coup" and "Batman's Waterloo." King Tut was played by my friend Victor Buono, one of the sweetest men I've ever known. I played Princess Neela, one of King Tut's concubines. Lee Meriwether appeared in the show as an heiress who is kidnapped by Tut to be his unwilling Queen of the Nile (she later appeared in a *Trek* episode, "That Which Survives").

I didn't have many scenes with Adam West (Batman), but we talked a lot on the set, having known each other from our days together at Warner Brothers. He was another one of those gorgeous Hollywood men I was extremely attracted to. Though

I never got involved with Adam, I was always aware of a powerful sexual electricity on the set.

Another show I worked on just before joining the cast of *Star Trek* was "Mona McCluskey," a short-lived NBC situation comedy about a Hollywood dancer-actress (Juliet Prowse) and her military husband. The producer of the show was George Burns—that's right, the cigar-chomping "Say goodnight, Gracie" half of the Burns and Allen comedy team. He was also an incredibly lecherous old man (maybe that's why he lived so long!). Like Desi Arnaz, he couldn't keep his hands off me—he would fiddle

In this shot from "Batman," I am Princess Neela, one of the harem girls of the villainous King Tut, played by Victor Buono—that wonderful, lovable ham!

with my costume, put his hands on me, and whisper lewd suggestions in my ear. Also like Desi, he wanted to see me get ahead (no doubt in the hope that I would be properly grateful and do something for him in return). I did one episode as Mona's perky blond girlfriend, and George wanted to add me to the series as a regular, but Juliet Prowse wouldn't stand for it. If anyone was going to provide the perkiness on that show, it would be her.

Shortly after "Mona McCluskey," I was selected to co-star in a pilot for a show called "Police Story" (not to be confused with Joseph Wambaugh's anthology cop show of the same name which came a decade later). My co-stars on that pilot episode were Steve Ihnat (who would later appear as Garth in a third-season episode of *Star Trek*, "Whom Gods Destroy") and DeForest Kelly (who would become Dr. Leonard

McCoy on *Star Trek*). I was cast as Police Sergeant Lily Monroe, a cross between the 1950s "Queen of the Strippers," Lili St. Cyr, and actress Marilyn Monroe. The writer, creator, and producer of the show was a man by the name of Gene Roddenberry.

I had previously worked for Gene in 1963, when he put me in an episode of his short-lived (one season) show about life in the United States Marine Corps, "The Lieutenant." The series starred Gary Lockwood as Lieutenant William Rice and Robert Vaughn as Captain Ray Rambridge. (Lockwood would later appear in the second pilot of *Star Trek*, as well as Stanley Kubrick's *2001: A Space Odyssey*, while Vaughn would be cast as Napoleon Solo in "The Man From U.N.C.L.E.") Remembering my work on "The Lieutenant," Gene Roddenberry brought me back to play the female lead in "Police Story." (Gene also remembered the work other alumni from "The Lieutenant," and later cast them in *Star Trek*: Leonard Nimoy, Majel Barrett, Nichelle Nichols, Walter Koenig and Ricardo Montalban.)

I remember going to Gene Roddenberry's office at Desilu to interview for the part of Lily Monroe. Gene and I just hit it off—he kept telling me how terrific I was for the part, and that he was looking for someone who was sexy, blond, and provocative, but with a kooky, comedic flair. "Police Story," he said, was going to be a tough-as-nails cop show, based in part on Gene's own experiences as a beat cop with the L.A.P.D. But Gene also wanted some sexy comedy to lighten the drama—and that was what I was there for. Gene had a twinkle in his eye as he described the role. My quirky character, he explained, would play off of the very serious tough-cop persona of Steve Ihnat. I would make funny, flirty comments to him to get him to lighten up a bit. The comic relief would be in this interplay between mischievous Lily Monroe and her stiff, straight-arrow boss. The double entendres really flew in the pilot episode. I think it would have been a very good show.

I was outfitted in a tight-fitting police uniform, and I wore my hair short and platinum blond. We filmed the exteriors on the city streets outside the Desilu Culver studio (not the Desilu Hollywood studio where *Star Trek* was later shot). We were in the middle of filming when the Watts riots broke out. Apparently, Gene was very concerned with security on the exterior sets, which were right on the streets of Culver City, because he hired guards with rifles to sit in cars or stand behind trees around the perimeter of the sets in order to protect them. There was some fear that the rioters might head our way, but it never happened.

After the "Police Story" pilot was completed, it was audience-tested by a Los Angeles research firm. A large L.A. theater, Preview House, was specially rigged with dials on the armrests of the seats, so that the audience could register favorable readings for things they liked about a show and unfavorable readings for the things they disliked. As the people turned their dials clockwise or counterclockwise, the readings were fed into a big computer that tabulated the results. After the "Police Story" pilot was tested, Gene told me, "Grace, when Lily Monroe came on the screen, you pushed all the buttons and rang all the bells."

"Police Story" didn't sell, but another pilot Gene produced at the same time was bought by NBC. It was a show called *Star Trek*. Gene took my character and the

This role served as my screen test for Star Trek—Sgt. Lily Monroe in the unsold pilot for Gene Roddenberry's "Police Story." The medical examiner in that show was played by DeForest Kelly—Dr. McCoy in Star Trek.

acerbic medical examiner out of the unsold "Police Story" pilot and put them into *Star Trek*, where they became Yeoman Janice Rand and Dr. Leonard McCoy.

When Gene Roddenberry beamed me aboard his new science fiction adventure series, *Star Trek*, I was thrilled. I didn't fully realize it at the time, but my life had just taken a sharp turn in a totally new direction. I was about to boldly go where no man (or female yeoman) had ever gone before.

Space, the Final Frontier...

I remember the waiting.

I remember sitting at home with my two kids, hoping that the phone would ring with the news that I was going to be a star. I had pinned my hopes to the "Police Story" pilot—I didn't even know what *Star Trek* was. So when the phone rang and I heard my agent's voice, my heart jumped into my throat.

"Grace," he said, "I've got great news—"

"Ohmigosh!" I screamed in his ear. "They sold the 'Police Story' pilot!"

"Uhhh—no, Grace. The network turned it down."

"No?!" My dream of stardom fell to the floor and shattered into a million pieces. "Then, what's this so-called 'great news' of yours? And it had better be good!"

"Oh, it's good, all right. Gene Roddenberry liked you so much in 'Police Story,' he wants to put in another show—a new show he just sold to NBC. It's called *Star Trek*."

"*Star Trek*? What's it about?"

"It's sci-fi. You know—rocket ships and bug-eyed monsters. Roddenberry wants to see you in his office tomorrow."

"I don't know. Do you think this will be good for my image?"

"It's a *series*, Grace. It's steady work. It'll be good for your bank account."

I brightened. "Well, then, that *is* great news, isn't it?"

So I went down to Gene's office at Desilu and he told me all about his new "wagon train to the stars" concept. He explained the part of Yeoman Janice Rand, and how she would fit into the overall chemistry of the show as the captain's yeoman and the object of his repressed desire. It was a sexy part, with lots of possibilities. I instantly loved it. I signed the contracts without a moment's hesitation. I couldn't wait to get started. That was in April 1966; we would begin shooting in late May.

Finally, I had what I wanted: a continuing role on a weekly series. It meant fame, money, security—and not just career security, but the kind of emotional security I had been searching for ever since I learned I was adopted. I felt accepted. I felt beautiful and wanted. I felt chosen. Finally, I was *home*—home aboard the Starship *Enterprise*.

In the book *Inside Star Trek: The Real Story* Herb Solow (who coauthored the book with Bob Justman) writes,

> When casting was discussed with Gene, the only performers he
> would stand up for were the actresses with whom he'd had a previous

personal relationship: Majel Barrett, Nichelle Nichols and Grace Lee Whitney.

The suggestion that Gene Roddenberry put me in *Star Trek* because of a "previous personal relationship" is flatly false (Sorry, Herb—you and Bob wrote a great book, but you got this one wrong.). It doesn't matter how you define the word "personal," it is simply not true. The fact that Majel was involved with Gene Roddenberry before *Star Trek* is well-known; in fact, they were married after the series finished its network run. And Nichelle talks candidly about her relationship with Gene in her book *Beyond Uhura*.

But I never had a romantic relationship with Gene Roddenberry before *Star Trek*, during *Star Trek*, or after *Star Trek*. In fact, until I started working with him on *Star Trek*, I scarcely knew him in any way that could even be remotely defined as "personal." When he cast me as Yeoman Rand, the only relationship I had ever had with Gene Roddenberry was a professional relationship: I had appeared in two shows he produced, "The Lieutenant" and the "Police Story" pilot.

Did Gene make passes at me? You better believe he did! Passes, innuendoes, double-entendres, the whole nine yards. But I wanted to keep our relationship on a professional basis and I was basically moral at that time (it wasn't until *after* I got written out of *Star Trek* that my sexaholism went off the scale). Who knows? Maybe if Gene had gotten me in the sack, I might have done all three seasons of *Star Trek* instead of only half a season!

Herb Solow goes on to talk about Gene Roddenberry's evolving vision of the role of the captain's female yeoman on *Star Trek*:

> Gene's version of the ship's yeoman role came straight out of old Hollywood movies: cute and shapely, and cute and bubbly, and cute and not too bright—and cute. Laurel Goodwin as Yeoman Colt fit Gene's vision for the first pilot, but she was swept away by the NBC broom. Model Andrea Dromm, also fitting the mold, came aboard for the second pilot as Yeoman Smith. Actually, it was a non-part. But during the casting process, director Jimmy Goldstone overheard Gene say, "I'm hiring her because I want to score with her." It was not only a non-part, I'm sure it was a non-score as well. ...
>
> Grace Lee Whitney was another refugee from Gene's unsold "Police Story" pilot. She had played the part of Police Lieutenant [*sic*—I was actually a sergeant] Lily Monroe. ...Gene liked Grace Lee. Unlike the two prior "model-type and cute" Yeoman actresses, she appeared to him as what she was—pretty, sexy, and vulnerable. Yeoman Janice Rand was piped aboard the U.S.S. *Enterprise*.[1]

If you watch the first two *Star Trek* pilots and notice the female yeoman in each of those episodes, you can see that Gene Roddenberry had not yet discovered the dramatic possibilities of the character. By the time he had cast me in that role for the

This big, bold smile is a very rare look for Yeoman Rand. We were usually in such dire circumstances aboard the Enterprise *that no one had time to smile! This was a promotional shot for* TV Guide's *preview of the 1966 debut of* Star Trek.

regular series, he had given a lot of thought as to how Yeoman Rand would fit into the chemistry of the *Star Trek* ensemble. He explained his vision of my character this way:

"Grace Lee," he said, "you're going to be like Miss Kitty on 'Gunsmoke.' Matt Dillon always comes back to the saloon and talks over his problems with Miss Kitty. She knows him better than anyone else. That's the kind of relationship I want Yeoman Rand to have with Captain Kirk. He will seek out your company, confess to you, draw strength and inspiration from you—and secretly, in his heart of hearts, he will love you. But he can never openly admit his love to you—or even to himself.

"You will love the captain the same way. You're to be as beautiful as you can be and as efficient as you can be, and you are to love the captain—but because of your duty, because of your career as a starship yeoman, you can never openly express your attraction toward him. There will always be an undercurrent of suppressed sexuality between you that will come out in very subtle ways."

That's how Gene sketched the outline of Janice Rand's relationship with Captain Kirk. But it was up to me to fill in that outline with colors and emotions and reality. I projected a lot of my own self onto the soul of Janice Rand. I really began to feel that I knew her, I understood her, I loved her as a sister under the skin. It was my idea to give Janice Rand an artistic dimension (we see her in her room with an easel and canvas in "The Enemy Within"), which was an extension of my own artistic and musical side. I saw her as a virtuous young woman who loves the captain but is utterly committed to the performance of her duties. Though she yearns for the captain in her woman's heart, her yeoman's sense of duty and honor demand that she keep her feelings to herself.

In the microcosm of the relationship between Kirk and Rand, Gene Roddenberry foresaw the tensions and problems in today's military, where we have so many women serving alongside men on bases, on ships, and aboard planes. The Kirk-Rand relationship asks the question, "How can you put an attractive female crewmember aboard ship with an attractive male crewmember and not expect nature to take its course?" It's a very timely issue.

In those first few episodes, the chemistry Gene described to me was really there. It was subtle, and it worked beautifully, just as Gene Roddenberry had envisioned it. Gene and the other writers, however, seemed a little unsure at first what the yeoman's duties were. In the first episode, she seems little more than a glorified waitress, bringing the captain his lunch on a tray, or bringing a carafe of coffee to the bridge. Later (notably in "Charlie X" and "Miri"), they put a tricorder in her hands and make her a more responsible, professional member of the crew. But even in that first episode, "The Corbomite Maneuver," the sexual-romantic tension between Kirk and Rand peeks through.

There is a scene in "Corbomite" where Captain Kirk and Dr. McCoy are in the captain's cabin. The good doctor is functioning in his role as Jim Kirk's friend, therapist, spiritual advisor and listening ear. I enter the cabin, set out the captain's lunch (to his mild annoyance: "Stop hovering over me, Yeoman!"), then I exit. After I leave, Captain Kirk grouses, "When I get my hands on the genius at Headquarters who assigned me a female yeoman—" Dr. McCoy grins knowingly and jabs, "What's the matter, Jim? Don't you trust yourself?" The irked expression on Kirk's face is priceless. Dr. McCoy had scored a direct hit—the captain is attracted to the yeoman and even the doctor has spotted it. As much to convince himself as to convince McCoy, Kirk counters, "I've already got a female to worry about. Her name is the *Enterprise*." But although the captain is in denial, the doctor and the audience know that Captain James T. Kirk is caught in the classic romantic dilemma, torn between two loves— between his love for the ship and his love for the yeoman.

Only in extreme circumstances does Janice Rand allow herself to express her normally repressed feelings for Captain Kirk. An example is in the episode "Miri," where the captain and I are trapped on a planet where a genetically engineered disease has infected us. We know this disease will gradually lead to our disfigurement, madness and death. In a private moment in a hallway, I tearfully open my heart to the captain: "Back on the ship, I was always trying to get you to look at my legs... Captain, look at my legs." And the camera pans to the gray patch of disease on my legs. The captain and I are both infected, both afraid, both aware of the doom that awaits us. That terrible knowledge overpowers our will to repress our feelings, and in that moment we embrace. My love for James Kirk and my need for his protection comes rushing to the surface. As he embraces me, Captain Kirk— always a tower of commanding strength in the storm of crisis—struggles to keep his emotions hidden, though it is subtly apparent that he truly cares for me. Later, when the crisis is over, the captain and I both stuff our feelings once more.

The chemistry between Captain Kirk and Yeoman Rand, between William Shatner and Grace Lee Whitney, was natural and unforced. When Rand was afraid, she would go to Kirk's side, and he would automatically reach out and hold her. The director never had to tell me to go to Bill Shatner's side, and the director never told Bill to put his arms around me. It was instinctive for both of us. We knew our characters and the electrical undercurrent that crackled between them, and we just responded to that as the situation demanded.

I loved Janice Rand. She became like a sister to me, someone I came to know very well, someone who was very dear and important to me. I wanted her to be an effective component of the *Star Trek* ensemble. I knew that I was not the star, that Janice Rand was not the main character. Her job was not to steal the show or upstage anyone, but to be one of the balancing and interacting agents in the overall chemistry of the show. I knew there were great dramatic, comedic and story possibilities in the character of Janice Rand, but only if she meshed well with the other characters.

I'm a method actress, and when I become involved in my character, I actually *become* the character. When I went in to work in the morning, when I got away from my house in the San Fernando Valley and the dishes and the washing, when I got into my makeup and costume and onto the set, *I was Janice Rand*. Despite all the seamy things I had seen and experienced over the years, I still considered myself an innocent kid from Michigan—and I put those aspects of myself into Janice Rand. I saw her as an innocent—sexy and efficient, but also very wide-eyed, honest and virtuous.

I'm often asked at *Trek* conventions what Yeoman Rand's role was aboard the starship. I tell everybody I was a space geisha! It gets a laugh, because people tend to assume that geishas are Japanese prostitutes, so my answer sounds a bit risqué. But in fact, geishas are not prostitutes—they are entertainers who are bound by contract to their "superior officer" or employer for a period of years. They serve the boss with song, dance, conversation and hospitality. I think that was really the yeoman's role—she was a virtuous geisha, a faithful servant, smart and resourceful, talented and artistic, loyal and duty-bound. It was a complex role embedded in a network of relationships with the captain and the rest of the crew. It would have been fascinating to explore the many facets of the role, and to develop new facets over several seasons.

But I never got the chance.

The cast and creators of *Star Trek* were plunged into a flurry of activity long before we shot a single frame of film. We were all brought together and introduced to each other. Our real costumes and phaser weapons hadn't even been designed yet, so they put *Flash Gordon* costumes on us and shoved flashlights with colored lenses in our hands. "Pretend they're gizmotronic space blasters," they told us. Then they snapped dozens of pre-production publicity stills of us. In those early shots, I didn't look like Yeoman Rand—I looked like Ann Francis in *Forbidden Planet.*

Gene Roddenberry devoted a great deal of time and attention to my visual trademark, my hair. He assigned our costume designer, William Ware Theiss, the job of designing it. It was composed of two Max Factor wigs woven together over a mesh cone, and the final result was beautiful, free-flowing—and heavier than a NASA space helmet. They practically had to nail it to my head to keep it on, and if you look closely, you can see it gets slightly off-plumb in some scenes. I often had to hold onto it because it was so heavy, especially if I was running down a corridor or if Bill Shatner was shaking me and roughing me up as he did in the episode "The Enemy Within."

The wig was meticulously created in stages, and at each stage I would go into Gene's office with Bill Theiss and say, "Well, Gene, what do you think?" Each time, Gene would study my hair with a critical expression, then say, "It's still not high enough." And he'd come over to me and fuss with it and pile more hair on top of it and squeeze it. "Like this, like this," he'd say. "Janice Rand is a woman of the twenty-third century. We want the viewers to know they're looking at a futuristic hairstyle. It has to be totally unlike anything in our world." If Gene was right, I pity all the poor women three centuries from now, going through life with the mass-equivalent of a bowling ball on their heads!

No one knows where that wig is today—it was stolen from the Desilu properties room sometime after I left the show. It was very expensive, and I have nightmares of it turning up somewhere. I go down to Skid Row to give talks at recovery groups, and I keep expecting to look out and see some bag lady wearing Janice Rand's hair!

Our makeup was designed and applied by Fred Phillips, a true master of the art. He created all the makeup on the show, from Spock's pointed ears to the faces of beautiful alien seductresses. He designed the most alluring eye makeup and shadow for me, and applied artificial nails that were always polished a stunning shade of red that went perfectly with my red uniform. Fred was an older man, and I think he had a crush on me. He was always making flirty comments—nothing serious, just light banter. We laughed a lot in makeup. I had known Fred for years, having worked with him at the ZIV studio on a show with Ron Ely called "The Aquanauts." He was also the makeup man on "The Outer Limits." I always enjoyed being made over by Fred Phillips.

Costume designer Bill Theiss created the uniforms that were so much a part of the unique look of *Star Trek*. People often ask me at conventions if I liked the mini-skirted uniforms the women wore on the show. My answer: Absolutely! I wanted to show off my assets, and Bill Theiss's uniform creations certainly did that (of course, my moral values are much different today than they were back then!). The red skirt of the uniform went over short red pants and sheer black stockings and black boots—a very sexy yet functional-looking uniform. The stockings were brand-new every day, and the uniform was always sparkling clean and freshly pressed daily. The velour material of the uniforms was soft and curvy. When these uniform designs finally appeared on film, they created a vivid sense of being transported to another time, another place—and a very sexy time and place at that!

After weeks of experimenting and redesigning and snipping and tucking here and there, with both the hair and the costume, Bill Theiss paraded me into Gene Roddenberry's office for final approval. Gene looked me up and down as I modeled the complete Janice Rand look for him. Then he clapped his hands, grinned broadly, and said, "That's it! Perfect! Wonderful job!"

I was ecstatic. We were edging nearer and nearer to the launch date for our maiden voyage.

It was an exciting adventure, creating a character and a world that no one had ever seen before. We were in a different galaxy, a different time—everything about this role was completely different than anything I had ever done before.

It was even more exciting when we first stepped onto the *Enterprise* sets, because nothing like this starship had ever been seen before. Most people are amazed to learn how few sets there actually were—the bridge, the sickbay, the transporter room, the conference room, the crew quarters, the turboshaft and so forth. When you see the ship on film, you get an impression of enormous size, of deck after deck, compartment after compartment, corridor after corridor. In reality, the same few sets were redressed again and again to create new sets. The captain's cabin would become Mr. Spock's cabin, which would become Yeoman Rand's cabin. The briefing room would become the chapel and on and on. Our brilliant production designer, Walter "Matt" Jeffries, created a spectacular starship on a considerably less-than-spectacular budget.

Another hero of the *Star Trek* production crew is Jerry Finnerman, the show's cinematographer. His contribution to the show has been greatly underestimated. His skillful use of color, backlighting and focus effects greatly enhanced the visual impact of the series. The men on the show always looked hard-edged and strong under Jerry's intense lighting and carefully positioned shadows. The women were often photographed in soft-focus with color gel backlighting, giving them an air of almost ethereal beauty and mystery. Color drenched Jerry's images, and gave the show a visual feel that has never been duplicated by any other show, or even by the *Star Trek* shows and movies that came afterwards.

Jerry Finnerman's vivid and skillful use of color in the show may well have been one of the deciding factors that kept NBC from canceling the show after the first and second season. Some network and studio insiders have suggested that the famous "Save *Star Trek*" letter-writing campaigns may have had less to do with the show's two renewals by NBC than the fact that NBC was promoting itself as the color network. In the mid-sixties, most TV shows were still broadcast in black and white. NBC was owned by RCA, so it was in the interests of both NBC and RCA to get as many people as possible to go out and buy color TV sets. NBC may well have kept *Star Trek* alive in

This preproduction still for TV Guide was shot in front of a backdrop at NBC in Burbank, weeks before we began filming. Instead of the miniskirted uniform Bill Theiss designed for the series, I'm wearing the unisex velour tunic and black pants from the first two pilots. And instead of real Star Trek hand-phasers, we're armed with—you guessed it!—flashlights with colored lenses.

large part because it was such a beautiful, vividly colorful series which showcased NBC's ability to deliver brilliant color images. In short, *Star Trek* probably sold a lot of RCA TV sets—thanks to Bill Theiss' colorful costuming, Matt Jeffries' colorful sets, and Jerry Finnerman's vivid cinematography.

A lot of fans seem to believe that Gene Roddenberry did everything by himself to get the show off the ground and into orbit. Fact is, Gene was a master delegator.

His genius was in selecting talented, hard-working people he could trust to make his vision a reality. He relied on skilled, experienced Desilu executive Herb Solow to sell the show to NBC, and Herb came through. He relied on Matt Jeffries and Bill Theiss to create the look of the show, and they delivered. Bob Justman ran herd on practically every detail of the production. And while Gene was fanatical about making sure his directors had quality scripts to shoot, it was Gene Roddenberry's largely unsung, uncredited line producer, Gene Coon, along with story consultant John D. F. Black, who ensured script quality from initial treatments to final rewrites.

The two Genes, Roddenberry and Coon, decided that the first voyage of the *Enterprise* should be a simple shakedown cruise. They wanted to get the cast and crew's feet wet with a very simple story—no exteriors or planet sets, no elaborate special effects, no convoluted plotting or film editing. They settled on a script by veteran TV writer Jerry Sohl called "The Corbomite Maneuver," in which most of the action takes place on the bridge. I remember sitting down at a conference table for the first time with Bill Shatner, Leonard Nimoy, De Kelly and George Takei for our first read-through of the script. It was exciting to open the cover of the script, turn the pages, and watch the unfolding of the *Star Trek* universe for the very first time. I felt so lucky to be a part of it.

In the story, the *Enterprise* crew is roadblocked in space by a glowing alien cube. When Kirk orders the cube destroyed, an incredibly huge alien ship appears, looking like a massive molecule. Its alien captain, Balok, condemns the *Enterprise* to destruction within minutes. Captain Kirk, a poker-player at heart, bluffs the alien to a stand-off by claiming that the *Enterprise* is rigged with a substance called "corbomite." The corbomite, he lies convincingly, will destroy the alien ship if the *Enterprise* is destroyed. In the end, it turns out that the alien was running a bluff of his own—a test to see if the *Enterprise*'s intentions were truly peaceful. Instead of the menacing being projected on the *Enterprise* viewscreen, Balok turns out to be a short, jovial being (played by child actor Clint Howard, brother of Ron Howard). The alien menace is happily dispelled rather than violently defeated—a very cleverly written surprise-ending tale.

Star Trek was such an advanced concept that we all worried if the public would get it. The average television viewer probably hasn't a clue what a light-year or a parsec is, or why we use a transporter instead of simply landing the ship on a planet, or what "warp factor six" means. This concept went far beyond the old video sci-fi conventions of having rocket ships land tail-first in a Venusian swamp. We worried about whether people would think Leonard Nimoy's Mr. Spock was actually the Devil. We worried that people wouldn't get it—and we were right to worry, because the average viewer *didn't* get it! The network audience for the show would turn out to be very small, and the show really would not be a major success until it was cancelled and syndicated.

But in those early days, months before our first airdate, as we were reading our scripts, rehearsing, shooting scenes and watching the dailies, I began to get the feeling that there was something very special happening with *Star Trek*. I felt there was a magic chemistry to the cast. We played off each other well, and demonstrated a warm and touching vulnerability toward each other. Even people who didn't have a clue what antimatter is could enjoy the simmering romance between Kirk and Rand, the amiable antagonism between Mr. Spock and Dr. McCoy, the emotionalism of Kirk in constant collision with Spock's unassailable logic, and Mr. Scott's inevitable "Captain, I canna change the laws o' physics!" just before he proceeded to do just that and pull the ship's fat out of the fire.

Once, when I appeared at a *Trek* convention in England, I asked Patrick Stewart (Captain Picard in *Star Trek: The Next Generation*) how he felt about the chemistry of the new *Trek* series, and if he missed the strong dynamic that existed between Kirk, Spock and McCoy in the original series. His reply was something like this: "There's no question, the chemistry of the new series is more subtle and less vivid than that of the original series. Captain Picard is not the swashbuckler that Captain Kirk was. Mr. Data is not Mr. Spock. We do not have any characters who match the emotionalism of Dr. McCoy. The chemistry of our show is different because the themes and the intent of the show are different."

And he's right. The chemistry of the original *Star Trek* series is something that happens once in a given era, and can never be repeated. It was special—no, it was *unique*. The interplay between the classic *Trek* characters is as engaging and entertaining as that of any other ensemble show on television. I'm sure it was that warm and vulnerable chemistry that gave me a sense of belonging on *Star Trek*, and part of the reason I felt so lost and cast adrift when my character was written out of the show.

At *Trek* conventions, I'm always asked, "Did you and William Shatner have a real-life romance going on during the show?" The answer is no, we were never romantically involved with each other. And yet—

I was always aware of a tremendous attraction between us that was never consummated. Part of that attraction has to do with the roles we played. The scripts and the series format called for Kirk and Rand to have a repressed attraction and fascination for each other, and our job as actors was to *become* James Kirk and Janice Rand, to feel what they felt, to behave as they behaved, to immerse ourselves in their identities.

I remember that Bill used to stand behind me in certain scenes, and he would hold me, and the back of my body would be absolutely on fire for him! That's lust, not love. I was very attracted to him. He was very charismatic, very sexy. There was a strong physical attraction between us, but we never did anything about it.

I also was intimidated by Bill Shatner. He was so powerful—and I don't simply mean that he is physically powerful, but he also possesses a very strong personality. He was my leading man, and actresses have a hard time not falling in love with their leading man. I would like to think that the reason I never became involved with Bill Shatner was that I was moral and virtuous and I wanted to be a good girl. But I don't know if that's altogether true.

This scene from the episode "Balance of Terror" typifies the Kirk-Rand relationship, as it was explained to me by Gene Roddenberry. The Captain is like a tower of strength and invincibility on the bridge, even though the viewscreen shows that the Romulan photon torpedoes are on the way and we are about to get clobbered. In a crisis, the Yeoman and the Captain instinctively reach out for each other.

I believe I resisted my attraction for Bill in part because I was always in character. Yeoman Rand wouldn't hop into bed with Captain Kirk, so neither would I. On some level, I'm sure I intuitively knew that if I became involved off-screen with Bill, it would ruin the on-screen chemistry between Kirk and Rand. I cared about the character too much to do that.

I thought Captain Kirk was the most exciting character I had ever seen on the screen. The volatile, bombastic, charismatic Captain Kirk was perfectly balanced by the logical, strong, reserved Mr. Spock. I loved being in the middle of that wonderful aura in episodes like "Charlie X" and "Miri."

Bill Shatner was trained as a Shakespearean actor, a stage actor. Stage performances have to be bigger and broader in order to reach the audience in the back of the theater. Bill was often accused of overacting and not bringing his performance in closer and smaller for TV. But I absolutely loved his bold, swashbuckling manner. His incredible energy was perfect for the larger-than-life captain of the U.S.S. *Enterprise—*

and when nuance was needed (as for example, when he became the stand-in father figure for troubled adolescent Charlie X), Bill could always supply that as well.

William Shatner has been criticized by some of his fellow cast members for being self-absorbed and inconsiderate on the set of *Star Trek*. In Bill's defense, there was a lot going on in his life. I remember him as being very sad and withdrawn during those early weeks of shooting. His father was dying at the time, his marriage was breaking up, and he obviously loved his two little girls and wanted to be a good dad to them, no matter what happened to his marriage. He didn't seem to have close friends to confide in, and he was under a lot of stress as the star of a network series. I suppose Bill was self-absorbed during that time—but given the way his life was disintegrating, I can't hold that against him. The wonder of William Shatner is that, with so much going on in his off-screen life, he was so engaging and commanding on-screen.

Leonard Nimoy was my best friend on the set of *Star Trek*. He probably saved my life when I was bitter and suicidal after being written out of the show. He is a very serious actor and filmmaker, and he coached me and helped me prepare for my role. Whenever I asked him for some insight into my character or advice in how to deliver a certain line, he would have the perfect answer.

I remember one day, a few weeks before the first episode of *Star Trek* aired, Leonard called and asked if he could drop by my house for some reason. Before he arrived, I told my boys that this nice man was coming over to the house, and that he was the star of the new TV show I was in. "He's going to be very famous," I told them, "because he plays a man with pointed ears who came from another planet."

When Leonard arrived, they looked him up and down and said, "He doesn't have pointy ears!" and "He isn't famous! I've never seen him on TV!" They didn't think that Leonard Nimoy was any big deal. I just laughed and laughed, because I knew what my boys didn't yet know—that this man was going to be a nationwide sensation.

Leonard is the exact opposite of the emotionless alien he played. While Mr. Spock is mysterious, cool and smugly logical, Leonard Nimoy is sensitive, vulnerable and attuned to the feelings of those around him. As an actor, he is the complete professional. He always cares about the character, the show, the quality of the performance. He's not interested in one-upping the other actors.

On one occasion, Fred Phillips was talked into making up Leonard's son, Adam, as a Vulcan—pointed ears, arched eyebrows and all. They put Adam in the captain's chair on the *Enterprise* bridge. When Leonard arrived for a late call to the set, there was Adam. It was adorable! They really looked like father and son—because *both* were made up as Vulcans!

Leonard enjoyed the joke, even though he normally kept his kids as far away from the studio as possible. He didn't want his children having anything to do with show business. We all tried to talk Leonard into letting his kids appear as extras in "Miri," along with my boys and Bill Shatner's girls, but he absolutely would not allow it. The only time Leonard would really allow his kids to come to the studio was around their birthdays. We always had birthday parties for the kids of the stars over at the studio commissary. We'd have a cake and ice cream and games and songs. Everybody on the show really loved kids and parties.

DeForest Kelly was a "bad guy."

At least that's what most Hollywood casting directors thought. He had played a hundred bad guys in TV westerns throughout the 1950s and '60s—outlaws, cattle-rustlers, gamblers and gunslingers.

But Gene Roddenberry saw a lot more in De Kelly than a cowboy with a black hat. He saw a spacefaring country doctor. Oddly, though De was Gene's first choice for the ship's doctor from the very beginning, Gene deferred to the advice of others in choosing John Hoyt as Dr. Boyce in the first pilot, and Paul Fix as Dr. Piper in the second. Only after NBC picked up *Star Trek* as a regular series did Gene rescue De (and me!) from the unsold "Police Story" pilot. It's impossible to imagine *Star Trek* without De Kelly's wonderful character, Dr. Leonard McCoy.

Part of the unique characterization and chemistry of *Star Trek* is DeForest Kelly's role as Captain Kirk's friend, personal bartender, confidante, counselor and priest. He was also a damn fine doctor. He will always be known for his famous tagline, "I'm a doctor, not a [fill in the blank]!" As in, "I'm a doctor, not a bricklayer!" Or, "I'm a doctor, not a mechanic!" Or, "I'm a doctor, not a magician!" Or, "What am I, a doctor or a moon shuttle conductor?" And then there's his other, equally famous tagline: "He's dead, Jim."

As an actor, De is unassuming, hard-working and professional. He doesn't get into ego-battles, studio politics or fighting over lines and scripts. He never creates problems or tension on the set. Instead, he goes quietly and professionally about the task of bringing his character to life. On *Star Trek*, he crafted a character who emerged as a major element in the chemistry of the show's ensemble cast. De's warm, wise, compassionate "Bones" McCoy became a critical balancing force to the forceful, emotional, action-oriented Captain Kirk and the steely, logical Mr. Spock. McCoy would often chide Spock for being too coldly calculating, or question Kirk for being too rash and quick to resort to violent means, often getting in the last word: "I hope you know what you're doing, Jim," or, "You're taking a big gamble, Jim." But when Captain Kirk experienced his Hamlet-like moments of self-doubt, McCoy would be there to help Kirk regain his self-confidence.

DeForest Kelly is such a sweet, decent, thoroughly *nice* man that you wonder how in the world he was able to play so many TV villains before *Star Trek* came along. He's a true southern gentleman. I just love DeForest Kelly—he and his wife Caroline have always been wonderful to me.

It was De who first brought me back into the world of *Star Trek* after I had been away for almost a decade. By the mid-'70s, all the *Trek* stars were appearing at *Star Trek* conventions—all, that is, except me. My *Star Trek* memories were so bitter and painful that I wanted nothing to do with *Star Trek*. I didn't even know what a *Star Trek* convention was.

One day in 1976, I was in line at the unemployment office in Van Nuys—a great place for actors to meet other actors. Just a few places ahead of me in line was DeForest Kelley. He spotted me and waved. We chatted for a few minutes, then he said, "You know, they're all asking for you at *Star Trek*."

"What do you mean?" I asked. "*Star Trek*'s cancelled."

"Well, haven't you heard about the conventions?"

"What conventions?"

So De told me all about *Star Trek* conventions, where the Trekkies and Trekkers gathered to meet the stars, trade memorabilia and fan magazines, watch screenings of old episodes and generally have a great time with fellow fans. "There's a big convention coming up in a few weeks," he said. "You really ought to be there."

So he told me whom to call, and I was added to the guest lineup at the big Equicon '76 gathering in L.A. *Star Trek* conventions have been a big part of my life ever since.

There was a great spirit of camaraderie on the set of *Star Trek*. I felt very close to the cast and crew. Jimmy Doohan and I were buddies. There was a bar Jimmy and I and some of the others liked to go to on the corner of the Desilu lot, a place called Oblath's. We would always end up there, or at another place called Sorentino's, after a day of shooting. We would laugh and carry on, and Jimmy would tell the most marvelous stories. We had a great time.

George Takei—the ship's dependable helmsman, Mr. Sulu—has also been a good friend over the years. I've worked with him in the original series, in the *Star Trek* movies, at conventions and even a 1996 episode of *Star Trek: Voyager*. Like De Kelly, George got his start playing bad guys, because that was, unfortunately, the most common sort of role being written for Asian characters back then. *Star Trek* gave George the opportunity to present an Asian character as a positive role model. George Takei is the only person I know who calls me "Gracie." Somehow our two names just go together: George and Gracie!

Nichelle Nichols (Lieutenant Uhura) was always very kind to me when I was on the show. Sometimes at the end of a day's shooting, she would come over to my dressing room and we'd share hot coffee and spicy talk. Like me, she was a singer before she was an actress, having toured extensively with Duke Ellington, Lionel Hampton and other jazz greats. We had a lot in common, and often compared stories about mutual friends in the music business.

I loved my new role, my new friends, my new adventure in "space, the final frontier." But at the same time my professional life was on the rise, my personal life was headed for a fall—and I didn't even know it.

I was the original conehead! The application of the Janice Rand beehive begins by securing a cone of lacquered netting, like an upside-down coffee filter, to my own hair, which is in pincurls. Once the cone is secured, the wig goes over it and is anchored to the cone. The wig took about a half hour to apply.

Right at the beginning, when I went in to be fitted for my uniform, Bill Theiss, the costume designer, said to me, "Grace, you're a little overweight. You really have to slim down a bit, or the costume won't look right. Why don't you call your doctor and have him give you some pills?"

So I did. I called my gynecologist and he gave me pills. He was a Doctor Feel-Good, and he had prescribed plenty of pills for me before. When I was on the L.A. stage as Lucy Brown in *Three Penny Opera*, I was told I was too thin, I needed to get a bit more fat on my bones. So I went to my gynecologist and he gave me high-dosage birth control pills. I put twenty pounds on with those pills in nothing flat. When Bill Theiss told me I was too fat for *Star Trek*, I just went to the same Doctor Feel-Good, and he gave me "uppers," amphetamines, and *voila*! I lost weight just like that.

That was the beginning of my problem with amphetamines. I would take amphetamines to keep the weight off, and to get me through the day. I had to be up at 4, at the studio by 5:30, in makeup by 6, and on the set by 8—and the amphetamines gave me the energy to keep going. I was going very fast with my feet in cement. The amphetamines would make me edgy and anxious, so at night, after I got home, I'd drink to take away the edginess and come down at night.

But I never drank on the set, I never let alcohol interfere with my performance on *Star Trek*. I was an evening and weekend drinker. And, of course, at the Friday night wrap parties on the set or over at Oblath's with my *Star Trek* castmates, I could get pretty high. Once you got me started, I never wanted to go home. I was the life of the party and I wanted to keep going.

Drugs and alcohol are a terrible combination. Together, they multiply the addictive properties of each other. They say it takes about 20 years to "cook" an alcoholic, to get him really hooked. I began drinking at 13 and I was a confirmed alcoholic by around 35 or 36. They also say that if you're doing drugs and alcohol together, you can cook in a fraction of the time. I began to show the symptoms of a confirmed alcoholic around the time I started doing uppers and booze at the same time.

I sometimes drank at wrap parties until I couldn't drive myself home. I'd start off in my car, then I'd have to pull off the road and sleep. There were times I spent half the night in the parking lot at Ralph's Market or Vons because I was seeing double. I could feel a blackout coming, so I'd pull into the lot and pass out. I'd wake up a few hours later when the early morning sun peeked through my windshield. Then I'd hurry home and quietly sneak into the house before my boys and the housekeeper would wake up.

Even so, I didn't have the slightest idea that I was an alcoholic. After all, I didn't drink on the job, I functioned just fine (so I thought). I just liked to get high every weekend like everybody else. An alcoholic? Me? The idea didn't even occur to me.

Even when I wasn't drinking, I had what is called the "ism" of the disease of alcoholism. The alcohol part of alcoholism is a self-induced illness, something the alcoholic self-inflicts every time she takes a drink. The ism part of alcoholism is emotional, and I believe it is genetic in origin. The ism is that gnawing sense of restlessness, depression, anxiety and guilt that the alcoholic feels. The ism of alcoholism makes us self-centered. All those feelings are part of the disease—that is, the disease, the sense of not being at-ease. Cancer is a disease, but alcoholism is a dis-ease. Having the dis-ease is the opposite of being at-ease.

When I became a part of *Star Trek*, I experienced moments of excitement and incredible happiness because of the newfound success I was enjoying. But there was also a strong emotional current of guilt and unease.

Why did I feel guilt? Because I had begun sabotaging my marriage to Steve. On some level, I had concluded that my marriage was holding back my career. As I moved into my new identity as Yeoman Janice Rand, I began escaping my identity as Steve's dutiful wife. I ordered him out of the house and filed for divorce. Secure in the belief that I was on the verge of becoming a star, I even turned down alimony. I didn't need his money. I was going to be *rich*!

I have to say this about Steve: He was never a deadbeat dad. Even though I turned down alimony, he willingly paid child support and he was never late, not even once. I never had to call him and ask for the money. Steve loved his boys and he showed it. I let Steve's attorney handle the whole divorce, and didn't bother getting my own attorney. So I got railroaded—but I made the choice to get railroaded, not Steve. It was my fault that I didn't get alimony, no one else's. We alcoholics are great at fighting for second best.

I knew I was doing the wrong thing by getting a divorce—that's not something a "good girl" does. But I did it anyway. I had very mixed emotions. I was enjoying the tremendous high of finally having something I felt a part of, a place of acceptance on *Star Trek*. But I also felt horrible over the fact that I was breaking up my nest. I had built this nest and I had these two wonderful children and this beautiful house—and I was trashing it. I wasn't even sure why I was trashing it. I just had this idea that there wasn't room in my life for both a marriage and a career on *Star Trek*.

I blame myself, not Steve, for the divorce. I think he really meant to do right by our marriage, but I was a very difficult character to live with. I could list a lot of Steve's flaws, but why? I was the alcoholic, not him. If he was hard to live with, I was even more so. He was not an abuser. He was good to the kids when we were together. He was even kind to my parents; he treated them with respect. So, looking back, I have to shoulder most of the blame for our failed marriage.

During the divorce proceedings, the attorney told me I needed a witness to come in and corroborate my identity—I'm not sure why, but that's what he told me. So I asked my mother, who was living in California by this time, to come into the divorce court and simply tell the judge who I was, that I was her daughter.

"But I can't do that," she said.

"Why not?" I asked, stunned. To my mind, it was such a simple request.

"Because you're not my daughter," she said. "I can't go into a courtroom and lie."

"I'm not asking you to lie," I said. "I just want you to go in and tell the truth. Just tell the court that you adopted me in 1930 and you raised me as your adopted daughter and my name is Grace Lee Whitney. I just want you to tell the court who I am."

"But," she responded, "I really don't know who you are."

Those words hit me in the face like a physical slap. "Of course you know who I am!" I said. "I'm your daughter! Your adopted daughter!"

"I can't go into a courtroom and say that!" she said, shaking her head. I could see she was not going to budge.

At that moment, I realized what she was really telling me. On one level, it was true that she didn't want to lie. My mother always had an unbending rule about telling the absolute, verbatim truth. I honestly believe that if she had been hiding Jews in her basement in Nazi Germany in the 1930s, and the storm troopers had come to her door and said, "Are there any Jews in your house?" she would have said, "I cannot tell a lie. Yes, they're all down in the basement."

At the same time, while she was stubbornly insistent on always being accurate and truthful, her refusal to help me in divorce court was really an act of monstrous denial, of *lying to herself*. What she really meant when she said, "I can't lie," was, "I can't tell the truth. I can't tell that courtroom that I was never able to bear a child, that I couldn't procreate. I can't tell anyone that you are my *adopted* daughter, because I am ashamed."

I once told this story to a friend of mine, and he said, "That is really bizarre!" I replied, "Of course it's bizarre! You don't think I got this nuts having a mother who's normal, do you?" My mother did the best she could. But there were some truths she just couldn't face, and some things that, emotionally, she just couldn't give me.

These are the issues I wrestled with as I stepped aboard the Starship *Enterprise* in mid-1966—the emotional upheaval of my self-inflicted divorce, and the ongoing struggle of wondering who I was, where I belonged and what was my place in the world. While Janice Rand was trekking through the galaxy, Grace Lee Whitney was free-falling to earth.

These are the Voyages...

. . . .

C aptain Kirk tried to rape me.

It happened in the episode "The Enemy Within." It happened in a TV show. It was fantasy.

But it was only a few weeks later that The Executive sexually assaulted me. Not a fantasy assault, not television violence. It was all too horribly real.

Throughout the late spring and summer of 1966, my life was a swirl of fantasy colliding with reality. The heights of exhilaration alternated with the depths of depression. From the moment I was beamed aboard the U.S.S. *Enterprise*, I was whipsawed up and down, back and forth, on the wildest emotional roller-coaster of my life.

Monday, May 23, 1966, was my first day of rehearsal with the entire cast of *Star Trek*. The next day, Tuesday the 24th, we began shooting the first regular season episode, "The Corbomite Maneuver." In fact, our associate producer on *Star Trek*, Robert Justman (who kept precise records), tells me that shooting began that day at precisely 8:22 in the morning.

Series television is an assembly line job—and the pressure to produce on-time and on-budget was fierce on the *Star Trek* set. Very often, we would finish shooting one show at noon, and we'd start in on the next show right after lunch. On many TV series, particularly half-hour comedies, you begin by gathering all the actors around a table to read through the script. We rarely had that luxury on *Star Trek*. Rehearsals were done on the fly. As we came to each new scene, the director would talk us through the staging of the scene, then the actors would walk through it a couple times, and we'd shoot it.

We spent eight days shooting "Corbomite"—it was a shakedown cruise and we needed to get our "space legs" under us. My old friend, Joe Sargent, directed the episode (his only *Trek* outing), and he turned in a very taut, suspenseful episode. Bill Shatner as Captain Kirk was in top form from the get-go, totally controlled and commanding, as he engaged in a high-stakes battle of wits with the alien commander.

In the early shows, Leonard Nimoy and the various writers and directors struggled to find the Spockish response to emotionally charged situations. We all know that the half-human, half-Vulcan Mr. Spock comes from a culture that exercises iron control over emotion. Yet, in "The Corbomite Maneuver," when the *Enterprise* is suddenly shaken by a force beam from the alien ship, Mr. Spock loses his cool and yells, "Tractor beam, Captain! Something's grabbed us! Hard!" He also shouts, almost panicky, when the engines are superheating. There are many such moments in the two pilots and the early regular season shows as Leonard and the creative staff struggled to find the consistency of the character.

But there was one moment in "Corbomite" where director Joe Sargent demonstrated a moment of brilliant clarity and insight into Spock's character. As the massive, molecule-shaped alien vessel fills the viewscreen on the *Enterprise* bridge, Sargent cuts from crewman to crewman, from Kirk to Sulu to Bailey—and each one registers alarm. But then Sargent cuts to Mr. Spock. The Vulcan's not afraid. He's *curious*. "Fascinating," he says, using a word that forever defines his character in the public mind.

Throughout the series, Leonard will deliver that same line with an even more cool and unperturbed raised eyebrow, an even calmer air of scientific detachment, and he will do so even while gazing into the jaws of some hideous death. That's the key to Spock's character—and the key to his phenomenal popularity on the series, especially among female viewers. We women are attracted to cool, strong guys. And no one is cooler in a crisis than Spock. When he can stare down a hypermassive alien starship and merely find it "fascinating," then we know that here is someone larger than life, larger than anything that can happen to him.

This first episode also shows that Mr. Spock's deadpan, logical nature can be the source of great comedic moments. After the initial crisis encounter with the alien cube, there is this exchange between Spock and the high-strung, neophyte navigator, Lieutenant Dave Bailey (Anthony Call):

> BAILEY
> Raising my voice back there doesn't mean I was
> scared and couldn't do my job. It means I happen to have
> a human thing called an adrenal gland.
>
> SPOCK
> Hmm. It does sound most inconvenient, however.
> I would consider having it removed.

I remember being a little baffled by my role in that episode. After having had many conversations with Gene Roddenberry about my character's function in the chemistry of the show, I was disappointed that this episode contained comparatively little hint of the "Matt-and-Miss-Kitty" dimension he had envisioned. The script presented me as a space-waitress. I brought the captain his lunch and his coffee—and the captain even stiffed me on the tip!

I did get to show a little yeoman-like resourcefulness in that episode. There is a scene where I appear on the bridge with a pot of hot coffee. Captain Kirk and Dr. McCoy are surprised because the ship has lost all power—even the ship's Mr. Coffee is out of commission. When McCoy says, "I thought the power was off in the galley," I perkily reply, "I used a hand phaser and zap! Hot coffee!"

We filmed a scene in which I went into the captain's cabin to lay out his uniform for him (so I was a maid as well as a waitress!). While I was up on a ladder, taking some articles of clothing down from an upper storage bin, Captain Kirk was below me, giving my fanny the once-over! A little risqué for 1960s television—and I'm sure that's why the scene was cut.

Speaking of risqué: Around the time *Star Trek* was going into production, I was approached to be interviewed and photographed for *Playboy*. Imagine, Yeoman Rand in the buff! I turned it down, just as I had always turned down offers to do film roles with nude scenes. More than anything else, I rejected such offers because of my kids. I didn't want my boys someday watching an old movie or opening a magazine and finding their mother looking back at them in the altogether!

One thing I vividly recall during our first couple weeks on the set was an overwhelming sense of pressure—pressure to perform, pressure to succeed, pressure to please the producers, the director and the other cast members. And it wasn't just me—we all felt it. Even my stand-in, Jeannie Malone,* felt the pressure. She told me that, during her first few days on *Star Trek*, she was so eager to please everyone that she never stopped smiling. "I smiled so much," she said, "I thought my face was going to crack." I was the same way—people-pleasing like crazy, doing anything and everything to be liked. *Star Trek* was my new adoptive family, and I wanted to stay aboard the *Enterprise* for the duration. I really wanted my new family members to like me.

I didn't appear in the next episode, "Mudd's Women," which was shot in early June, but I did come to the studio and watch the filming. I wanted to soak up everything I could about the show, the characters, the storylines. I was very conscientious about being the best I could be, about contributing everything I could to the show.

We began shooting the third regular season episode, "The Enemy Within," on Tuesday, June 14. The show was written by Richard Matheson and directed by Leo Penn (Sean Penn's father). In the story, a survey team led by Captain Kirk lands on a planet of subfreezing temperatures. When Kirk beams back to the ship, a transporter malfunction splits him into two identical men. One is aggressive, uncontrolled and evil—the "dark side" of Captain Kirk. The other is kind and good, but weak, indecisive and lacking in command ability—the "good side" of Captain Kirk. Until the transporter can be repaired, Sulu and the rest of the landing party are stranded on the killer-cold planet. It becomes a race against time to repair the transporter, reunite the "dark" and "light" halves of Captain Kirk, and beam the landing party back to warmth and safety.

I loved watching William Shatner portray these two sides of Captain Kirk. He went wonderfully crazy in that episode—it was the classic, bombastic, over-the-top Shatner, and he was very charismatic in the dual role.

---

*A stand-in is someone who is physically similar to the actor he or she stands in for. The stand-in is costumed like the actor and takes the actor's place on the set while the cinematographer and other technicians light the set and position the cameras for the next shot. This allows the actor to stay fresh and out of the hot lights until needed for the actual filming of the scene.

This was the show in which the evil Kirk attempts to rape Yeoman Rand. There's a lot of truth in that scene—and I think it is significant that when he appears, he is swigging from a bottle of Saurian brandy. What happens to Captain Kirk when his good self is stripped away and the evil underside is exposed is much like what happens to a man who has been drinking heavily. His inhibitions, his judgment, his caring, his compassion, his concern for others, his spiritual side—all of that is stripped away. What's left is the evil underside of a man—his animal self, his hunger and naked lust, his self-will-run-riot. The flesh always wars against the spirit—and when the spiritual aspect of Kirk is stripped away, the raw, pulsating flesh reigns supreme in the evil Kirk's body.

In the scene, the evil Captain Kirk is already lurking in my cabin when I enter. (Trivia buffs take note: This scene reveals that Yeoman Rand's cabin was designated Compartment 3C 46.) As I enter, I don't see the captain at first—then he comes out from behind a partition. Seeing him, I'm startled and frightened. Even after the initial fright passes, there is apprehension and confusion on my face as the scene develops:

> ME
> Captain! You startled me— Is there
> something that you— Can I help you, Captain?

> EVIL KIRK
> Jim will do here, Janice.

> ME
> *(surprised and alarmed)*
> Oh!

> EVIL KIRK
> *(advancing toward me)*
> You're too beautiful to ignore.
> You're too much woman.
> We've both been pretending too long.
> *(He grabs me roughly.)*
> Let's stop pretending.
> Come here, Janice! Don't fight me, Janice!

And then he is all over me. It's a violent, scary scene. Bill is a very physical actor and extremely strong. Because I had been on diet pills for so long, I was very lightweight, and Bill picked me up like a twig and threw me around the room. He really got into the part!

At one point, he gets on top of me, and I fight him and scratch his face. Then I get to my feet, hide behind my artist's easel—and as he rushes me, I push the easel at him, then run to the door and yell to a passing crewman, "Call Mr. Spock!" The evil

Two out of three falls, Captain? In "The Enemy Within," I did my own stunts—and acquired the bruises to prove it!

Kirk lunges at me, throws me across the room, then dashes out the door and pummels the crewman as he is trying to use the intercom to call for help.

We did endless takes of that scene—and some of the retakes were due to the fact that my beehive wig wouldn't stay on through all that tossing and shaking. Again and again, Kirk jumped on top of me and tried to kiss me, and each time I pushed him away. Finally, during one take where we were struggling together, practically in the "missionary position," I stopped struggling. I just let him kiss me!

There's a very famous still from that scene which has appeared in all the *Trek* magazines and calendars—a picture of Kirk on top of Rand while they wrestle on the floor. When the fans ask me about that picture at conventions, I tell them I have that same picture hanging on my wall—only I have it turned upside down so that Janice Rand is on top of Kirk! That especially gets a laugh from the female fans—they think that's a terrific idea!

It took us the better part of a day to shoot the rape scene. By the end of the shoot, I was a mass of bruises. For days afterward, you could see the prints of his hands on my arms where he grabbed me and threw me around.

After the attempted rape, there is a scene involving me, Mr. Spock, Dr. McCoy and Captain Kirk. It's a crucial scene which draws upon the subtle attraction between Kirk and Rand for its emotional power. The evil Kirk referred to that attraction when he said, "We've both been pretending too long." In this scene, I am telling Spock and McCoy what the captain did to me in my cabin. Because the captain—the good Kirk—is standing right there as I tell my story, I'm intimidated and it's hard for me to get the words out. I'm traumatized, tearful, hurt and confused because I've been attracted to Captain Kirk, and now he has done this terrible thing to me and I can't understand it.

I remember that we were shooting the scene just before the lunch break and everybody was in a hurry. Although Bill Shatner was in the medium and wide shots of that scene, at that time we were only filming my close-up. In that shot, I didn't have any lines with Bill, so he didn't need to be on the set. I noticed as they were setting up the shot that Bill was there, standing behind the cameras. I remember thinking, *I wonder what Bill is doing here.* Leonard Nimoy was also there, because I was delivering my lines to him.

The director said, "Action!" Instantly, Bill came out from behind the camera and *smacked* me right across the face! It stung and shocked me, and tears welled into my eyes, causing my mascara to run. Instantly, the pain and confusion began to pour out of me.

"He kissed me," I began, "and he said he was the captain. And he said he could order me to— I didn't know what to do! When he mentioned the feelings we'd been hiding and he started talking about us— Well, after all, he is the captain…"

When I finished, the director yelled, "Cut! Print it!" The cast and crew applauded, and Leonard gave me a hug. I looked at Bill, and he smiled at me and said, "Beautiful!" Then we all went to lunch.

We had shot the rape scene a day or two earlier, and sometimes it's hard to get back into the emotions of a previously shot scene when some time has passed. Bill just knew that a surprise slap across the face would put me right back in that frame of mind, that painful sense of having just been violated by the captain. He knew that it would provide just the right emotional impact to motivate me to do the scene. As a result, I gave a terrific performance in a single take.

That was my reputation—"One-Take Whitney." My first take was always my best.

The theme of good versus evil in "The Enemy Within" is fascinating. The message of the episode is that all of us have our good and evil halves, and these forces are constantly at war within us—the flesh at war with the spirit. But more than that, this episode suggests that we all *need* our dark side—that we can't live as whole human beings without it. And that's just plain *wrong!*

The story is a science fictional parable of the ancient Chinese dualism of *yin* and *yang*—the idea that wholeness can only be found by embracing both opposite extremes: male and female, north and south, winter and summer, shadow and light, life and death, good and evil. According to this view, good and evil should not be seen as opposing each other, but complementing each other. The one is as necessary as the other. This is also the concept behind the "good side" and the "dark side" of The Force in *Star Wars*.

The message of "The Enemy Within" is that by managing our passions, character defects and emotions with reason and logic, we can be whole and well-balanced as human beings. That's why the good Kirk tells the evil Kirk, "Hold on! You won't be afraid if you use your mind! Think! Think!" In other words, we shouldn't try to destroy the evil in us, but to embrace it, master it and harness its raw power with our intellect and reasoning ability. But as Mr. Spock would say, "That is not logical."

After all, what was this evil thing that was unleashed in Kirk by the transporter malfunction? A *beast*—a thing of pure appetite, lust, cruelty, and self-will-run-riot. And the good Kirk? He was the one who was kind, caring, compassionate—in short, he was *human* as opposed to bestial. He was the best of what is human in all of us. The script placed the ability to command and make decisions in the evil Kirk—and I believe that's wrong. All of Kirk's higher functions—his ability to reason, to logically think his way to a decision—belong to the human side of Kirk, not the animal side. His ability to lead and command should have been within his good side, not his dark side.

I do not believe we need our evil side. It is the source of our weakness and cowardice, our selfishness and lust, our hate and intolerance, our self-will-run-riot. Kirk ended up embracing his dark half and receiving it back into himself. In reality, we must continually purge that darkness by filling ourselves with light and truth.

After the evil and good Jim Kirks are reunited, Dr. McCoy asks the captain how he feels. "How?" responds the captain. "I've just seen a part of myself no man should ever see." Wrong. That is the side of ourselves that we must face squarely and unflinchingly. To avoid the truth of our own evil is an act of denial. The evil in us is more powerful than our will to do good. The only way to defeat it is to make a searching and fearless moral inventory of our lives, to admit the exact nature of our evil, and to allow God to remove the evil from us—day by day and piece by piece.

At the end of "The Enemy Within," there is a badly botched attempt at humor. In a poorly motivated and out of character moment, Mr. Spock needles me about my feelings toward the evil Kirk (who came to be called "the Imposter," even though he was supposedly every bit as much a part of the "real" James T. Kirk as the good Kirk). There is almost a nasty leer on Spock's face as he says to me, "The Imposter had some very interesting qualities, wouldn't you say, yeoman?" My response was to ignore the jibe.

I can't imagine any more cruel and insensitive comment a man (or Vulcan) could make to a woman who has just been through a sexual assault! But then, some men really do think that women want to be raped. So the writer of the script (ostensibly Richard Matheson—although the line could have been added by Gene Roddenberry or an assistant scribe) gives us a leering Mr. Spock who suggests that Yeoman Rand *enjoyed* being raped and found the evil Kirk attractive!

This scene is doubly ironic in view of how wonderfully caring and compassionate the *real* Leonard Nimoy was a few weeks later after the *real* Grace Lee Whitney was sexually assaulted and violated by The Executive.

We finished filming "The Enemy Within" the morning of Wednesday, June 22. After lunch, we came back and began filming "The Man Trap"—the "salt vampire" episode, the very first *Star Trek* episode the world would see. Marc Daniels (a veteran of everything from intense television dramas to "I Love Lucy") came aboard as director. He would eventually direct more *Trek* episodes than any other director. The episode, written by George Clayton Johnson, is filled with plenty of horrific and suspenseful moments. It was a great debut episode for the series.

One of my favorite moments in the entire series is the scene in "The Man Trap" where Sulu (George Takei) and I are in a botanical garden filled with alien plants. George has always been wonderful to work with—a very lighthearted, fun-loving soul—and this episode was no exception. I enter the botanical garden—actually the sickbay set redressed and filled with outlandish plants—with a tray of food for Sulu (how do you like that? I'm a space-waitress again!) One of the specimens in the botanical garden is a woman-groping alien plant named Beauregard—actually an animated puppet operated from below by one of the stagehands. I was right in front of the table with my short skirt, and the stagehand was down there looking up my skirt. Throughout the shooting of that scene, the plant kept reaching for me and trying to get personal!

The scene was a bit of comic relief to break the tension as the "salt vampire" stalked me and other crew members aboard the *Enterprise*.

There were a lot of dirty remarks going on as we shot that scene, and it was very funny. We had to do several retakes because either George or I would lose composure and burst out laughing.

On Thursday, June 30, we again finished one show in the morning and started another show after lunch. The next episode we shot was "The Naked Time," written by John D.F. Black and directed by Marc Daniels. In that episode, a landing party returns to the *Enterprise* from investigating a collapsing planet—and they have unwittingly brought aboard a fast-spreading infection that causes madness and death. It's interesting that, at one point in the show, Dr. McCoy observes that the disease "acts like alcohol—it depresses the centers of judgment and self-control," something I know a little bit about!

The alcohol-like disease affects each infected crewman differently. One crewman, Lieutenant Kevin Riley, locks himself in engineering and sabotages the ship's engines. Captain Kirk loses the ability to command. Sulu takes up a sword believing himself to be all three Musketeers rolled into one. Nurse Chapel confesses her love for Mr. Spock. Even Spock becomes infected, triggering the release of Spock's suppressed human emotions in a very moving scene. Spock weeps—and the tears he sheds are tears of remorse: "My mother—I never told her I loved her."

The tension of this very suspenseful episode is occasionally broken by moments of humor. Some of the funniest lines in the episode go by so quickly that many viewers miss them, such as the brief exchange when Sulu, crazed by the alien disease and waving his sword all about, grabs Uhura and shouts, "I'll protect you, fair maiden!" To which Uhura replies, "Sorry, neither!"

Happily for me, in this episode Yeoman Rand gets to do more than wait tables and serve coffee, so that the character begins to fulfill Gene Roddenberry's original vision of the role. At one point, for example, after Lieutenant Sulu has gone mad and abandoned his post, Captain Kirk roughly orders me to take the helm of the starship. All right! Yeoman Rand in the driver's seat of the Starship *Enterprise*. Let's put the top down and floor it!

There is a scene between Kirk and Spock that dramatically reveals Captain Kirk's inner struggle and repressed love for Yeoman Rand. After the infected Mr. Spock pours out his grief over his Earth-born mother's tragic life on Vulcan, a world without love, Captain Kirk responds:

"Love—you're better off without yours, and I'm better off without mine!" Spreading his hands, indicating the *Enterprise*, Kirk adds, "This vessel—I give, she takes. She won't permit me a life—I have to live hers. ...That beautiful yeoman—have you noticed her, Mr. Spock? You're allowed to notice her. The captain's not permitted a woman to touch, to hold... a beach to walk on, a few days with no braid on my shoulder—"

Later in the story, the captain is on the bridge, and I am standing beside the command chair. Captain Kirk reaches out for me—but his hand stops short, not quite touching me, but wanting to. "No beach to walk on..." he murmurs.

"Sir?" I asked, bewildered. I remember that as we played that scene, Bill Shatner seemed so lost and lonely, so full of pain, that I just wanted to reach out and hold him. It was a powerful, emotional moment.

By fadeout, we see that the hero-captain is also a tragic figure. James T. Kirk is a man who in his heart of hearts wants to be loved and to give love. But he cannot. He is trapped by his sense of duty, and by the demands of that most jealous lover of all, the Starship *Enterprise*.

After we finished shooting "The Naked Time" on July 11, we started right in on "Charlie X" with director Lawrence Dobkin. Screenwriter Dorothy Fontana wrote a beautiful part for me as the object of a troubled young teenager's first crush. When I opened the script for the first time, I was struck by what a tender, sensitive, yet powerful tale it was. The story wrings every emotion out of you—fear, horror, sympathy, laughter. Seventeen-year-old Charlie Evans, the "Charlie X" of the title, is easily the most frightening yet sympathetic character ever presented on television.

Charlie is discovered marooned on the planet Thasus. He is the sole survivor of a ship that crashed on the planet when he was an infant. Transferred from his rescue ship, the *Antares*, to the *Enterprise*, he is a mystery to Kirk, Spock and McCoy. They cannot understand how he managed to survive all those years alone on a desolate planet. A teenager with all the healthy teenage drives, but without any social skills, Charlie tries to understand human relationships—and his own strange feelings of attraction (he calls it feeling "hungry all over") for Yeoman Rand.

Soon, Captain Kirk learns that the reason Charlie survived on Thasus all those years was that he was not alone—there are Thasians with incredible powers, and they taught those powers to Charlie so that he could survive. Now Charlie has all these raging adolescent hormones, emotions and frustrations. But unlike normal teenagers, he also possesses *unlimited power*, and that makes him an enormous threat to everyone aboard the *Enterprise*. Charlie even uses his power to make people "go away," and to destroy the rescue ship, the *Antares*, from long range.

Seventeen-year-old Charlie was played—brilliantly and convincingly—by 36-year-old actor Robert Walker, Jr. Already quite accomplished in theatrical films (he played the title role in *Ensign Pulver* with Jack Lemmon), Robert Walker was a stroke of casting luck for *Star Trek*. It's impossible to imagine anyone else in the role—he captured the perfect balance, projecting vulnerability, innocence and horrifying menace all the same time. A lesser actor could not have handled the range and depth of the character.

At times, Charlie is a child, looking to Captain Kirk, Dr. McCoy and Spock with an almost puppy-like need to be liked, to be instructed, to be validated, to be told that he is okay. The first time Charlie meets me, he eyes me with astonished fascination and asks, "Are you a *girl?*"

Later, Charlie sees two crewmen talking in a hallway. "See you in the rec room, eh?" says one. "You've got a deal, friend," says the other, delivering a slap to his buddy's bottom (it's a guy thing). Taking this in, Charlie figures a slap on the rear is how people demonstrate friendship to each other. So, a couple scenes later, when I say to Charlie, "I'm off at fourteen-hundred—why don't you join me in recreation room six?" he just copies what he has seen. "You've got a deal, friend!" he says, administering a socko slap to my posterior. Poor guy! He has no clue why I'm so offended and angry!

From childlike vulnerability, Charlie can switch to deadly menace in a heartbeat. At one point, he uses his alien power to unlock my cabin door. He enters, finding me in a pink nightgown. He holds in his hands a single rose he has created with his godlike powers. "Pink is your favorite, isn't it?" he asks hopefully, offering me the rose.

By this time he has become such a pest that I decide it's time to give him the cold shoulder. "You don't walk into a room without knocking," I respond icily.

"Don't ever lock your door on me again, Janice. I love you." His words are a plea—but his tone is a threat.

"I'll lock it when I please," I reply. "What is it you want, anyway?"

He advances toward the camera, and we know what he wants even before he says it: "You."

As he advances, I use a hidden button to signal the bridge. Soon they arrive: Kirk and Spock, the two larger-than-life stars of the show—and with a mere glance, the 17-year-old boy tosses them like rag dolls across my cabin, breaking their legs. At that moment, this "boy" has become the most sinister and powerful monster ever seen on *Star Trek*.

I reach out and slap Charlie across the face—and he instantly sends me off into the Nth dimension. Then he smirks at Kirk and Spock, gloating, "Being grown up isn't so much! I'm not a man and I can do anything! You can't!"

Near the end of the episode, I reappear on the bridge in my pink negligee—the Thasians have arrived and are putting everything back the way it was, including all the people Charlie "made go away." They explain that they didn't realize that Charlie had been taken from the planet, and they regret the loss of life aboard the ill-fated *Antares*.

And poor Charlie! He pleads with Kirk, "No, please! Don't let them take me! I can't live with them anymore! I'll be good! I won't ever do it again! I'm sorry about the *Antares*! I'm sorry! Help me!"

Even hard-bitten Captain Kirk is moved. "The boy belongs with his own kind," he appeals. "If he could be taught not to use his power—"

But, the Thasians explain, they gave him that power so that he could survive on a hostile world. He will always use it, and would inevitably destroy again—or be destroyed.

Then Charlie turns to me. "Please! Don't let them take me! I can't even touch them! Janice, they can't feel, not like you!"

I try to go to him, but Dr. McCoy, with his hand on my arm, pulls me back. I remember that as Charlie pleaded with me for help, I was absolutely overcome with pity and hurt for this poor boy who was about to be ripped away from his own kind and taken back to a world without people, without companionship. He was about to descend back into the hell in which he had been raised, without another living soul to touch and love—or to love him back. And the tears just welled up in my eyes and spilled down my cheeks.

"Please," Charlie begs one last time. "I want to stay—" And he fades away—yet his last, heartbreaking words continue to echo: "stay… stay… stay…"

And Charlie is gone, returned to a planet of solitary confinement, where he can't hurt anyone ever again.

Throughout the week that Robert Walker spent with us as Charlie X, he completely avoided the rest of the cast. If he wasn't on the set, he holed up in his dressing room. Understand, that's not because he was stuck up—it was because he is a method actor and wanted to stay in character. The cast and crew of *Star Trek* were a very happy, loud, rambunctious lot—always laughing and joking and pulling pranks. If Robert Walker had spent time with us and gotten to know and like us, it would have affected his performance. He explained to us when he arrived on the set that he wanted to remain alien and apart from us—and it worked. You can see it in his performance, a subtle yet persistent air of estrangement from the *Enterprise* crew, and indeed from the rest of humanity. His careful effort to stay in character added a convincing dimension to his performance.

On Friday of that week, he finally relented and joined the cast and crew at our weekly "wrap party." Though we still had two more days of shooting the following week, we had a weekend ahead of us—plenty of time for Robert to work himself back into character. At the party, he told us he was crazy about all of us, and loved working on the show. We had plenty to celebrate that night, because we all knew that "Charlie X" was a very special episode. To this day, it is one of my all-time favorites.

On July 20th, we began filming "Balance of Terror," a science fictional tribute to the WWII submarine movies, such as *Run Silent, Run Deep* and *The Enemy Below*. Written by Paul Schneider and directed by Vincent McEveety, the story opens during a wedding ceremony in the chapel of the *Enterprise*—probably the only time there is ever any indication of religious practice aboard the *Enterprise*. As Captain Kirk is about to finalize the nuptials ("…in accordance with our laws and our many beliefs…"), the ceremony is interrupted by an alarm: A Federation outpost is under attack.

Rushing to the aid of the outpost, the *Enterprise* finds itself engaged in a cat-and-mouse chase with a Romulan Bird of Prey, which is shielded by a new cloaking technology and armed with an incredibly destructive plasma energy weapon. A furious battle ensues, and the *Enterprise* suffers serious damage. In the end, of course, the *Enterprise* prevails. Captain Kirk offers to rescue the vanquished Romulan commander and his crew. The Romulan commander (played by Mark Lenard, who appeared in later *Trek* installments as Spock's father) refuses Kirk's offer, salutes the victor, and destroys himself and his ship. When the casualties are counted aboard the *Enterprise*, there is only one fatality: the bridegroom-to-be, Lieutenant Tomlinson.

The episode concludes where it began, in the chapel. The bereaved almost-bride, Angela, is found contemplating, perhaps even praying. Kirk enters and tries to comfort her. "It never makes any sense," he says, looking even more helpless than she. "We both have to know that there was a reason." And the unspoken question hangs in the air: What reason could there possibly be for the senseless death of a young man who, hours earlier, was about to be married? All in all, this episode is a strong statement on the futility of war.

I recall that as we were filming this and other episodes, actors Martin Landau and Barbara Bain would occasionally come over to our set and watch us work. Their hit show, "Mission Impossible," was shooting on the stage next to ours. Barbara thought *Star Trek* was the most exciting thing she had ever seen, and she often talked about wanting to do a *Trek*-like series. She and Martin Landau were both impressed with how much fun we were having romping around the galaxy—and they wanted in on the fun. Almost a decade later, they got their wish, filming two seasons of "Space: 1999" in England, with my friend Barry Morse (from "The Outer Limits" episode "Controlled Experiment").

I had the next week off during the filming of a Robert Bloch-written episode, "What Are Little Girls Made Of?" As with "Mudd's Women," no part had been written for me. However, I had seen the script for the following episode, "Dagger of the Mind" by Shimon Wincelberg, and was ecstatic that I had a very big role in that episode.

In "Dagger of the Mind," Captain Kirk and I beam down to the planet Tantalus Five. On Tantalus, Dr. Tristan Adams runs a progressive penal colony where criminal tendencies are treated as curable disorders. Dr. Adams gives us a tour of the facility, including a demonstration of an experimental treatment device called a "neural neutralizer." Captain Kirk becomes suspicious about the purpose of the device when he learns that an escaped "patient" from Tantalus, who smuggles himself aboard the *Enterprise* in a cargo container, is not an inmate at all, but Dr. Adams' assistant, Dr. Simon van Gelder. The captain and I sneak into the room housing the neural neutralizer and test it, discovering that it is a diabolical mind-altering, mind-controlling device.

In the end, I risk my life to cut the facility's power, turning off the power to the neural neutralizer, saving Kirk's life. The power outage also turns off the penal colony's force shield, so that Spock and a security team can beam down and rescue us. While the power is off, Kirk and Dr. Adams struggle—and at the end of the struggle, Kirk has knocked Dr. Adams out, leaving him in the chair under the beam generator of the neural neutralizer. When Spock restores power to the facility, the neutralizer comes on—and Dr. Adams is killed by his own devilish machine.

That is how the script was originally written. If you've seen the episode, you know that this episode was not filmed that way. The week before we were to begin shooting "Dagger," I was told that I would not appear in that episode at all (as I recall, it was Bob Justman who broke the news to me). My part had been rewritten for a character to be called "Dr. Helen Noel," and would be played by actress Marianna Hill.

I was very upset about losing such a juicy part. It involved a romantic flashback scene in which Jim Kirk and Janice Rand meet at a Christmas party, dance, kiss and make love—a scene built around the repressed attraction between Kirk and Janice Rand, brought to the surface by the neural neutralizer. But even though this part had been given to another actress, there was never any hint that the producers or directors were in any way unhappy with my work or with the development of the character. I had no clue that I was approaching the end of my run with *Star Trek*.

In his book *Star Trek Memories*, William Shatner and his co-writer, Chris Kreski, talk about the diet pills I took and the fact that I sometimes drank to take the edge off the nervousness caused by the amphetamines. That much of my story is exactly as I related it to him in our phone interview, and as I related it here in this book. But after that point, inaccuracies and misinterpretations begin to compound themselves in Bill's version of my story. He writes:

> Even during our first few weeks of production, Grace had become
> noticeably distracted, visibly ill, and as a result her performances suf-

fered terribly. By the time we were filming our tenth episode ["What Are Little Girls Made Of?"], Grace's condition had worsened to the point where her scenes were consciously being given to other characters or completely written out of episodes. For example, Grace was to have co-starred with Captain Kirk in our eleventh episode, "Dagger of the Mind," but her deterioration forced Roddenberry and Justman into a decision to rewrite the episode, adding the guest character of Dr. Helen Noel and entirely deleting Yeoman Rand. Further, in Grace's final episode, "The Conscience of the King," her performance consisted solely of walking onto the bridge in the background of the scene, taking a quick look at a particular piece of equipment, then exiting. She was let go the following day.[1]

No, I wasn't let go the following day. I was informed of being written out over a week *before* we began filming that episode. I vividly remember how horrible and humiliated I felt, going in to shoot that final six-second walk-on, knowing that my *Star Trek* career was already over.

I was not "noticeably distracted" in *any* of my *Star Trek* appearances. I never drank on the set, nor would I have allowed alcohol to interfere with my performance in those days. I drank on evenings and weekends, at our wrap parties, but never on the set, never when I was working.* In fact, it was being written out of *Star Trek* that actually tipped me into full-blown, falling-down drinking. It wasn't my drinking that caused me to lose the part on *Star Trek*. It was losing the part on *Star Trek* that really sent my drinking off the scale! I look at those *Star Trek* episodes today, and I'm as proud of them as of any work I've ever done. Fans continually tell me how much they loved my work in those episodes.

Star Trek Memories says I was consciously written out of "What Are Little Girls Made Of?" Wrong. No part was ever written for me in that episode, just as no part was written for me in "Mudd's Women." The only actors whose contracts put them in every episode were William Shatner and Leonard Nimoy. The rest of us were guaranteed so many episodes out of thirteen (except Nichelle Nichols, who was hired in the first season as a day player, with no guaranteed number of episodes). Jimmy Doohan didn't appear in "The Man Trap," "Charlie X," "Miri," or "Dagger of the Mind." George Takei wasn't in "Charlie X," "Miri," or "Dagger of the Mind." Nichelle does not appear in "Miri." Not only was I missing from "What Are Little Girls Made Of?," but so were DeForest Kelly, George Takei and Jimmy Doohan. Does that mean the *all* of these actors turned in such poor performances that they were consciously written out of

---

*When I say I never drank on the *Star Trek* set, I don't count my six-second walk-on in "The Conscience of the King." By that time, I had already been written out of the show. I did the scene sober, but after shooting my walk-on, I went out to a liquor store, bought a bottle of wine, and brought it back to my dressing room. That day, I drank. I couldn't deal with the fact that I wasn't going to be on the show anymore, so I drank to anesthetize the pain. That was the only time I ever brought a bottle onto the studio lot.

these episodes? Of course not. Neither our contracts nor the storylines required that we be in every episode.

Pardon my immodesty, but I think my performances on *Star Trek* were *terrific*!

Was I written out of "Dagger of the Mind"? Absolutely. Was it because my performances were poor? Of course not. In fact, Bob Justman, who was present when the decision was made to put Dr. Helen Noel in place of Janice Rand, has told me that it was a creative decision, based on the needs of the storyline and the characters. He told me it was not a reflection on me.

The very week after "Dagger of the Mind" was shot, I came back to the studio and had a very important role in "Miri." If my performances were so completely inept that I could not be trusted anywhere near a script or a camera, then they certainly wouldn't have given me such a strong part as the one I carried off (and carried off well I might humbly add) in "Miri." They could have replaced me with Uhura. Or better yet, Nurse Chapel could have been in that episode, assisting Dr. McCoy in his search for a cure—that would have made a lot of sense in terms of the plot. Instead, I played the strong, substantial part that was written for me precisely because the producers knew I could handle it—and I had never given them any reason to doubt me.

So why was I written out of "Dagger of the Mind"? I believe it was because the episode, as originally written, brought the repressed attraction between Kirk and Rand too much out in the open. The Christmas party scene where Kirk and Rand flirt, dance, kiss and go to bed together is so overt that it really would have painted Captain Kirk into a corner. Certainly such a scene went far beyond the Matt Dillon-Miss Kitty chemistry that Gene Roddenberry had initially envisioned for the captain and the yeoman. After a scene like that, how could Kirk and Rand ever go back to the way things were? How could the viewers *not* be furious with Jim Kirk's cheating heart as he wooed Lenore Karidian in "The Conscience of the King," or fell head over heels for Edith Keeler in "The City on the Edge Of Forever," or gave his heart to Miramanee in "The Paradise Syndrome"?

In the very next episode, "Miri," there is a scene in which the Kirk-Rand attraction is again glimpsed, but subtly so. It is the scene where I tell Jim Kirk, "Back on the ship, I was always trying to get you to look at my legs. ... Captain, look at my legs." It is not nearly so overt as the scene in "Dagger." The Kirk-Rand/Matt-Kitty dynamic remains intact in "Miri," whereas it was blown sky-high in "Dagger." As painful as it was for me to lose the part in "Dagger of the Mind," I know the decision to remove Janice Rand from that episode was a creative decision—not the result of any problem with actress Grace Lee Whitney.

While "Dagger of the Mind" was being shot, I had the week off. "Dagger" finished shooting on Wednesday, August 17, and then there was a break in production for a few days. On Monday, August 22, we all returned to the studio to begin shooting my favorite episode, "Miri," written by Adrian Spies and directed by Vincent McEveety (I remember that Vincent McEveety directed that episode from a wheelchair, having broken his leg in a skiing accident a few days earlier).

Two of Jimmy Doohan's sons and one of my sons, Scott, appeared as extras in Star Trek: The Motion Picture. *Jimmy's sons were Earth medics while Scott was a Vulcan medic. The Paramount hairstylists cut off Scott's big afro and slicked his hair down to the Spockish look you see here. After filming, he had to return to classes at California State University Northridge—and to a merciless ribbing from his friends.*

"Miri" is the story of an earth-like planet where the entire adult population has been wiped out by a genetically engineered disease, leaving only children—children who are hundreds of years old. The disease, it turns out, was the result of experiments to artificially prolong human life. While the aging process has been slowed down in these children, it accelerates when the child finally reaches puberty, causing madness and death. Kirk, Spock, McCoy and I are stranded on the planet, racing against time to find a cure for the disease before it kills us. Meanwhile, one of these children, an adolescent girl named Miri who is just entering puberty, develops a massive crush on Captain Kirk—and a bad case of jealousy against me!

(A personal aside: There is a point, late in the episode, where Miri observes Captain Kirk giving me a hug to console me—and Miri happens to see us locked together in an embrace. In a fit of adolescent jealousy, she refers to Captain Kirk as "Mr. Lovey-Dovey." Today, I have three cats named Trouble, Tribble and Mr. Lovey-Dovey.)

The role of Miri was played by beautiful young Kim Darby (*True Grit, Bus Riley's Back in Town, The People*). Like Robert Walker, Jr., Kim is a serious method actress. She kept her distance from the rest of the cast during the week because the *Star Trek* cast was so crazy and raucous that she couldn't have been around us and stayed in character.

We were so loud and crazy that we used to drive our assistant director crazy. *Star Trek*'s a.d. was Gregg Peters, and it was his job to make sure everything was ready on the set so that the director and the actors could do their job. He was supposed to keep order on the set. All of us in the cast were loud and outrageous—but I was the most unruly of all.

My best friend on the set was our hairdresser, Virginia Darcy, and she and I used to go into my dressing room, tell stories and laugh till our sides split. She had spent several years working with Esther Williams, the famed swimmer-actress and star of numerous "splashy" musicals—and Virginia had dozens of outrageous stories to tell. I was such a loudmouth that Gregg would come running in, absolutely furious, and say, "Will you shut up in here! You just spoiled a take on the set!" And I would try to stifle my laugh and keep quiet—which was very hard for me to do!

Years later, after I got sober, I felt terrible about all the trouble I caused Gregg Peters—but I had no idea how to reach him to tell him how sorry I was. It happened that, purely by chance while I was working on this book, I was in L.A. and happened to be talking with a man who knew I had been in *Star Trek*. He said, "You know, you have a lot in common with my neighbor out in Pacific Palisades. He used to work on *Star Trek*, too."

"Oh?" I said. "What's his name?"

"Gregg Peters," he replied.

"Ohmigosh!" I exclaimed. "Gregg Peters is your neighbor? I need to call him and make amends for being so terrible to him on the show! What's his phone number?"

And the man gave me Gregg's number, and I called him. After 30 years, I was on the phone with Gregg, telling him how sorry I was that I had caused him so much grief on the set of *Star Trek*. I told him I was clean and sober, and he was thrilled to hear it— and very happy to hear from me.

"Miri" is a sentimental favorite for me because my two sons appear in it. They are in all the child "gang" scenes with guest stars Kim Darby and Michael J. Pollard, and they also accompany Pollard when he sneaks into the laboratory and steals the communicators. For insurance purposes, the studio had to pick up my kids in a limo. I couldn't drive my own kids to the studio! So there they were, sitting in the back of the limousine, waving at me through the back window, while I followed along in my old Buick.

They arrived at the studio at 6 in the morning, where they were made up as grimy little street urchins. Then director Vincent McEveety let all the kids do what comes naturally: run wild around the lot and play mean tricks on the grown-ups!

I remember one scene that required endless retakes. Dr. McCoy (DeForest Kelly) is speaking into a communicator, relaying data about the disease organism to the computers aboard the *Enterprise*. I'm in the shot, along with De and Kim Darby. De has a line of technical gobbledygook to say, and it's such a tongue-twister that, try as he might, he can't get the line out: "...tubular with multiplicability ... appear to have an affinity for nucleic acids..." And can you blame him for flubbing the line? Just try saying "multiplicability" three times fast—it's almost as bad as "rubber baby buggy bumpers." Every time he stumbled over the word, the entire cast and crew exploded in laughter. When De finally got the line delivered correctly, we all wanted to applaud—but we couldn't because the camera panned from McCoy to Kirk and Spock, and the scene went on from there. Lines like "...tubular with multiplicability..." are part of the risk you take in doing a science fiction series.

The final scene in the episode is an absolutely priceless exchange between Captain Kirk, Dr. McCoy and myself on the bridge of the *Enterprise*:

> ME
> They were just children. Simply
> to leave them there with a medical team—
>
> KIRK
> Just children! They're 300 years old
> and more. I've already contacted Space Central.
> They'll send teachers, advisors—
>
> McCOY
> And truant officers, I presume.
>
> ME
> Miri— She really loved you, you know.
>
> KIRK
> Yes. [*thoughtful pause*] But I never get
> involved with older women, yeoman.

The horrible incident with The Executive took place on Friday night, August 26, 1966, near the end of our work on this episode. The following Monday, The Executive came into the makeup room and gave me a small gift, a polished stone. On Tuesday, we finished shooting "Miri." A couple days later—probably on Thursday, September 1, I was in the kitchen of my Sherman Oaks home when the phone rang. It was Alex, my agent. "Grace," he said, "are you sitting down?"

And that's when my entire universe turned upside-down.

After all these years, after looking at all the evidence and hearing the different theories as to why I was dropped from the show, I still don't know the answer for sure. There are certainly a number of possible answers. But it seems to me that the answer which best fits the facts is The Executive. When he took me into his office, it was supposedly to discuss an enlarged role for Janice Rand—and if I had played along with him, perhaps he would have worked behind the scenes to steer things in my favor. Certainly, my substantive role in "Miri" indicated that I was headed for a bigger part on *Star Trek.*

All of that came to an abrupt halt immediately after the assault by The Executive. From the night of the assault till the day I got a call from my agent, telling me I had been written out of the show, no more than a week had passed. It's possible, but unlikely, that the timing was purely coincidental. It makes a lot of sense that, after what he had done to me, The Executive couldn't stand to have me around the studio anymore. He didn't want to look at me and be reminded of what he had done to me that night. So, in a production meeting or wherever the decision was made, The Executive could have steered the discussion of Janice Rand's future in the direction of her extinction. It's a scenario that fits all the facts.

So without any explanation, Janice Rand abruptly disappeared from the crew manifest of the Starship *Enterprise.* But while Janice Rand ceased to exist, Grace Lee Whitney had to go on living.

Star Trek made its network debut on Thursday, September 8, 1966, at 8:30 p.m. with the episode "The Man Trap." The notice in *Variety* was typical of the critics' response, calling *Star Trek* a "dreary mess of confusion" that might possibly appeal to "a small coterie of the small fry." Although a great many fans were ecstatic over what they saw, the mass audience response was as disappointing as the critical response.

The following week, I made my last trek to Desilu as a member of the *Star Trek* cast. I put on my Janice Rand uniform, I put on my Janice Rand hair, and I went onto the set and did my walk-on in "The Conscience of the King." Or as one fan magazine termed it, my "walk-off."

It was not my last time on the Desilu lot, of course. I came back to audition for other shows, and later did an episode of "Mannix" at Desilu. I was invited back for cast parties now and then. I even came back to Stage 9 and watched my old friends create new *Trek* voyages. I was on the set, for example, watching in awe and fascination as Mr. Spock mind-melded with the Horta in the episode "Dweller in the Dark."

My visits to the studio became less and less frequent with time. It hurt too much to be around *Star Trek* without being a part of *Star Trek.*

I soon acquired a bad reputation in the industry. I would show up at interviews reeking of alcohol. I would show up drunk on the set. I'd go home and try to put my emotions back together, but the amphetamines weren't working anymore and the alcohol made me depressed. The drinking and the drugs didn't fix it anymore.

Nothing worked.

My Cookies and Milk Days

. . . .

I kept running into Harlan Ellison.

I had met Harlan years before on the set of "Cimarron Strip," performing in an episode he had written. Then, while I was working on *Star Trek*, I kept seeing him around the Desilu studio. He spent a lot of time there, working on his script for "The City on the Edge of Forever." Harlan and I would wave and smile to each other, and sometimes we'd stop and chat. I found him absolutely charming.

Harlan and I had a lot in common. We were both Jewish, we were both involved in *Star Trek*—and we both grew to hate Gene Roddenberry! I was angry with Gene because I had been written out of the show. I knew that, whatever the real reason I was written out, Gene had a hand in the decision. I was always aware that one little word from Gene could have kept me on the show.

Harlan was angry with Gene Roddenberry because he felt Gene had butchered his script for "The City on the Edge of Forever." As long as I can remember, Harlan had a running feud with Gene—and he was very disappointed that I had been written out of *Star Trek* and out of the script for "City." Even while Harlan was feuding with him, Gene Roddenberry was able to talk him into heading up the "Save *Star Trek*" campaign. As Harlan recalls,

> Gene had an astonishing ability to tell people what they wanted to hear, to charm them into doing his bidding. ...I went for the okeydoke and believed (what is generally acknowledged now to be utterly untrue) that there were idiot monsters at NBC who were trying to scuttle *Star Trek*.
>
> Despite my lingering animosity at what Gene had done, and had allowed to be done, to my script, I volunteered to help save the show.[1]

Harlan organized an "advisory board" called The Committee, consisting of himself and fellow sci-fi writers Poul Anderson, Robert Bloch, Lester del Rey, Philip José Farmer, Frank Herbert, Richard Matheson, Theodore Sturgeon and A.E. Van Vogt. Though all these legendary masters of science fiction lent their names to the letterhead, the business end of The Committee consisted entirely of Harlan Ellison. He personally assembled a Rolodex of names and addresses from sci-fi conventions and fan clubs. He personally cranked out thousands of mimeographed letters at the Desilu office. He put the stamps on the letters and personally carted them to the post office.

Harlan was very upset when Gene and many of the fans later gave sole credit for saving *Star Trek* to Bjo and John Trimble. Clearly, Bjo and John deserve a lot of credit for the letter-writing campaign they organized after the first season, because their efforts helped ensure that *Trek* would go on to a second and third season. But before Bjo and John had ever seen *Star Trek*, before an episode was even aired, Harlan was busy working on a "Save *Star Trek*" at Gene's behest. Yet, after seeing the telecast version of his script, Harlan wished he had let *Star Trek* die.

Without question, Harlan Ellison's one and only *Star Trek* episode remains the most popular and beloved of all 79 shows. His original script was revised and rewritten by many hands. He did several drafts himself, then the story was further rewritten by Gene Coon, Dorothy Fontana and Gene Roddenberry. Harlan's *original* script (not the heavily restructured and rewritten version that was telecast) earned him one of his four Writer's Guild of America awards.

In the telecast version, Dr. McCoy goes psychotic after accidentally receiving an overdose of a mind-altering medication, cordrazine. In his crazed state, McCoy beams down to an uncharted planet where he enters a time-travel device called the Guardian of Forever. The Guardian takes McCoy to Earth in the 1930s, where he changes history, so that even the *Enterprise* has ceased to exist. Kirk and Spock, who have followed McCoy to the planet surface, enter the Guardian in order to undo the damage McCoy has done and restore the original timeline. While they are on Earth in the 1930s, looking for McCoy, Kirk falls in love with a visionary do-gooder, Sister Edith Keeler. Then, to his horror, Kirk discovers McCoy has altered history by *saving* Edith Keeler's life—and the only way to restore the original timeline is to allow the woman he loves to *die*.

There is a haunting beauty to the basic outline of the story, whether it is Harlan's original script or the greatly altered televised version. The tragic ironies of the story echo in the heart long after it is told. Here is a good, noble, self-sacrificing woman, Edith Keeler, who preaches and practices a Christ-like love for all mankind—but in order for the greatest good to take place, this good woman has to die. If she is allowed to live, her pacifist message will take root in American society of the 1930s, delaying America's entrance into the approaching Second World War. As a result, Hitler will win the war and the future will be forever changed. It is not because Edith Keeler is evil that she must die, but rather because she is so very good! All of the rich emotional texture of the story flows from this tragic, cosmic irony.

In Harlan's original version—the version that won the WGA award—there is a very strong part for Yeoman Rand. She is one of the members of the landing party that beams down to the planet and discovers the Guardians of Forever—living beings, not a time portal device. The Guardians dwell in a city near the Time Vortex of the Ancients. The Vortex is a thing of "light, height and insubstantiality" where "the million pulse-flows of time and space merge" and "the flux lines of Forever meet." The city of the Guardians (which does not appear in the telecast version) is the source of the title.

After the flow of time is altered, Kirk, Spock and Yeoman Rand beam back to the *Enterprise*—only to discover that, in this altered timeline, the starship is now a renegade ship called the *Condor*, manned by cutthroat pirates (this unused incident from Harlan's original script was probably the inspiration for the second-season episode "Mirror, Mirror"). As Kirk, Spock and Rand materialize on the transporter platform of the ship, they are confronted by the menacing renegade captain. Kirk quickly sizes up the situation, then sees that Yeoman Rand has her tricorder console with her. Here is what happens next:

> KIRK
> *(to Rand, softly)*
> Yeoman ... give that console full feedback!

37 CLOSE ON JANICE RAND

as she hesitates a fractional beat to understand his order. Then CAMERA TILTS DOWN SLIGHTLY to show us the console still strapped on her, and her hands moving to two big calibrated knobs. She suddenly twists them as far as they will go. There is an ABRUPT PIERCING WHINE.

38 SAME AS 33—HAND-HELD

As the Transporter console erupts in a shower of sparks and a WHAMMMM! and the Technician is thrown half across the room. The Renegade Captain and his men naturally turn with a start, and in that instant, Kirk leaps off the Transporter stage.

> KIRK
> *(yells)*
> Go!

And Spock joins him in a flying leap. ... There is a pitched battle in the cramped confines of the Transporter chamber and the tactic resolves itself into forcing the remaining members of the *Condor's* crew out the hatch, and sealing it behind them ....

(Later...)

> KIRK
> We have to change things back.

> SPOCK
> Then all the possibilities come back
> to a single course of action.

> KIRK
> *(nods understanding)*
> Yeoman Rand ... can you
> hold this chamber?

RAND
(unsure)
How long, sir?

KIRK
Indefinitely.

There is a beat of silence. Everyone knows what he means. She nods. Kirk looks at Spock.

KIRK
Let's get back.

They hasten to the Transporter stage, get on. Rand moves to the main control panel that her feedback exploded.

RAND
I'll have to cut in alternate
circuits, Captain. My feedback burned
out the central sources.

KIRK
Do your best, Yeoman.

As she works, rehooking circuits, moving hurriedly, Spock moves off his Transporter plate to Kirk's side. ...

(Later...)

RAND
Ready, Captain. It's
jerry-rigged, but it ought to hold.

KIRK
Energize!

43 ANGLE ON KIRK, SPOCK IN CHAMBER

The dematerialization EFFECT—they become transparent...

RAND
Hurry back, we might not be
here when you—

they dissolve. A few faint sparkles fade. Empty chamber.[2]

This is Harlan's excellent book about the favorite episode of many Trekfans. The cover shot depicts Harlan as I remember him from my cookies and milk days—along with a couple of other old friends of mine.

As Harlan wrote the part for me, Yeoman Rand was strong, capable, coura-geous, heroic. She caused the transporter malfunction as a tactical diversion, then she repaired the transporter so Kirk and Spock could return to the planet. Most heroic of all, she single-handedly held off the renegades on the other side of the door to the transporter room. After playing Janice Rand as little more than a waitress in early episodes, and seeing her true strength and competence just beginning to emerge in stories like "Charlie X" and "Miri," I would have loved a chance to portray Yeoman Rand as Harlan Ellison envisioned her in "The City on the Edge of Forever."

Harlan has a reputation (particularly among book editors and TV producers) as being impossible to deal with, a loose cannon, and barely housebroken. To me, he was always a perfect gentleman, a truly lovely man. Those who found him difficult or temperamental simply could not deal with the fact that Harlan is a demanding perfectionist who fights for the truth and purity of his ideas. In television—the ultimate medium of compromise—that kind of demanding idealism is rare. And it is resented.

Whenever Harlan felt one of his scripts had been violated in the editing and rewrite process, he would yank his own name from the project and substitute the pseudonym "Cordwainer Bird." It was his way of saying, "There is some nugget of Harlan Ellison's creativity buried in here somewhere—but on the whole, my work was raped." Harlan wanted to put his "Bird" pseudonym on "The City on the Edge of Forever," but when Gene Roddenberry found out, he personally called Harlan and promised to blackball him in Hollywood if he ever tried to embarrass Gene and *Star Trek*.

So Harlan relented. And later, he even helped save *Star Trek*.

But in the years that followed, the feud between Gene Roddenberry and Harlan Ellison became legendary. Gene would give media interviews or talks at conventions and say the most outrageous things. It usually started with a backhanded compliment: "I think Harlan Ellison is a genius, but he's completely undisciplined, and he never understood the *Star Trek* format and characters. So I had to step in and save Harlan's script." And then Gene would usually launch into the bizarre claim he repeated dozens, perhaps hundreds of times: "I mean, Harlan even had Engineer Scott dealing drugs!" Every time Harlan heard that Gene had used that line, he called Gene up and told him to knock it off. Gene would be apologetic, promise it would never happen again—then go right out to a convention the next weekend and repeat the same line!

Where did Gene get such a crazy idea? In Harlan's version of "City," there is an evil crewman named Beckwith who deals in illegal dream-narcotics, the Jewels of Sound. But Mr. Scott, an interplanetary dope pusher? Ha! Scottie doesn't even appear in Harlan's script!

There were numerous casualties along the way as this beautiful story made its way from Harlan's typewriter to the TV screen. Yeoman Rand was one. Another was one of Harlan's favorite supporting characters, a paraplegic war veteran named Trooper, who disappeared in the rewrite process. The actual "city on the edge of forever" which inspired the title didn't even make it to the screen, prompting many viewers to scratch their heads and wonder, "Why did they call it *that*?"

Perhaps the greatest loss of all was the loss of Harlan Ellison's involvement with *Star Trek*. Even altered as it was, the "City" episode that made it to the screen retained so much emotional power and depth that it is still everybody's favorite *Trek*. The show continued on for two more seasons after "City" was aired. Imagine what those seasons would have been like if, instead of clinkers like "Spock's Brain" and "The Way to Eden," we could have had more stories by Harlan Ellison.

In 1997, I appeared at a convention with Harlan—the first time I had seen him in years. He hugged me and we talked about old times. Afterwards, I telephoned my firstborn son, Scott, and told him I had seen Harlan.

"Really?" he said. "I remember when we used to play at his house. He had all those pinball machines and everything—what a blast we had!" By this time, Scott was 40 years old, but he vividly remembered going to Harlan's house when he was only 10. My two boys just loved Harlan Ellison.

Harlan and I started dating after I left *Star Trek*. He would come over to my house and pick us all up and take us out to Pacific Ocean Park. We would buy Oreo cookies and ice cream, and we'd all walk along the beach and go on the amusement park rides, then we'd go to Harlan's place and my kids would play with Harlan's toys. His house was full of toys. It was like walking into a penny arcade. In fact, the sign on the mailbox read "Ellison Wonderland"—and that's exactly what his home was, a wonderland.

From the outside, Harlan's place was an ordinary-looking house in a middle-class L.A. suburb. Inside, the house was as eccentric and eclectic as Harlan himself. Books were shelved, stacked and tucked everywhere, from floor to ceiling. If there happened to be a patch of wall or a tiny alcove without books, you might find an exotic statue, some photographic memorabilia, a limited-edition print, or one of his many Hugo and Nebula awards. Then there was his game room, filled with all sorts of machines and gizmos with flashing lights, jangling bells and rolling balls.

I call my time with Harlan my "cookies and milk days." Always with Harlan, it was Oreos and milk, or Oreos and ice cream. I always wanted a drink, but Harlan would screw up his face and say, "How can you drink that stuff? Alcohol tastes horrible! Worse than medicine! Here, have another cookie."

When he'd say things like that, I would look at him like he was crazy! I couldn't see how anyone could have a good time without a drink! At the same time, I found Harlan's abstinence very attractive. I was initially attracted to that same quality in my first husband. When I dated Harlan, I had the same idea about him that I did about Steve: *Maybe if I marry him, I'll stop drinking. I'll be a good Jewish girl.* I saw Harlan Ellison as another nice Jewish boy who could help me to be good.

Sometimes I would hang out at Harlan's house when he was writing. He never showed me manuscripts, but sometimes he would talk about different projects he was working on. I remember him telling me about a story he was writing about a boy and a telepathic dog making their way through the post-apocalyptic world. He said that the story had its roots in his childhood, and his boyhood love for his own dog. That story, "A Boy and His Dog," was later made into a movie starring Don Johnson.

One time, I hosted a party for composer André Previn at my home in Sherman Oaks. Harlan came and co-hosted it with me. André was there and a lot of other people from the L.A. entertainment and arts community. One of the guests was a famous broadcast news personality, and in his loud, broadcaster's voice, he began telling a story about some kids he had seen alongside the road wearing funny hats. He was laughing and making fun of those little kids, and as his story went on, I realized that the kids he was ridiculing were little Jewish kids wearing yarmulkes. The reason they were alongside the road is because, being orthodox Jews, they couldn't ride in cars on Shabbat (Saturday, the Sabbath).

I got so mad at this loudmouth that I picked up a plate of food and dumped it over his head. I mean, I got him good! It went all over his jacket and everything. Then I threw him out of my house. I was as Jewish as they come, and I wasn't going to have anyone in my house making fun of the Jews!

And Harlan? He was doubled up laughing! He just loved it. Harlan never knew what I was going to do next.

One of the biggest regrets of my life is the way I sabotaged my relationship with Harlan, just as I sabotaged so many other relationships in my life. I regret that I didn't stay with Harlan, because he was terrific with my two boys, and they loved him. My kids would have had a great life with him.

I look back on the time when I was dating Harlan, and I think, *What a fool you were, Whitney! What a special, rare gem this man was!* I didn't really appreciate how lucky I was to be in the company of this talented, kind, generous man. I couldn't see it because I was too caught up in my own self. I was full of self-pity because I had been written out of *Star Trek*.

During that time, I was not only drinking, but I began smoking dope. I knew that Harlan was very pure when it came to mind-altering, mood-altering chemicals. He absolutely wouldn't tolerate it in his presence. And he was right—but I just thought he was a prude.

One day I was at his house, waiting to go out with him somewhere. He was in another room, finishing up some work, and I was sitting on the floor in the living room, waiting for him. I figured, *While I'm waiting, I'll smoke a joint and relax. There's no alcohol in this house, so what else is there to do?* I had my stash with me, so I took it out, rolled a joint, and lit up.

A few minutes later, Harlan came into the room and saw me sitting there, blowing smoke. He stared at me speechless for a couple seconds.

"What's the matter?" I asked.

He pointed to the joint between my fingers. "Is that marijuana?"

"Of course it is," I said.

That's when I saw the whites of his eyes. "Get out!" he said.

I thought he was joking. "What?"

"Get out! Get out!" He was definitely *not* joking. He grabbed my purse off the floor, put all my stuff in it, then lifted me bodily to my feet and prodded me toward the door. "You're not gonna smoke that dope in my house!"

I thought, *My gosh, where is this guy living—the dark ages?! Everybody smokes dope!* I got in my car and drove to the nearest bar, completely mortified. I thought Harlan had gone totally meshuggenah!

Today, I know that I was the crazy one, not Harlan. I sabotaged the relationship, not Harlan. I knew how he felt about drugs and alcohol—and I had provoked the confrontation. At that time, I didn't know why I did such things, though I know now that it's a classic trait of alcoholics. We alcoholics can't have healthy relationships. If a relationship is going too well and seems to be healthy, then we have to find some way to wreck it. We're like tornadoes in the lives of others. Everyone we touch gets hurt.

Harlan was 100 percent right to do what he did. But I didn't see it until years later, when I got sober.

That incident ended our relationship. We never dated after that.

However, we did see each other over the years at *Star Trek* conventions. By then, of course, time had passed and all was forgiven. We never mentioned it—we just looked at each other, laughed, and had a good time at the convention.

To this day, I'm still crazy about Harlan Ellison. I wish I had been a good girl with him.

A Woman in Free-Fall

Nichelle Nichols likes to say that fantasy is something that hasn't happened yet. I say fantasy has a life of its own.

Fantasy is just as real as reality—but fantasy is not true. A thing can be real and not be true. Many people live their lives according to an illusion. Many people get fantasy and reality mixed up. I have always had a hard time differentiating between reality and fantasy. That was especially true right after I was written out of *Star Trek*, and I was so deeply mired in my pain. It wasn't until many years later, when I finally got sober, that I began to see life as it really is.

When *Star Trek* costume designer Bill Theiss told me I needed to lose weight, I began working out at the Gym And Swim on Fulton and Moorepark in Sherman Oaks. While I was working out, I got to be good friends with a young woman I'll call Shirley, a pretty blond who had been married for 10 years, with children the same age as mine. We had lots of time to talk there among the exercise machines, and we got to know each other very well. I told her about my career, my kids and my ex-husband.

She kept telling me about this wonderful psychologist she was going to. "I just adore my shrink," she said. "He's fabulous! He's into all the newest stuff in psychology! He conducts a group class for women, and you should come, Grace. All his women patients are nuts about him! He's not only brilliant—he a gorgeous-looking guy! Best of all, he's recently divorced, so he's *available!*"

That was when I was busy working on *Star Trek*, so I kept telling her, "Why would I want to go to a shrink? I've got a TV series, I'm happy, I'm on top of the world!"

But Shirley kept telling me I needed to go to her therapist—"Just go see him one time—I guarantee you'll thank me if you do!"

Time passed. A few months after I was written out of *Star Trek*, I was again at the Gym and Swim—and there was Shirley. As we worked out on the leg press, she once again urged me to go see her shrink. Well, at that point, I was hurting so badly from losing *Star Trek*, I figured I could use a shrink. So I said, "All right, all right! Get off my back, Shirley! Give me the guy's name and I'll go!"

So she gave me his name.

And my jaw dropped on the floor. I was so shocked I could hardly speak. "You can't be serious!" I finally sputtered. "Shirley! Don't you know who that is? That's my ex-husband!"

And her jaw dropped on the floor. "But your ex-husband's a drummer, not a psychologist!"

"Yes, he's a drummer. But he took the money I earned in movies and television, and he put himself through school! He's a drummer on weekends—but now he's a therapist, too!"

"Oh, no! It can't be! That means *you're* the woman he talks about in class! *You're* the 'crazy drunk' he told us about!* And you're not like he says at all! I believed everything he told us, and— Oh, no! Oh, Grace! I'm planning to leave my husband for this guy!"

"Shirley, you can't do that!" I said. "He's not worth it! You have to stay with your husband!"

"Oh, Grace, I don't know what to do!"

A few days later, I got a call from Shirley's husband. He was completely shaken up. "Shirley's in the hospital," he said.

"Why? What happened?" I asked.

"She took a lot of pills and tried to kill herself. Grace, Shirley talks to you all the time. She won't talk to me. Can you tell me why she would do a thing like that?"

I felt terrible. I couldn't tell Shirley's husband that the reason she tried to kill herself was because she was disillusioned over the guy she was planning to run away with! I just hemmed and hawed, and pretended to be ignorant. Inside, I blamed myself for pushing Shirley over the edge.

She had been living with a fantasy—that her shrink was a terrific guy who had once been married to the Wicked Witch of the West. And she had also been living with a reality—the reality of her friend Grace, someone she had learned to know and trust. When the fantasy and the reality collided, and could not be reconciled, the conflict nearly destroyed her.

I realize now that Shirley needed to know the truth—even though it almost killed her. After all, what if she had left her husband and her children to chase after this man, only to discover too late that she had made a horrible mistake?

Truth can be a hard thing to face. But only the truth can set us free.

---

*I heard from others that my ex-husband used to bad-mouth me all over town— and to be fair, calling me a "crazy drunk" wasn't that far off the mark. In those days, I bad-mouthed him just as badly.

Actor Roger Smith, who is married to singer-actress Ann-Margret, was a good friend of mine. My ex-husband was Ann-Margret's drummer. One time my ex-husband was talking to Roger and Ann about this nasty, drunken shrew he had married—and he didn't know that Roger and I had been friends since we worked together on "77 Sunset Strip." Roger knew me very well and couldn't put the evidence of his own eyes together with the stories Steve told about me. "Are you sure you're talking about Grace Lee Whitney?" Roger asked. "I know her and she's nothing like you say she is."

Of course, that's the Jekyll-Hyde nature of alcoholism. When I was around Roger on the set, I was competent and professional, and I wasn't drunk—he saw the Jekyll side of Grace Lee Whitney. Steve saw the Hyde side—and the stories he told were my drunken, Mr. Hyde stories. The fact is, Steve knew me better than Roger did.

Well, after the incident with Shirley, I figured I really *did* need to see a shrink—but not the one Shirley had recommended! I found a therapist who came highly recommended, and one of the first things he zeroed in on was the trouble I had differentiating fantasy from reality. He told me that much of the pain I felt after being written out of *Star Trek* came from my inability to distinguish between my real self, Grace Lee Whitney, and the character I played in a TV show.

He held up a picture me in my *Star Trek* uniform and said, "This is not you. This is a *picture* of you playing a part in a TV show. The only you that is *really* you is the person sitting in your chair right now."

I looked at him like *he* was the one who was nuts! "No!" I said. "You're wrong! This is me right here, but that's me in the picture, too!"

"But you need to see that when the part of Janice Rand was written out of *Star Trek*, it wasn't directed at you, at Grace Lee Whitney. That was a creative decision about a fictional character. You are not Janice Rand. You are Grace Lee Whitney."

"No! When I was on *Star Trek*, I *was* Janice Rand! When they got rid of Janice Rand, they got rid of Grace Lee Whitney! Don't you understand? I'm me, but that woman on the screen is me too! They didn't fire a name in a script. They fired *me*, Grace Lee Whitney!"

My therapist was unable to get me to budge from that point of view, because I knew who was in the room with The Executive that night. It wasn't Yeoman Janice Rand. It was Grace Lee Whitney.

❖ ❖ ❖

In 1970 and '71, I made some big changes in my life. I took another hostage. I married a bass player named Jack (I was married two times, to a bass player and a drummer—I like to keep it in the rhythm section). I also put the plug in the jug and stopped drinking. Was I finally clean and sober? Hardly. I just switched from drinking to smoking dope. It's called "switching seats on the Titanic." I stopped drinking but I didn't get sober—I only switched addictions. I was a dry drunk. I avoided alcohol and only smoked marijuana for the next eight years or so. I used to roll joints that were as thick as cigars, trying to get as high on weed as I used to get on the bottle.

I gave up the pursuit of my acting career and focused on singing, as well as being more of a full-time mother and housewife. I devoted myself to something I had been neglecting for a while: building a good nest for my children. I bought a female Great Dane and bred her. We raised nine puppies, sold six, and ended up with four Danes plus a collie we took in—a whole houseful of dogs.

I became a workaholic during this time. I had so much nervous energy, and no alcohol to dampen it with. I was always on the go, always doing something, anything, everything.

I became obsessive about being healthy and thin. I practically *killed* myself trying to be healthy! I became fanatical about vitamins—so fanatical that I overdosed on vitamins and broke out in a terrible rash. I abstained from sugar and flour and went on the Atkins diet. I quit smoking. I became anorexic and malnourished. My hair was bleached white and I began to get wrinkles everywhere. The thinner I got, the more wrinkles I got.

In later years, an actress tends to look better if she gains a bit of weight, because the fat fills in the wrinkles. There's a saying: "It's either your face or your fanny after forty." If you put on weight, your face looks great. If you take weight off, your fanny looks great. But rarely can a middle-aged woman have it both ways. Because I had become anorexic by this time, I looked *terrible*—but I thought I was beautiful. All anorexics do.

My mother and father had moved to Southern California in 1957, so I saw them fairly often. I could never fool my dad. He knew when I was in trouble, even if I didn't. He told me, "Grace, you look like a cadaver! You're too thin! What are you doing to yourself?" He would tell me that for the next 10 years, because I was anorexic from about 1970 to 1979.

In 1971, I had breast augmentation surgery—or, in common parlance, a boob job. In fact, I've had so much plastic surgery over the years that I often tell people, "My boobs are thirty, my face is forty, and my ass is fifty-one!" (Sorry if that line offends you—my problem is that I'm too dirty for church people and too religious for everybody else!)

When I'd go to Western Costumers for fittings, the dresser used to tell me, "You have the most beautiful body, absolutely perfect—if only your boobs were bigger." And I would feel absolutely horrible.

When The Executive had me in that office and made me disrobe and told me to dance for him, the reason he said he couldn't get aroused was "your boobs are too small." It wasn't enough that he violated me, he had to criticize me too! Those remarks hurt me so much I was willing to go under the knife to keep from having to hear them again. In fact, if I could have won that man's approval and kept my job on *Star Trek* by getting a boob job, I would have gone right out and done it. I would have made an appointment the next morning, and after it was done, I would have gone right back to the studio to show my beautiful new body to the man who had violated me! That's how desperate I was.

You can fix the outside all you want, but the inside is still in pain. I spent so much money trying to fix the outside, trying to feel good about myself—and I just kept getting sicker and sicker. When I got into recovery, I learned that fixing the outside doesn't solve anything. Becoming a whole, healthy person is an inside job.*

People wonder how I can go out and tell people I've had all this cosmetic surgery. I've told it in meetings and even on television, and people are always shocked!

---

*This is not to say that physical health and fitness are unimportant—only that making yourself beautiful on the outside does not make you emotionally and spiritually healthy on the inside. To this day, I still exercise and keep physically fit. Any casting directors who might be reading, pay attention: I'm going to keep fit into my seventies and beyond, so if you have a show or commercial to cast, just call me! Use me as proof that a woman can stay fit—even with a few wrinkles!

"Shut up, Whitney!" they tell me. "You're embarrassing yourself!" Well, yes, in the beginning, it was embarrassing to talk about it. But I learned something very important when I went into recovery: You're as sick as your secrets. Once a secret isn't a secret anymore, it loses its power over you. The more secrets I kept, the sicker I got. The more truthful I became, the healthier I got.

Another thing that amazes people is that I'm totally honest about my age. I was born April 1, 1930—you can do the math. Women often ask me, "Why do you tell people your age? You don't look your age, so why tell people?" I say, "Because, if I start lying to you by the sin of omission, if I don't tell you how old I am and what I've done to my body to make me look good, then I'm conning myself. If I'm not honest with you, I'm not honest with myself. And if I'm not honest with myself, then sooner or later, I'll find myself in a bar someplace. I can only keep my sobriety by facing and telling the truth."

The alcoholic mind is insidious. I've been plagued by that kind of mind all my life. Even before I drank, I had an alcoholic mind. Alcohol is only a symptom of the real disease. The "ism" of alcoholism runs much deeper than alcohol alone.

The same year I had my first surgery, 1971, I got pregnant—and I really wasn't ready to take care of a newborn again. I immediately sent Jack out to get a vasectomy. A few months later, I had a miscarriage. The doctor who did the D and C procedure was a Dr. Feelgood who kept me well supplied with pills—a dope dealer with a diploma on his wall. I was still using amphetamines at the time—part of the reason I was so thin.

When I got my boobs done, I finally felt *zaftig*, luscious, round and physically perfect. Suddenly, 10 years of mileage just melted right off my body. But I still wasn't satisfied. I had to go out and show everybody! I had to go out and attract some attention! My plastic surgery was so successful, it nearly ruined my life. In large part, it triggered my sex addiction.

My second husband, Jack, didn't push me toward getting cosmetic surgery. I told him I felt perfect except for my breasts, and he encouraged me to do whatever I needed to feel better about myself. Little did I know that the procedure would be so successful I would want to run out into the street and into the bars to show everybody my new perfect body!

My first few years of marriage to Jack, I was faithful to him. But I began to feel that this beautiful new body of mine was going to waste, being saved for only one man. So I started acting out my fantasies. I did many things I'm ashamed of today.

During those post-*Trek* years, people often stopped me on the street or in stores and asked, "Aren't you that blond yeoman from *Star Trek*? Whatever happened to you? Where have you been?" And I would smile politely and say, "Captain Kirk was too old for me. I've been out on *Antares* with Charlie X, because I like younger men." I signed an occasional autograph, but for the most part, I wanted nothing to do with *Star Trek*.

By 1976, the series had been out of my life for 10 years. The last thing in the world I wanted to see or hear about was *Star Trek*. I felt that The Executive had ruined my life, and *Star Trek* only reminded me of all that pain.

But then something happened that changed all that: I ran into DeForest Kelly at the unemployment office in Van Nuys. He told me that the fans were asking about me and wanted to meet me, and he gave me the number of the organizers of an upcoming *Trek* convention, Equicon. The organizers happened to be Bjo and John Trimble, and ever since Equicon, Bjo and John have been wonderfully supportive friends (Bjo has always told me I should write a book!).

I couldn't believe that people were actually holding conventions about a cancelled TV show—and that they were asking about *me*! But when I arrived at Equicon '76 at the Hilton Hotel in L.A., I discovered it was all true. The fans were overwhelming in their enthusiasm when I came out onto the stage. I had written my first two *Trek*-oriented songs, and when I performed them, I got the loudest, longest ovation I have ever received in my life. I think it was the first inkling the fans had that I was a singer and songwriter, so my songs "Disco Trekkin" and "Star Child" (which I wrote for my son, Jonathan) really knocked 'em out.

After that first taste of *Trek* fandom, I was hooked. The hurt and the resentment of the past decade began to wash away, replaced by the thrilling realization that I had been a part (however short-lived) of something very special to many people. At Equicon and all the other conventions I went to, I felt loved and appreciated as I never had before. I am so grateful to all you fans who kept *Star Trek* and Yeoman Janice Rand alive in your hearts—I can't tell you how much you mean to me!

After Equicon, I went home and immediately began writing more songs for *Star Trek*—13 songs for 13 episodes. I read the old *Trek* scripts for inspiration, and wrote the lyrics, while Jack composed the music. Then I performed my songs at the conventions and sold tapes to the fans. Jack was my partner and my manager. He set up the sound equipment at the conventions and took care of all the details for me, so that I could go onstage and do my thing.

One of my favorite songs is "How Will He Love Me," the story of the repressed love of Yeoman Rand for Captain Kirk:

How will he love me when he's near me
How will he look into my eyes
Will he ever see me as a woman
Eager to please his every sigh

How will he hold me when he's wantin'
And will his arms enjoy the show
Will he take his time to kiss me oh so slowly
Will I ever, ever really know

Is there a chance, could he care
Will he romance me everywhere
Or am I foolin' myself
Down to my very soul

A sad affair am I, alone here in the sky
Am I a dreamer ever so lonely
Playin' my own starship charade
How can I go on another day without him

Oh, I don't know
I need, I need him so
Well, I don't know
I need, I need him so

Waitin' for you, wantin' you
Needin' you baby, I'm wantin' you
Come look at me, baby, I'm lovin' you
Wantin' you, baby, I'm needin' you

That's Janice Rand's heart, poured into a song. That's the feeling she expressed to Captain Kirk in "Miri" when she confessed that she had always tried to get him to notice her when they were roaming the galaxy together. Another song, "The Enemy Within" expresses the dark side of *Star Trek*. Here's how that song begins:

Oh Lord, take away the pain
Oh Lord, here it comes again
The Enemy Within, don't fight it
You can't win

It sneaks around the corners
Up and down your spine
Like a spider creepin'
Laughin' all the time

Turns you into Satan
It makes you scrutinize
Starts your blood a-boilin'
Puts daggers in your eyes

There were other songs, some based on specific episodes ("Miri" and "Charlie X"), some that were just fun ("Disco Trekkin" and "From Venice to Balboa"), and some that were deeply personal, written to my boys ("Star Child" and "Spaced-Out Pilot"). The fans really responded to these expressions of my heart and of the *Star Trek* legend in song. To this day, they still ask, "When are you going to sing your songs again?"

❖ ❖ ❖

In the last few years of the '70s, I developed an absolute craze for roller skating. I would go to Cher's skating rink on Monday nights (that was Screen Actor's Guild night—you could only get in by showing your SAG card). Sometimes Cher would come with her daughter, Chastity (who was just a toddler then, but she would get out and skate, too). There would be many other stars there, like Ed Begley, Jr., and LeVar Burton. Sometimes, a big limousine would pull up and the door would open, and there would be John Huston, delivering his daughter Angelica to the rink.

Skating was my release. I had all this energy to burn off from not drinking. I was hyper all the time. My husband, Jack, thought I was crazy, going skating at all hours of the night. "Why don't you grow up?" he asked. Of course, the last thing in the world I wanted to do was grow up and act my age!

One time at Cher's rink, I met a skater named Bill Turner who used to be Sonja Henie's ice-skating partner (Sonja was the Norwegian Olympic gold medalist who made a number of Hollywood movies such as *Thin Ice* and *Sun Valley Serenade*). Bill was a great skater, and he had a friend named Kevin LeRoy. We began skating up and down Sunset Boulevard at dusk. We did this practically every night for months. I loved it!*

I always parked my MGB hatchback in the lot of the Huntington Hartford Theater (now called the Doolittle Theater), and I'd open the hatch, sit on the rear of the car, and strap on my skates. Then Kevin, Bill and I would skate along the sidewalk on Sunset from Vine out beyond Doheny, to the Rainbow Cafe. It was about three or four miles there and the same distance back again. I'd wear my shorts and my braided Bo Derek wig, and Bill would have his boom box on his shoulder. We were a sight!

One night, I was sitting on the back of my car, putting my skates on as the theater was letting out—and who should come walking out of the theater but Bill and Marcy Shatner! I hadn't seen Bill Shatner in years. I called out to him and waved, and he looked up and said, "Would you look at that! It's Grace Lee Whitney!" The traffic was so bad that they could hardly get out of the lot and onto the street. Meanwhile, my two friends and I took off down the sidewalk on our roller skates, boom box blaring. Pretty soon Bill and Marcy were pulling up alongside us in their car. Marcy was laughing, and Bill was calling out to me in his Captain Kirk voice, "Yeoman Rand! I *order* you to stop this nonsense immediately!" Bill talks about this incident at con-

---

*An aside: I wrote a roller-skating song, "From Venice to Balboa," and I mentioned Bill and Kevin in the song. I went to Herb Alpert at A&M Records and showed him the song and told him I wanted to do it as a music video. The video would have me singing the song as I skated along the sidewalk at Venice beach, with my two Great Danes out in front of me. The video would end with me beaming up to a starship—and there would be Robert Walker, Jr., Charlie X, and I would sing "Charlie X" to him as we skated around each other aboard this starship. Although VCRs were just coming on the market at that time, it was a few years before the advent of MTV. Herb listened politely to my song, then said it would never work, putting music and video together. People liked to *listen* to music—not watch it. I was just a few years too early for the MTV generation!

This is my Bo Derek look, circa 1980. I wore this red wig with beads and braids when I roller-skated up and down Hollywood and Sunset. In fact, this is the wig I wore when I entered recovery. I remember one guy in the meeting would see me and call out, "Here comes old rope-head!"

ventions sometimes, and he says he thought I was just as far out to lunch as anyone could get!

On another night, I came back from skating up and down Sunset, and it must have been about 10:30 or 11:00 when I got back to the theater parking lot. I noticed that the marquee read JACK LEMMON IN "TRIBUTE." I thought, *I haven't seen Jack since Irma La Douce! I'm gonna go say hi!* The show was over, but the lights were all on, so I went right into the theater on my roller skates, rolled right up to the stage manager and said, "Is Jack Lemmon still here?"

"He's in his dressing room?" the stage manager replied. "Does Mr. Lemmon know you?"

"You bet!" I said. "Tell him Grace Lee Whitney is here."

I followed the stage manager to the foot of the stage and waited. I heard the man say, "Mr. Lemmon, there's a lady out here on roller skates. Says her name is Grace Lee Whitney."

And I heard Jack exclaim, "The hell you say! Grace Lee Whitney on roller skates! Well, tell her to roll on in and have a drink!"

So I skated across the stage of the Huntington Hartford Theater, and my skates rumbled like thunder in that big, empty theater. I skated right into his dressing room, and he just couldn't believe it was me. I sat down and he offered me a drink. "No, thanks," I said, "but I'll have a glass of that selzer." This, of course, was my dry period.

"Sure, sure," he said, and he poured me some sparkling water, and we sat back and talked for the longest time—stories about Billy Wilder and Tony Curtis and *Some Like It Hot* and *Irma la Douce*. It was fabulous. What a lovely man.

I skated almost every night. The lights and the noise and the smell of the city on Sunset Boulevard really got my blood pumping. The night life in Hollywood was garish and rude and unbelievably bizarre—and you never knew who you might meet or what you might see. I loved it. I loved being on wheels, rushing at warp speed through the neon galaxy at twilight, my braided hair flowing behind me like the energy flux from a starship drive.

I was so proud of my body and my skating ability that I jumped at the chance to audition for the movie *Skatetown USA*. I had gotten all this cosmetic surgery done, I was in great shape from all the skating I did, and I envisioned myself as young. But when I went to the audition, I found myself up against skaters in their twenties. I looked great—but I sure wasn't in my twenties. I was approaching the half-century mark!

Once again, fantasy and reality came into collision in my life. The fantasy was my illusion of youth. The reality was that I wasn't young anymore. That was very hard for me to accept, or even recognize.

Jack ,my husband, was my soulmate. We were born a month apart, which means we were both in the womb at the same time. He used to tell me that the stars were aligned before we were born. Jack was a very likable, kind, generous guy with a great sense of humor, and I had a lot of fun with him. He took my boys camping and worked hard to be a good stepdad to them, teaching them to be responsible.

Once, when one of my boys was being bothered by a bully on his paper route, Jack and I got in the car early one morning and laid an ambush for the kid. As my son came along on his bike, there was the bully on his own bike, chasing my son, trying to tip him over. Jack was out of the car like a shot, and I was just a few paces behind. Jack grabbed the bully, yanked him off his bike, and got him on the ground. He was like a tiger—but he didn't hurt the kid, just scared him and chased him off. I thought it was wonderful—and my son was never bothered again.

I loved getting stoned with Jack, but our shared addiction had its definite downside. Our marriage was a typical alcoholic relationship—unhealthy and sometimes violent. Jack and I had our good times, but we also fought a lot. When we would start up, my children would hide under the beds and the dogs would run at the sound of our voices. We had some real knockdown drag-out fights, and sometimes we called the police on each other. That was a terrible thing to inflict on my boys.

Jack always wanted to restrict my behavior and make me be good—but I didn't want to be good! One time I got so mad at him that I took all the beautiful gold-rimmed porcelain dishes with gilt-edged black flowers that my mother had given us for our wedding, and I stood in the kitchen and threw every last one of those dishes against the wall. I did it right in front of Jack because I was angry with him, I was totally self-willed, and I wouldn't let *anyone* make me be good! (Defiance is an outstanding characteristic of alcoholics.)

Jack and I had a beautiful house on a half-acre in Van Nuys, with a swimming pool and tennis court. In 1976, we built an eight-track recording studio in the cabana by the pool (we named the studio The Epic Blunder). Jack composed the music and I was the lyricist. Even though I had performed most of my life as a singer, I became obsessed with becoming the best I could be. I took singing lessons and recorded with my husband for six years, practically every hour Jack was not at his day job.

Jack and I had our big, grandiose plans for our recording studio, our house, our future together. We hired an architect to create plans for enlarging the house. Even before the loan was approved, we started tearing out the walls of the enclosed patio, breaking up the concrete to put in new plumbing, and ripping off the roof. When the bank told us the loan was turned down, we were stunned. Suddenly, we had a ripped-up house and no money to fix it with. We just had to live with this awful torn-up patio in the back of the house. When Jack's union called a strike, we went through all my savings in a few weeks, then had nothing to live on. Naturally, we started fighting over money.

To top things off, Jack's ex-wife decided to take him back to court for more alimony because he had married (her words) "a rich actress," he owned a "sailboat," and he could obviously afford higher alimony payments since we were living the high life. Well, clearly, I was not rich. And the "sailboat" was a six-foot Sabat—a little rowboat. Jack went into court, and he got up and produced a picture of the "sailboat." When the judge saw it, he broke out laughing! Case dismissed.

We eventually refinanced the house and paid off a lot of debt. But I was sinking deeper into the self-will-run-riot aspect of my disease. I was still not drinking, but I was stoned on dope and high on amyl nitrite. Being a dry drunk undoubtedly slowed

In addition to my Bo Derek look, I also had a Farah Fawcett look. This is often how I looked while roller-skating with my friends and our boombox. I was a menace on wheels! By the way, I was 50 years old when this was taken, a year before I got sober.

my free-fall toward destruction. Alcohol will take you down fast. Pot's a slow burn, but with alcohol, you're down the toilet.

I wanted fun. I wanted passion and excitement. I was tired of housewifery, I was restless and discontented, and I was getting ready to divorce again (another relationship sabotaged).

At this point in my life, I felt I had been sexually preyed upon and exploited by men (such as The Executive)—so I decided to turn the tables. I figured Hollywood would be a safer place if I could become the predator instead of the prey. So that's what I became: a sexual predator. I preyed on men and I preyed on women. My sexuality knew no boundaries. I didn't only need to get sober—I needed to get *sexually* sober. It wasn't just alcohol that was destroying me—*all* my obsessions were destroying me.

When I say I was a sexual predator, I don't mean I preyed on others the way The Executive preyed upon me—using physical force, or the threat of it, to obtain sex. When a woman behaves in a sexually predatory way, she uses her sexuality, not force. She teases, she comes on, she even comes across—but she does it all to control and manipulate her sex partner. She gives what the other person wants, to get what she wants.

I would leave Jack at home and go dancing at Studio One all night. I'd end up in a hotel room or a hot tub with a person (or persons, plural) I had never met before. During that time, I plunged to the absolute depths of my sex addiction. I urged my husband to view our marriage as an "open marriage," and I got involved with mate-swapping. I reached a point where I no longer viewed sex as being about connecting with or giving pleasure to another human being. It wasn't even about receiving pleasure in the form of closeness, foreplay and sexual release. To me, sex was *power*, no more, no less. I could make people want me, and I could make them do what I wanted. I was no longer the victim. I had the power.

But sex didn't satisfy me. In fact, I discovered that when I acted out my sexual fantasies, it made me sick. I would engage in these orgiastic debaucheries, and at the end of it all, I was actually physically sick to my stomach. On some level, I knew I was violating and defiling myself—yet I couldn't stop, because I craved the power that came with sexually manipulating and controlling others. I knew that my lifestyle was dirty and degrading. Even though I didn't know God at the time, I realize now that he was trying to reach me through the nausea of my sin. He was saying to me, "Don't do this, my child." But I did it anyway, and I suffered terribly because of it.

People think that sin is glamorous. But at some point, usually when it's too late, they discover that sin is a slow-acting poison. People think that God punishes us for our sin because he doesn't want us to enjoy life. They see God as a cosmic killjoy who wants to squash our fun. But no, God truly loves us and wants us to enjoy life. He wants us to enjoy our sexuality within the protective enclosure of a covenantal commitment called marriage. "You will show me the path of life," says the ancient

Jewish Psalmist. "In your presence is fullness of joy. At your right hand there are pleasures for evermore."[1] God doesn't hate us for our sins. He *aches* for us when we wound ourselves with our sins. I believe we are punished not so much *for* our sins as *by* them.

I sinned, willfully and deliberately. And my sins nearly killed me.

By the late 1970s, the "isms" of my disease were becoming very advanced. I still wasn't drinking—but I wasn't sober, either. The symptoms of the disease of alcoholism were still with me and growing worse, even though I was dry. The obsessions I practiced were smoking dope and wild sex. I look back on who I was and how I behaved, and it's hard for me to believe that this totally out-of-control woman was really *me*. It was as though I had lost my mind. In a way, perhaps I had gone insane.

Though I was still Jewish in my mind, I had completely thrown the God of Abraham, Isaac and Jacob out of my life. I had become an atheist. Not a doubting, inquiring, skeptical agnostic, but a hardheaded, self-willed atheist. I was also a complete hedonist. I was totally selfish, pleasure-seeking and thrill-seeking. Everyone I came in contact with got hurt. My husband suffered terribly—he lost 15 pounds living with the crazy woman I had become. My kids were terribly hurt by the things I did and said.

I was approaching the "crash and burn" stage of my disease. Approaching—but not there yet. I still had a lot more pain to suffer—much of it self-inflicted.

But a lot of my pain would come from an old, familiar source. *Star Trek* was about to put the knife in me again—

And twist it.

In 1977, I was in a bookstore and happened to notice a book by Gene Roddenberry's executive assistant, Susan Sackett. The book was called *Letters to Star Trek*. I flipped the book over and saw that the back cover listed the 10 questions most frequently asked by *Star Trek* fans. Question number three read, "Whatever happened to Grace Lee Whitney?" As soon as I saw that, I rushed home and called Susan at Paramount and said, "You want to know what happened to Grace Lee Whitney?"

"I sure do," said Susan. "Do you know where she is?"

"Of course I do," I said. "*I'm* Grace Lee Whitney!"

Susan screamed into the phone, "Ohmigosh, where have you been?!"

"Susan," I said, "let's have lunch. I've got a lot to tell you."

We met over lunch at the Paramount commissary, then Susan took me to Gene Roddenberry's office. Gene wasn't back from lunch yet, so Susan let me wait in his inner office. I was sitting on the corner of Gene's desk when he walked in, took one astonished look at me—then picked me up in the air and whirled me around. He was so glad to see me, he was jubilant. He said, "I wanted to see you and make it up to you! Grace, we're bringing *Star Trek* back as a weekly series—*Star Trek: Phase II*. Everyone's going to be in it. Bill Shatner, George, Nichelle, everyone! Leonard, too, if we can iron out the contractual details. And Janice Rand is going to pick up right where she left off! Hey, we might even give her a promotion!"

I was so thrilled to hear it. Just as he had said he would, Gene got the entire cast together, except Leonard Nimoy. Spock was going to be replaced by a young Vulcan officer named Xon. We all had contracts, we were to get paid up-front, the scripts were written, the sets were built, and there was even a new version of the *Enterprise*. It was even more exciting than the first time around. Gene guaranteed that Janice Rand was going to be a major part of the ensemble. I played my *Star Trek* songs for Gene, and he just flipped out over them.

Gene and I talked about my removal from the original series, and he told me it was the biggest mistake he ever made. He blamed the decision on the network, claiming that the edict to remove me came from NBC. Supposedly, the network had wanted Captain Kirk to be unencumbered by a girlfriend back on the ship as he went from world to world, leaving a trail of broken hearts in his wake. I believed him then, though I've since learned that it was typically Gene's pattern to use the "evil network" as a scapegoat.* The fact is that Gene could have put his foot down and kept me aboard, but he didn't do so—and he later apologized to me for it. That's all that counts.

"I should have kept you aboard the *Enterprise*," Gene told me, "so that when Captain Kirk came back from having affairs with all these other women on all these other planets—he'd have to deal with you. What a great plot-thickener *that* would have been! And I never even thought of it. Losing you was the dumbest mistake I ever made." Although I was happy that he finally saw my ejection from the series as a bad move, it made me sick to know that I had gone through all that hell, all that humiliation, all that drinking, because of Gene's so-called "dumb mistake."

For months, everything went sailing along smoothly for *Star Trek: Phase II*. Then, just two weeks before we were to begin shooting the first episode of the new series, word came down from the Paramount studio heads, Michael Eisner and Jeff Katzenbaum, that *Star Trek: Phase II* was being scrapped. There would be no new TV series. Paramount had decided to revive *Star Trek* as a theatrical film instead.

The theatrical film would be an enlarged version of the pilot script for *Star Trek: Phase II*,** a story called "In Thy Image," written by producer Harold Livingston from

---

*For example, Gene conned Harlan Ellison into spearheading the first "Save *Star Trek*" letter-writing campaign by claiming NBC wanted to shut down the series even before it aired; all the evidence indicates that NBC really wanted *Star Trek* to succeed, because it was a brilliant sales tool for parent company RCA's color TV sets.

**Though it never got off the ground, the aborted *Star Trek: Phase II* series managed to spin off not one but *two* successful projects—*Star Trek: The Motion Picture* and the TV series *Star Trek: The Next Generation*. Many of the ideas that would have gone into *Phase II* (including entire scripts and storylines) were later adapted for *Next Generation*.

a story by Alan Dean Foster. The story that emerged as the script went through various revisions and was strongly reminiscent of an original series episode, "The Changeling," in which an old Earth-launched space probe is picked up by the *Enterprise*. The probe's mission: to seek out its creator.

Film legend Robert Wise was brought aboard as director of the movie. His screen credits included *The Sand Pebbles, The Sound of Music, Run Silent, Run Deep* and *The Day the Earth Stood Still*. He had assisted Orson Welles as film editor on *Citizen Kane*. I was in awe of this man. He was movie history personified.

Gene Roddenberry had a habit, whenever new people entered the tight little world of *Star Trek*, of playing a practical joke on them. His idea was that *Star Trek* is a fun place, and he wanted people to be loose and relaxed, not stuffy. For example, there was the time that Gene tricked newly hired associate producer and story consultant John D. F. Black into interviewing an "unknown young actress" for him. This was in April 1966, before the cast and crew of the series had been set, and Black had no idea that the "unknown young actress" was Gene's girlfriend, Majel Barrett. So Majel went into John's office for the interview, shutting the door behind her, and John began interviewing her. As the interview progressed, Majel began disrobing and coming on to John. She was down to her underthings and sliding onto the lap of a very terrified John D. F. Black, when the door burst open and Gene walked in. "What's going on here?" Gene demanded, while poor John blushed and stammered and protested his innocence. Then a whole crowd of people rushed in—with cake and champagne for the party. John realized he'd been set up. A typical Gene Roddenberry prank.

Gene decided he was going to play a practical joke on his new director, Robert Wise—and he roped me into it. I told him I didn't think it would work, but he assured me it would be funny—after it was all over, Robert Wise would never forget me. I wanted to please Gene, because I desperately wanted to maintain my connection to *Star Trek*, so I agreed to it. I was so grateful to be in the movie, I would have done anything.

Gene had me dress up like a real floozy, with my hair piled high on my head, with lots of makeup and a short skirt. I looked like a two-dollar hooker. Gene had me sit on the desk in Wise's new office and wait for him to come in. So when our new director entered, he found me sitting there, filing my nails and chewing gum. His jaw dropped, he sputtered incoherently, then he spun on his heel and dashed off down the corridor. "Gene! Gene!" I heard him calling as his footsteps receded. "What is *that thing* in my office?"

I heard Gene say, "That's your new secretary."

"I don't believe it!" he roared. Then I heard the stamp of his approaching footsteps, and as he walked through the door the second time, I said (just as Gene instructed), "Welcome to your new office, Mr. Wise. I'm here to serve you in any way I can. Of course, I won't be here long today—I have a doctor's appointment. I'm going to have a bunion removed from my right foot, see here?" And I put my foot out in front of him—

And he freaked. He absolutely freaked. He spun around and yelled, "*Gene!*"

A 1978 preproduction shot of the cast of Star Trek: The Motion Picture, *gathered on the bridge before the start of shooting. We had just gotten our uniforms, and this was the first time we had all been together since the original series. Director Robert Wise is at far left, Gene Roddenberry at far right.*

I left the office, and just hid out for a while. When I came back in to find Gene, he said, "I think you'd better tell him."

I said, "Me?"

"Yeah," he said. "Tell him it was all a joke."

"Well, you come in with me, Gene! It was your idea!"

So we went into the office together, and Robert Wise was sitting at his desk, fuming.

Gene said, "Bob, it was all just a joke. This is really Grace Lee Whitney from the original series. You know, practical jokes are sort of a tradition on the *Star Trek* set. We had no idea you'd be so upset. It was all my idea. I sent Grace in to do this."

Wise looked right at me. If his eyes had been phasers, they would have been set on KILL. "Not very funny," he said in a voice that could freeze a solar flare.

Well, Gene promised that Robert Wise would never forget me—and he was right. Throughout the making of *Star Trek: the Motion Picture*, Robert Wise was very cool to me. He always called me "Sara Lee," as if I was a frozen cheesecake! He issued a direct order to the makeup department: "I want very little makeup on this woman." I can't pretend to know his mind, but my impression at the time was that he was deliberately sabotaging me. I felt he did not want me to look glamorous, as I did in the original show (how I missed Virginia Darcy, Fred Phillips and Jerry Finnerman!). It seemed that he wanted me to look plain and old—and it just about killed me. I was horribly upset, practically suicidal, throughout the picture. It didn't help that I was so thin and anorexic—just 113 pounds.

I would come into the studio looking good—and by the time I got through in makeup, I looked like my own grandmother! People on the set would look at me and say, "My gosh, Grace! What have they done to you? You're a pretty woman! Why are they screwing up your looks in this movie?" Actress Persis Khambatta, who played Lieutenant Ilia, the "bald-is-beautiful" Deltan, said to me, "Grace, I would not allow myself to be photographed that way. Why do you let them do this to you? It's your face! They should make you look beautiful!" I would go home at night, comb my hair out, and cry.

On one occasion, I went to Robert Wise and told him I at least wanted to put a little mascara on. "If you wear any eye makeup," he replied, "you will not be allowed in the shot." End of discussion.

I was so distraught, I almost got a face-lift in the middle of the movie. I actually made an appointment with the surgeon, and I would have gone through with it except Jack, my husband, said, "You can't do that! You'll look like two different people in the movie!" I was so manic and panic-stricken at the thought that this movie was going to make me look horrible, I could hardly live with it.

I got so frantic about my looks that I went from being anorexic to being a binge eater during the making of the film. I would see myself in the dailies, and I looked so thin that I would go to the food cart on the sound stage and I'd wolf down a dozen donuts at a single sitting. Then, on the way home, I'd stop and buy a box of donuts and stuff myself all night long, trying to put on weight by the next day. The emotional pain I felt was horrendous—hour after hour, day after day, of intense, unrelieved panic.

But nothing worked. Nothing would fix it.

I had gone into *Star Trek: The Motion Picture* thinking it would mark my joyous return to the world of *Star Trek*. Instead, the experience nearly destroyed me.

For a long time afterward, I blamed Robert Wise for the way I looked in that movie, and for making me feel so terrible about myself. I viewed him as a vindictive, tyrannical sadist who used his power to get even with me for Gene's prank. Once, when I complained about the incident to Beverly, my sponsor in the recovery program, she said, "You have to stop blaming Robert Wise for what happened to you. In fact, you need to make amends to him."

I was stunned. I couldn't believe what I was hearing. Robert Wise humiliated *me*—and I owe *him* an amends?

"Absolutely," she said. "You allowed yourself to be used in a practical joke to embarrass and humiliate another human being. Now you need to make amends to Robert Wise." And, of course, Beverly was exactly right. It's a very alcoholic thing to blame other people for our problems. My problems aboard *Star Trek: The Motion Picture* were self-induced.

I haven't seen or talked to Robert Wise in the years since we finished making the movie, so I haven't yet made amends. But Mr. Wise, if you read these words, contact me and I will say it to you in person: I apologize from the bottom of my heart for the hoax Gene and I played on you.

❖ ❖ ❖

I don't want to give you the wrong idea. *Star Trek: The Motion Picture* was not a completely miserable experience. I also have some wonderful memories of making that movie.

I wrote a song called "U.S.S. *Enterprise*" while the movie was being filmed. It has a strong melody set against a throbbing bass line (suggesting the booming, soul-shuddering power of the starship's antimatter-powered engines). I brought a tape of the song to Paramount and gave it to Stephen Collins, who played Captain Will Decker in the movie. Stephen is a great bass player in his own right, and had his electric bass with him on the set. He put the tape on his portable tape recorder with his head-phones, and he picked up his bass (which wasn't plugged in, so you had to be very close to hear it unamplified). It was such a thrill for me to watch him close his eyes, smile, and play along with my music—he just loved that song.

So then I brought him another song—"Ilia's Theme." It's the story of Decker and Ilia and their eternal love for each other. Stephen loved that song, too, because the lyrics told such a beautiful story:

Ilia, creature from a star
You are so beautiful
Ilia, tell me who you are
Are you a fantasy, a fantasy
Do you remember
He came into your life
He was so tender
Time after time, remember
He tasted so sweet
A celebration, strawberry wine
Oh, surrender

You gave him all your love
And then he vanished
Into thin air
Leaving you crying
In the dark nowhere
So now you're searchin' for love

The entire experience of making the movie was a dazzling, awe-inspiring jour-ney. The sets were so detailed and high-tech compared to the sets of the original series. Back in 1966, our sets were made of plywood and painted Styrofoam and Radio Shack switches and knobs. The computers in the movie were real, working computers with actual video displays that were programmed to produce convincing computer images. We had technical advisors from NASA and Apple and Hewlett-Packard. Everything was perfect to the last detail.

There's a scene near the beginning of the film where I'm operating the transporter. As I'm beaming up two crewmen, there's a transporter malfunction. The crewmen end up dying horribly as their atoms are scrambled by a computer glitch.

To prepare me for the scene, one of the NASA technicians, who was on loan to Paramount as a technical advisor, showed me the schematic of how the transporter works, what controls to manipulate, and the proper sequence to make it work. "You do this to set the coordinates," she said, "and you do this to energize, and you control the power level with this," and so forth. She explained it with such complete seriousness, and I was so mesmerized and caught up in the complexity and seeming reality of the thing, that I asked her, "Do you mean this thing is real? Does this transporter really beam people from place to place?" Technology has advanced so much in my lifetime that I didn't find it incredible at all that we might actually be able to dematerialize people and beam their atoms around like sending a fax!

Once again in my life, I was finding it hard to differentiate fantasy from reality. And I wasn't the only one who was awestruck by the seeming reality of the fantasy world we were in. At one point, the cast was gathered on the bridge for some publicity shots. I was standing next to Majel Barrett Roddenberry, and she looked around with wonder in her eyes, then turned to me and said, "It almost seems like this thing could really fly!"

After we finished filming, I hosted a party at my home in Van Nuys for the cast of *Star Trek: The Motion Picture*. A few days before the party, I was skating at Cher's rink when I saw someone I hadn't seen in years: Robert Walker, Jr.—Charlie X himself! I skated up to him and said, "Hi, Charlie!" He was so surprised to see me. I told him we were had just finished shooting *Star Trek: The Motion Picture*, and we were having a cast party at my house. I invited him to come, and he did.

It was a fabulous party. Everyone was there, and we all sat around in our big backyard and we ate and talked and laughed. My roller skating friends were there, and we skated around the deck of the pool.

Jack played the backup tracks for the *Star Trek* songs over the big speakers we had around the pool, and I sang the songs I had written from the original *Trek* and the movie. I sang "Ilia's Theme" to Stephen Collins and Persis Khambatta, and I sang "Charlie X" to Robert Walker. The backup musicians on those recordings were unbelievable—Greg Matheson on keyboard (Donna Summer's accompanist); Peter Donald on drums; Tim May on guitar; and Abraham Laboriel on bass (possibly the finest, most in-demand session bassist in the world—he's played with Stevie Wonder, George Benson, Barbara Streisand, Elton John, Quincy Jones, and Michael Jackson, to name a few). A&M Records came close to putting that song on record.

Shortly after we finished making the movie, I ended an eight-year dry spell and began drinking again. I threw a lot of parties at my house in those days. I served a lot of wine—and I drank a lot, too. I would roller skate around the pool, totally out of control, and I embarrassed people by the horrible things I said and did. The first drink or two would loosen me up, so that I was having a good time. But after the first drink, I could never stop. I had to keep going until I became angry, obnoxious and abusive.

The next morning, I would be awakened by the phone ringing, and I'd be afraid to answer it, afraid to hear what horrible thing I had done the night before. Long before I got sober, people tried to tell me I was not a good drunk, not nice or fun to be around at all. I remember an incident before my second marriage, when I dated a wonderful actor friend, Paul Smith. He really liked me, and I liked him, and he took me to a fabulous, posh garden party in Beverly Hills. During the party, I got loaded and pushed Paul in the pool with all his clothes on. I thought it was funny, but it wasn't funny at all. No one else laughed, least of all Paul. I don't think he ever forgave me (I still need to make amends to him). We never dated after that.

When I was drinking—especially when I started drinking again after being eight years dry—I was a nasty, pathetic drunk. Alcoholism is a progressive disease, and it progresses even when you aren't drinking.

Both of my boys moved out of the house around that time. My younger son moved all the way across the country to go to school in New York. It was around this time that Bjo and John Trimble came to my house to do an article on me called "Amazing Grace." They saw my house and were just amazed at the 62 plants I had in my living room (it was a full-time job just keeping that jungle alive!), plus my four Great Danes and my collie. I showed them the recording studio Jack and I had built, and played all my music for them—they were very impressed. And I remember standing in my kitchen with Bjo, and telling her how depressed I felt. On the one hand, I had all these wonderful things to keep me busy—my music and the *Star Trek* movie and convention appearances—yet I couldn't settle down and just be quiet without becoming very sad and even suicidal. I felt restless and dissatisfied with my life.

"Well, I know what causes that," Bjo said. "You've got empty nest syndrome."

"Empty nest syndrome? What's that?"

"You've spent twenty years raising your two boys, and now they've gone away. You're used to having your children with you, and now you have no one to mother. Your little birds have flown, and that can be very hard to deal with."

I thought about it, and realized that Bjo was right. I did miss being a mother to my two boys. Having an empty nest was certainly part of the sadness and restlessness I felt. Part—but not all.

Star Trek: The Motion Picture premiered in theaters across the country in December 1979. Many critics found the movie slow and ponderous, too enamored of its own gadgetry and special effects wizardry, and lacking in the kind of broad humanity, warmth, and humor that characterized the original series. Robert Wise had redefined the *Star Trek* universe in many ways, toning down the brilliant colors of the original series with sets and costumes of muted beige, gray and off-white, and toning down the bold sexuality of the original series with unisex costuming styles.

Many *Trek* fans complained about the new look and feel of *Star Trek: The Motion Picture*—but they paid their money and they came and came and came again. Box-office receipts topped $100 million—a respectable return on Paramount's investment which paved the way for the *Star Trek* films and TV series that followed.

Paramount flew the *Star Trek* cast to Washington, D.C., for an appearance at the Smithsonian, where we had our pictures taken with the original *Enterprise* model that's on display there. That night, we all went to a theater in Washington for the premiere. It was a packed house, a "star-studded event," as they say in Hollywood. One reviewer later commented on the cast members who were there in the theater for the premiere, noting that "also in the audience was Grace Lee Whitney and her Dolly Parton wig." Yes, I was there in my wig, my face-lift, my new body parts, eager to watch this movie I had appeared in about a year earlier. Over the past few months, I had forgotten some of the horror and panic I went through during the filming, and I was actually looking forward to my first experience of the completed film.

My first scene came early in the movie—the scene where I am operating the transporter when it malfunctions and scrambles two crewmen. About 10 or 15 seconds into the scene, I heard a collective gasp and a murmur go up around the theater. It had taken that long for the audience to realize that the woman on the screen was Janice Rand from the original series! They didn't even recognize me!

I wanted to shrink into that theater seat and completely melt out of existence. I couldn't wait for the movie to be over. I needed a drink.

During my eight-year dry spell, I had picked up a lot of substitute addictions to take the place of the bottle: amphetamine pills, sniffing amyl nitrite, wild sex, workaholism, skating and more. When I started drinking again, I didn't throw out my other addictions—I just added booze to the list. When I broke my dry spell after the filming of *Star Trek: The Motion Picture*, I chose a very high-class place to have my first drink: La Dome, a very expensive restaurant on the Strip. Three months later, I was drinking in restaurants on Western Avenue. Four months after that, I was drinking in bars on Alvarado. Nine months after that, I was drinking straight from the bottle at Sixth and Main. That's Skid Row, as far downtown as it gets.

Once I started drinking again, I was in free-fall, headed all the way down.

Sobriety is not for Wimps

*T*he year *Star Trek: The Motion Picture* was released was also the year my father died.

I had grown up thinking of Dad as a rigid perfectionist who would never let me forget that one B in a report card full of A's. In my selfishness, I easily forgot that he truly loved me and that he was totally loyal to me. Though I had hurt him and my mother very deeply, he would have done anything for me. It wasn't until he lay dying of bacterial endocarditis in Veterans Hospital in Los Angeles that I realized how much he loved me—

And how much I loved him.

We visited a lot and got very close during the last few weeks of his life. Eventually, he was placed on a respirator, and he could no longer talk. They had a tube down his throat, and he fought it. It was horrible, and I could scarcely stand to be there, watching him struggle for life on a hospital death row.

The last day of his life, my mother and my son Scott went up to see him, but Jack and I stayed downstairs in the lobby. I couldn't go up to his room. I was in such pain and fear, I just couldn't function. After a while, my mother came back down to the lobby and said, "Grace, you have to go up there and say goodbye to your father. They're going to take him off the respirator and he's going to die. You have to see him one last time."

"I can't, Mother," I whimpered. I was a quivering mass of self-pity and self-centered pain.

"Grace," she pleaded, "if you don't go up there and say goodbye to your father, you're going to regret it for the rest of your life."

"I can't," I insisted. My mother turned and went to the elevator without me. She and Scott were with my dad when they took out the respirator tube. And me? I went outside, sat down among the bushes by the front steps, and smoked a joint.

For months afterwards, whenever I looked at my mother's face, or my son's face, I thought I could read a look of utter disapproval and disappointment in their eyes. It may have only been my own guilt and shame, projected onto their faces, but it haunted me for a long time.

I was drinking and smoking dope and going so fast that Jack couldn't keep up with me. I drove him to depression and I drove him to another woman. He lost so much weight and looked so terrible, I thought he was going to die. But I couldn't stop doing the things I did. I was restless, irritable, impossible to live with. I was insane. I became even more insane when I started smelling perfume on him.

I cleaned out our bank account and left Jack, and began living with another man. I look back at the way I was living in those days, and it's like an out-of-body experience. I can't believe it was really *me* doing all those insane, destructive things! I had tumbled deep into the worst of my alcoholism, my sexaholism, and my drug abuse. To top it off, I added a new addiction: gambling.

I got involved in a big pyramid game that was spreading all across the San Fernando Valley. The idea is that you come into the game with $5,000, then you bring in more people with $5,000 each, and they bring in more people, and it just grows and grows, and the money starts flying around, until finally the thing collapses of its own weight. Some people get rich, but most lose their shirts. It's also totally illegal.

I borrowed $5,000 from my mother and put it all on this game. We'd go to these big Hollywood homes to trade the money. You never saw such a feeding frenzy in your life. The only other frenzy I've ever seen like it is a sexual frenzy. It was an orgy of greed, it was humanity at its very worst.

For me, the pyramid game was an incredible high. I arrived with $5,000, and I went home with $15,000, then I went again and turned it into $30,000. I came home with all that money in my pockets, and then I couldn't find a place to put it. I ran around the house, trying to hide the money. I was totally paranoid because I was smoking dope. I was obsessed with the idea that someone was going to come into my house and steal all my money.

There were some men with the pyramid group who were supposed to come to my house the next day, and I was going to take the $30,000 and *triple* it! These guys had some connection with organized crime, and they had guns. I was dealing with some very dangerous people—and finally I just wimped out. I couldn't take being that scared all the time, no matter how much money I made in a single day. I just flipped, I told the men with the guns to take their money, the whole $30,000—including the $5,000 I had borrowed from my mother. They could have it all if they would just let me out. But at first they didn't want to let me out! Finally, they decided I was too chicken to go any further, so they took their money and left.

I did guest shots in a couple TV shows in 1980 and '81—"Cannon" with William Conrad, and "Hart to Hart" with Robert Wagner and Stephanie Powers. On the set of "Hart to Hart," I became friends with an actress named Susan. Without realizing it, Susan was about to become the instrument of my sobriety. God used her to save my life.

Susan introduced me to her friend Sandy, who befriended me when I was nearing the end of my drinking. Later, after I got sober, Sandy told me, "Grace, if you ever think about taking a drink again, call me first. I'll tell you exactly what you're like when you drink, and I guarantee that'll keep you sober!" It was Sandy who introduced me to Buzz Aldrin, the second man to walk on the moon.

If the most famous line ever spoken on the moon was Neil Armstrong's "That's one small step for a man..." then the *second* most famous line was that of Armstrong's Apollo 11 partner, Colonel Edwin "Buzz" Aldrin, who stood upon the moon and said, "Beautiful! Beautiful! Magnificent desolation!" Even before he went to the moon in July 1969, Buzz set a space record with a five and a half hour spacewalk during the Gemini 12 earth orbital rendezvous mission in November 1966 (less than two months after I took *my* involuntary spacewalk off the Starship *Enterprise*!).

When Sandy first introduced me to Buzz, I didn't know he was an Apollo astronaut—Sandy didn't tell me! Later, when I met him again at a *Star Trek* convention and realized who he was, I said to him, "So you walked on the moon, did you? Well, don't think you're such hot stuff! I was touring the galaxy two years before you were on the moon!" He laughed, and he just loved me. Soon, we began dating.

I was drinking heavily, and Buzz knew it. He told me I should go to a Twelve Step* recovery group for alcoholics. But I was very slippery. I had all my defenses up and my denial was as impenetrable as the force shields on the Starship *Enterprise*. I was not yet ready to give up my drinking and my excuses, but Buzz did give me a nudge in the right direction. He was one of the influences in my life, nudging me toward sanity and sobriety. Buzz and I dated both before and after I got sober, in 1980 and '81.

---

*The Twelve Steps are a spiritual path to sobriety and recovery from alcoholism and other addictions, originally formulated by Alcoholics Anonymous in the late 1930s. Today, the Twelve Steps are used by literally hundreds of different recovery organizations, including Overcomers Outreach, which was one of my principle support groups early in my sobriety. The Twelve Steps are (italics are in the original):

1. We admitted we were powerless over alcohol—that our lives had become unmanageable.
2. Came to believe that a Power greater than ourselves could restore us to sanity.
3. Made a decision to turn our will and our lives over to the care of God *as we understood Him.*
4. Made a searching and fearless moral inventory of ourselves.
5. Admitted to God, to ourselves, and to another human being the exact nature of our wrongs.
6. Were entirely ready to have God remove all these defects of character.
7. Humbly asked Him to remove our shortcomings.
8. Made a list of all persons we had harmed, and became willing to make amends to them all.
9. Made direct amends to such people wherever possible, except when to do so would injure them or others.
10. Continued to take personal inventory and when we were wrong promptly admitted it.
11. Sought through prayer and meditation to improve our conscious contact with God *as we understood Him*, praying only for knowledge of His will for us and the power to carry that out.
12. Having had a spiritual awakening as the result of these steps, we tried to carry this message to alcoholics, and to practice these principles in all our affairs.

When I did "Hart to Hart," my girlfriend Susan had the lead and I had a small speaking part. Susan and I would go out to lunch, and I would tell her about my problems while she listened and watched me drink through my meal. One time she said to me, "Grace, I don't think there's anything really wrong with you, except that you're an alcoholic."

"Me? An alcoholic?" I laughed. "Why do you say that? I'm only having a couple of drinks."

"Well," she said, "you drink just like an alcoholic. My husband's an alcoholic. He used to drink like you, but he's been in recovery for two years."

Secure in my denial, I shook my head. "I would know if I'm an alcoholic," I said. "And I'm *not* an alcoholic!"

But, of course, I was.

I didn't resent it that Susan called me an alcoholic. I thought it was funny. We got to be very close friends, and we ran around together all the time. I went to her house and met her husband—an actor who worked largely in commercials. We went to parties together and had a great time. Susan was a great party girl, but she didn't drink.

One time, Susan was having a party at her home, and there was her husband, the recovering alcoholic. It really bothered me that he didn't drink. I couldn't stop my own drinking, and it infuriated me that here was a guy who used to be a drinker, and now he was sober. I took it as a personal insult. I had a bottle of Scotch, and I went up to him, waved it under his nose, and told him I was going to entice him to drink. He got away from me, ran to the back of the house, and locked himself in the bedroom. I followed him and tried to push the door in. I pounded and pounded on the door with my fists, but I couldn't get the door open. I can't remember if Susan tried to stop me, or if she just thought it was funny. I was so drunk, the only thing I knew was that I couldn't stand the fact that there was a recovering alcoholic in that bedroom, making me feel bad about my own drinking!

Sometime after that incident, Susan invited me to go to a party with her—but she made a tough stipulation: "Come to the party," she said, "but don't drink."

I was horrified! "Oh, no! I can't do that! Go to a party and not drink? You've got to be kidding!"

But she was serious. "You can have fun without drinking. You can eat, talk, dance, anything you want—just don't drink."

I couldn't believe anyone could have fun without drinking—but for my friend Susan, I was willing to give it a try. I didn't realize what a strange experience lay in wait for me at the party, or how dramatically my life was about to change!

Susan and I went to the party, and there was a psychic doing readings with cards, drawings and other paraphernalia. I noticed immediately that he looked a lot like Mr. Spock. He was tall and dark, with arched eyebrows like Mr. Spock—but without the pointed ears. He looked at me and said, "Aren't you Grace Lee Whitney from *Star Trek?*"

I said, "Yes."

"I see an aura all about you," he said.

"An aura?" I asked. "What's that?"

"A soft golden glow. It emanates from within you and casts a glow all around you."

"And no one else can see it but you?"

"Well," he said, "I do have certain mystical powers."

"If it's a golden aura," I said, laughing, "then it must mean money. It must mean I'm going to get rich." I didn't take any of this seriously—and the psychic seemed to think it was as funny as I did.

"Miss Whitney—may I call you Grace?—I would like to perform a mind-meld on you. I'll show you what is going on inside your psyche. Will you allow me to do that?"

The Vulcan mind-meld was a technique used by Mr. Spock to read minds on *Star Trek*. Spock would place his hands on the person's face, and his touch enabled him to "tune in" on the other person's thoughts. "That would be fun," I said. "How do you do it?"

"Turn around and face the wall," he said. "I'll put my hand on your head while you draw something on a piece of paper." He gave me a pencil and a paper napkin and told me to draw a geometric sign.

"A geometric sign?" I asked.

"Sure," he said. "Geometric shapes—rectangles, squares, whatever comes into your mind to draw."

"Okay," I said. "I can do that."

"Good. And while you draw a geometric sign on your paper, I'll draw one on mine. Now, we have plenty of witnesses here. Everyone can see that I'm not looking at your drawing. Now, go ahead and draw."

So I drew a couple geometric symbols on my paper napkin while he placed his left hand to the back of my head and drew something on his paper napkin with his right hand. I drew a triangle inside a circle. When I had finished my drawing, the psychic showed me the drawing he had made during our "mind-meld." It looked exactly like mine. I was amazed—but I assumed it was some sort of parlor trick. I had seen other such tricks before, and there was always some rational explanation.

I didn't think much about it for the next two weeks.

Meanwhile, my life continued its downhill slide—sex binges, drinking binges, drug binges, all interspersed with bouts of suicidal depression. I was desperate to fill up all the holes in my soul. The wind that blew through these holes was getting colder and colder, killing me inside.

Around the beginning of 1981, I left the guy I was living with, then moved to my mother's house for a while, then went back home to Jack for a few weeks and tried desperately to put my life back in order. I was hoping Jack would forgive me and I could start over and start living right. But by that time, I couldn't stop drinking. The hell of it was that I drank and drank, but I couldn't get drunk anymore. But if I stopped drinking, I couldn't get sober, I couldn't clear my head. When an alcoholic drinks but can't get drunk, or stops but can't get sober, then that is the end of the line, one way or the other. There is no way out if you get to this point and can't get sober. You either go insane from a wet brain, end up in prison, or kill yourself.

The point I had reached is the very bottom of the downward spiral of the alcoholic. Alcoholics in recovery call it "pitiful and incomprehensible demoralization," or P.A.I.D. for short. It's the absolute lowest point, the black hole. At that point, you either begin to pull out of your nose dive—or you accelerate right into the ground.

I was accelerating.

My health was collapsing. I was taking shots of thiamine for my nerves, while drinking gin mixed with wine. My hair was coming out in clumps. I was incontinent, because everything inside me was liquid. I was bleeding at the gums. Alcohol and drugs were eating me up inside. It was just a short time after the party with the psychic that I was admitted to the hospital with delirium tremens, hallucinations, blackouts, dehydration, and incredible anxiety and fear. The fear was cold and stabbing, like an ice pick through my heart.

The doctor who examined me said my liver was enlarged and distended. He also found that I had developed a hole in my esophagus, because the gin was eating the flesh inside my throat. "If you don't stop drinking," he told me, "and I mean stop *right now*, you are going to be dead very soon." But how could I stop drinking? I had no clue. An obsession is something you do against your own will.

Nor did I see any way out of my obsession with sex. I was so obsessed that I actually tried to seduce the doctor in my hospital bed. "I'd love to go to bed with you," he said, "but I think you may have AIDS."

"What's AIDS?" I asked. This was back before AIDS became a household word.

"It's a new disease that's just coming on the scene," he said. He didn't tell me the disease was incurable and fatal.

As it turned out, I didn't have AIDS—but I was dying. My alcoholism was killing me. Amazingly, even though I was dying, I looked good—just like a glamour girl. You'd never know how sick I was to look at the pictures taken of me during those weeks. The reason my hair looks so great in those pictures is that it's not my hair—I wore wigs.

Despite all the evidence, I still could not accept the obvious fact that I was a dying alcoholic. I was Cleopatra, Queen of Denial.

At the time, I was working in downtown L.A. for a businessman I'll call Ray. On weekends, Ray would take me out to clubs for drinking, dancing and sex orgies. Every once in a while, I would get a hysterical call from Ray's wife, pleading with me to leave her husband alone. "He's a good man, and you're leading him astray!" she said. It made me laugh. A good man! Leading him astray! Good grief, he was conducting a guided tour of the lower reaches of hell—and I was along for the ride! But I later learned that what Ray's wife did is a very common feature of alcoholic relationships. The seamy life of the alcoholic is a hidden life—and the spouse helps keep it that way.

One time, Ray took me to a nightclub in a hotel in Apple Valley. He had me dance and flirt with the customers, then steer them to a hotel room upstairs where he and some other guys were waiting, loaded on alcohol, or pills or hard drugs. Then the orgy would begin. Everything you can imagine went on that night—and maybe a few things you can't imagine. It was the most dirty, degrading night of my entire life. It was so horrible that one of the men looked at me in disbelief, almost in pity, and asked me, "Why are you doing this?" I had no answer. I really didn't know why I was doing what I was doing. Lust addiction takes on a life of its own—it runs you and you have no defense.

I had reached absolute bottom. I had come to the end of myself. I was ready to reach out and grab something beyond myself, even though I had no idea what that something might be.

God bless Harvey P.

For four months, Harvey had been badgering me to go to a recovery meeting. Fact is, I had actually tried a couple Twelve Step meetings a few years earlier, but I walked out of both of them. The people in the meetings were too straight, too clean, and I was still in my perverted lifestyle. I hadn't reached absolute bottom at that time. Even worse, going to those meetings was like going to church. I hated church, I hated God, and I hated Jesus Christ. I was not an agnostic—no way, I was too hard-nosed and extreme for agnosticism. I was a hard-shell, confirmed atheist—a Jewish atheist if one can be such a thing. If anyone had mentioned the name "Jesus" to me in a Twelve Step meeting, I *never* would have gone back!

It wasn't until I reached absolute bottom and had nowhere else to turn that I finally was ready to listen to Harvey, go to a meeting, and sit through it from beginning to end. I had to have every last prop kicked out from under me, every last drop of pride and self-respect wrung out of me, before I could reach out to God or to another human being and say, "Help me!" I reached that point in April of 1981. My father had died, and I had not said goodbye. I had reached the absolute abyss of self-degradation. My health was rapidly failing. I couldn't get drunk anymore, and I couldn't get sober. I was drinking in porno joints on Skid Row—my disease had taken me all the way downtown.

Another devastating experience I went through at that time was the loss of my dogs. One of my Great Danes, Heathcliffe, got cancer of the throat, and another of my Danes, Citizen Kane, attacked Heathcliffe. Both dogs had to be put down. In fact, I came home from my dad's funeral, picked up Heathcliffe, took him to the vet and had him put down the same day my dad was buried. Over a period of a few weeks, I lost all five of my dogs to various causes—and the loss of those animals nearly destroyed me. I had a crazy obsession with my animals—and I later learned that this is very common with alcoholics. We often begin to think more of an animal than we do of people, or God, or even our own lives.

My life had become a no-win scenario. In *Star Trek II: The Wrath of Khan*, there is a training simulation that Starfleet officers undergo to determine how they respond to completely insoluble problems. It's called "the Kobayashi Maru simulation," and

These were my Great Danes— (clockwise from front right) Christmas Jingles (the mother), Heathcliffe, Heathcliffe's Cathy, and Citizen Kane.

among *Trek* fans it has become the classic metaphor to describe a no-win situation. That is where I was on the morning of April 13, 1981. I was facing the Kobayashi Maru test, my problems had become completely insoluble, my life had become completely unmanageable. This was no simulation, this was no drill. It was literally a matter of life or death.

But you know what? Even the prospect of dying was not what actually drove me to recovery. The last straw was not the loss of my health or the loss of my father or the loss of my dogs or the loss of my dignity. I was so incredibly self-centered that the last straw was *vanity*, pure and simple. One morning, I looked in the mirror and saw the veins in my face. Recovering alcoholics call that having your wiring exposed. When I saw that my alcoholism was sabotaging my beautiful face-lift—*that's* when it finally hit me that my life was over!

That morning, I went to Harvey, sat down in front of him with my head in my hands, and moaned, "Harvey, I'm dead, I'm finished, I don't care what happens to me anymore. I'm such a horrible person, Harvey—the absolute worst person in the world. I'm just sick and tired of being sick and tired."

"Grace," he said, "you're not bad. You have a disease. I've been trying all along to tell you that you have a disease called alcoholism."

"It must be an incurable disease, because I just can't shake it."

"It's treatable, Grace," he said, "but you have to want to get well. You have to go to a meeting."

"I've been to meetings—twice. They gagged me. It was like church. I couldn't stand it."

"You weren't ready then. Now, I think you're ready."

"What if I go to the meeting and it doesn't help?"

"I'll tell you what," he said. "You go to a meeting with me and see what we have to offer. If you don't like what we have, we will gladly refund your misery."

I had to laugh. "Okay, Harvey," I said. "I'll go with you to a meeting."

He looked me up and down and said, "Good. But first, put a safety pin in your blouse and cover up that cleavage. You can't go in there with everything showing—you look like a tramp!" As you can see, Harvey was quite the diplomat!

That night, he took me to a meeting in Beverly Hills—and he couldn't have introduced me to a better group. The meeting was filled with actors, directors, producers, show biz people of all kinds. God must have known that if I could see people who were like me, but who also embraced this program, then I would want the program, too.

My surrender came the moment I walked through the door. Even though I had walked out of two previous meetings, this was totally different. *I* was different. I was ready. I had reached the very bottom. Now that I had been completely destroyed, I was ready to do anything, pay any price, make any sacrifice if only I could be reconstructed and made new.

The first thing I noticed when I walked into the room was how *good* everyone smelled. I had come from Venice, California, where the debris meets the sea. When I breathed in the clean fragrance and the smiles of these people, when I felt the absolute serenity in that room, it was like I had crossed over to the other side of the universe. The veil had dropped from my eyes.

A man stood up and said, "Are there any newcomers here with less than thirty days of sobriety?" I raised my hand, along with several others. Each was called on and said, "My name is John, and I'm an alcoholic." Or, "My name is Janet, and I'm an alcoholic." Or, "My name is Ben, and I'm an alcoholic." Finally, the man at the front nodded to me, and I stood and said, "My name is Whitney—and I don't know what I am." The room erupted in applause.

Can you believe it? After all I had been through, after being reduced to drinking out of a bottle on Skid Row, after having a hole eaten in my esophagus from all the gallons of gin I had consumed, I *still* couldn't admit I was an alcoholic! But I was in a complete state of surrender. I threw myself on the mercy of the group, and I was ready to accept whatever happened next. And I knew I was home.

Home. It was a feeling I hadn't felt in a long time. It was a feeling I remembered from when I was a little girl—a feeling I lost the day my mother told me she was not really my mother after all. I had spent a lifetime trying to recapture that feeling. I had experienced it when I held my baby boys in my arms—the only blood relatives I had ever known. And I had fleetingly experienced it when I was part of *Star Trek*—only to lose it again when I was written out of the show.

Home. I had finally reached a place where I was safe and loved, accepted and understood. I hadn't introduced myself the way the others in the room had—I hadn't said, "I'm an alcoholic." But that didn't matter. The people in that room knew I had surrendered and I had come for help. They had been there themselves. They knew who I was and what I was—and that was okay. They knew that no one ever gets to a meeting by mistake. You may not know you're an alcoholic yet, but the people in that room know that if you're there, you belong there, whether you are in denial or surrender. My surrender came before I ever raised my hand. The people in the room could see that.

They identified with me. They nodded. They smiled. They applauded me. It was a wonderful thing they did for me that night. It was as if they could see right through me, as if they knew I had spent my whole life seeking applause. This was the first applause I had received in my life that was so truly genuine and satisfying. It warmed me to the core of my being.

In the years since then, I've experienced that warm feeling many, many times. I've stood before Twelve Step recovery groups and shared my experience, strength, and hope, and I have received the applause, I have seen the nodding heads and the knowing smiles, I have been awash in a truly joyful, heavenly laughter, I have felt wave upon wave of empathy and understanding and love. To identify with an alcoholic is to love him. There is no other place on earth where I have felt as completely loved and understood as I have felt in those meetings.

The speaker for the evening got up and told her story. She talked about getting up on the bar, dancing on the bar with a rose between her teeth, seeking attention, wanting to be noticed, hoping that the admiration of drunken men could somehow fill all the holes in her soul. I totally identified with her.

I loved the entire meeting, from beginning to end. I wanted what those people had—and for the first time in my life, I believed I could have it too. Throughout that evening, I was awash in laughter. I needed to hear that. The music of recovery is laughter. I had come into that room thinking I would never laugh again. I had always thought you needed alcohol to laugh. Here was a roomful of sober people—and they were laughing more genuinely, more sincerely, than I ever had when I was drinking!

At the end of the meeting, we all said the Lord's Prayer together—something I hadn't done since I was a 14, something that I, being Jewish, didn't think was possible for me to say. My parents had raised me as a Christian, and once I had gotten out of their house, I had rejected anything and everything that was in any way related to Christianity, including the Lord's Prayer. I didn't understand that the Lord's Prayer is actually a Jewish prayer, originally spoken by a Jewish rabbi, Y'shua ha Mashiach. But it didn't matter. I was surrendered. I was willing to do anything, say anything, believe anything if I could just have what those people in that room had—freedom from slavery to alcohol.

So I bowed my head and began saying the Lord's prayer, "Our Father, which art in heaven...." And as I said the prayer, I looked up and *bingo*! I knew that God himself was hearing that prayer. In that moment, my atheist's heart was instantly changed. I had the total assurance that there really was a living God—the God of Abraham, Isaac and Jacob. And I also knew that my obsession with drinking was removed! I have never had the obsession to drink or use drugs since that moment. It was all taken away because I simply turned and recognized that God was there. In my heart, it was as if I looked at God for the first time and said, "Oh, it's *you* I'm looking for!"

Suddenly, my eyes were opened to something I had never understood before. When I was a child, my parents had taken me to church every Sunday, where we recited the Lord's Prayer together. One of the phrases in that prayer had always been a meaningless jumble of sound in my ears, almost as if it was a single nonsense word: *thywillbedone*. I wondered what it meant, "thy will be done"? Thy *what* will be done? It was as if the word *will* was a verb without a subject—and the sentence never made sense to me.

But that night, as I prayed the Lord's Prayer in the meeting, I suddenly realized that it talked about "thy *will*," and that the word *will* was a noun. I realized that "*thy will*," God's will, was in contrast to *my* will. In praying that prayer, I was asking that God's will, his decision for my life, his plan for my life, would take complete precedence over my own self-will.

Instantly, I knew why so many events in my life had converged to move me to that place, to that meeting, to that decision. I suddenly understood that God had been steadily drawing me to a place of surrender. He wanted to squeeze the last vestiges of my own will out of me so that he could do his will through my life.

When that realization broke over me, I was delivered from alcohol and drugs. Not by my will, but by God's will. And because God did it, not me, I was delivered to the max. I had gotten to God and to that meeting through the process of elimination. God was the last thing on my list. I tried everything else first, and when I got to the end of the line, God was the only thing I hadn't tried. So I took the faith that was offered me in the meeting. The moment I reached out, I knew I was connected to his infinite heart of love.

When the meeting was over, a number of women came to me, and congratulated me for the first step I had taken. They gave me their phone numbers and told me to call them if I ever felt I needed a drink or needed someone to talk to.

One woman volunteered to be my sponsor—to be available to me at all times. "And to get started," she said, "read this." She placed a book in my hands—a big, thick book with a dark blue cover. It was the "Big Book" that is the basis of the Twelve Step recovery movement. I looked at it closely and could hardly believe my eyes. There was a symbol on the cover of the book. Just two weeks earlier, at the party where the psychic had done the mind-meld with me, the party where for once I didn't drink, I had drawn that same symbol—a triangle inside a circle—on a paper cocktail napkin. I was absolutely astonished. I thought, *My gosh! I'm right where I'm supposed to be. God has been leading me here all along.*

I don't know how it all works. In my life today, I would certainly have nothing to do with psychics, mediums, ouija boards, tarot cards or anything else having to do with divination. The ancient law of Moses is clear: "Let no one be found among you who sacrifices his son or daughter in the fire, who practices divination or sorcery, interprets omens, engages in witchcraft, or casts spells, or who is a medium or spiritist or who consults the dead."[1] I believe that there are spiritual forces in the world, both dark and light—and the dark forces are dangerous, and to be shunned at all costs. All I know is that this is what happened in my life, which tells me that, sometimes, God can use any tool—even a psychic—so that his will may be done on earth as it is in heaven.

At the end of the meeting, I noticed a young woman, practically a girl, standing in the doorway. She was too ashamed to come all the way into the room, and she was crying. I went to her and she told me she had been nine months sober—then she went out and drank. She smelled like an alcoholic, just like I did. And I, with my scant

60 minutes of sobriety, put my arms around her and said, "Why don't you come back in? Just start fresh, right here, right now. Everything's going to be all right." I reached out to her—and I've been reaching out to alcoholics ever since.

Somehow, I instinctively understood that a Twelve Step recovery program is based on the Christian principle that, in order for a man to get well, he has to help someone else. After receiving so much kindness, love and understanding from everyone in that meeting, I immediately wanted to give it away to others.

That night, as I got into my old Chevy and pulled onto the street, I saw a full moon in the sky. And I thought to myself, *I can't believe it! I'm actually sober!* I went home and before I went to sleep, I got down on my knees beside my bed and prayed—the first time I had prayed since I was about 10 years old. I thanked God for my sobriety, for my release from bondage to alcohol. Then I got into bed. I felt very peaceful. It was, I realized, a sense of serenity—the first real serenity I had felt in my entire adult life.

But as I lay there, I noticed a rattling sound. *What is that?* I wondered. Then I realized that the bed was shaking. It wasn't an earthquake. It was me. For months afterward, every time I went to bed, the bed shook. The noise was so loud I had to move the bed away from the wall. Eventually, about nine months into my sobriety, I noticed that the shaking had stopped. I also noticed that I no longer woke up in a rigid, curled position. Most of my life, I had slept with my feet curled up, as if I was holding on to the bed in my sleep, fearful of letting go. Around the same time the bed stopped shaking, I noticed I was no longer sleeping in such a fearful position. For the most part, my sleep was relaxed and serene.

Some alcoholics need medically supervised detoxification in order to safely stop drinking, followed by an intense Twelve Step recovery program. Perhaps God granted me a miracle in allowing me to stop drinking without being hospitalized, and without the withdrawal symptoms that can accompany quitting cold turkey. All it took was three meetings a day, every day.

Even now, I go to several meetings a week, because I am never "cured," I am always an alcoholic. I renew my recovery one day at a time. This disease can only be arrested on a daily basis—never cured. It's sleeping inside me—it's not dead. It will never be dead until I am. And when I die, I want to die sober.

I continued to experience fear and anxiety attacks long into my sobriety. In fact, I was 15 years into my sobriety before I stopped waking up in the middle of the night with an attack of blind, unreasoning fear. I don't know where that fear comes from, nor if it is a cause or a consequence of alcohol abuse. But I do know that there is a cold spot in the heart of every alcoholic that often causes panic attacks, night sweats, insomnia and other sleep disorders.

I fear this thing inside me that makes me want to do the things I don't want to do. I don't mean I'm continually terrified. The fear I feel is *respect*. I have to be so careful with everything in my life, because drinking is not the problem, it's only the symptom of the real disease. I can easily switch from drinking to something else. The

Here, I'm singin' and shakin' my tambourine with the Keith Williams New Big Band, sometime in the late 1970s. I maintained my singing career continuously from the time I was 18 until I got sober.

real disease is that sense of emptiness and worthlessness, that feeling of "What's the use?" You can fill the holes in your soul with a lot of things besides alcohol—addictions to food, drugs, sex, money, power, gambling, so many things. I suspect that some people even fill it with an unhealthy obsession with *Star Trek*. None of those things can truly fill the holes in the soul. You have to fill those holes with a strong sense of the existence of a greater power, with other people who have this same sense and with accountability and personal responsibility.

My biological birthday was April 1, 1930—but I never celebrate it. That's April Fools Day. I'd much rather celebrate the day I wised up. My *real* birthday is the day I became sober. The obsession to drink was taken away from me at 9:00 p.m. on April 13, 1981.

Sobriety is not perfection. It is a gift. I still had a lot to learn—and a lot of alcoholic thinking to unlearn—as I journeyed deeper and deeper into this new life that had been revealed to me. For example, there was a time, not long into my sobriety, when I was complaining to my sponsor about my boss, who used to take me on wild drinking and sex binges. After listening to me call him every horrible name in the book, she looked at me and said, "Whitney, I'm sure everything you say about this guy is true. But understand this: You attract what you are."

That statement shook me to the core. Yes, my boss was a slimeball. But what was I? That statement forced me to take a good hard look at myself, and what I saw was appalling. I had to face the fact that I was a trashy, brassy floozie. After the way I had lived, I had no right to point the finger of damnation at any other human being.

One of the big changes I had to make after I got sober was to literally get out of the dark and into the light. That meant I had to turn my back and walk away from my music. I had begun my career in the dark, singing in nightclubs. Throughout my career in movies and TV, including the time I was involved with *Star Trek*, I worked in nightclubs with various bands, singing every weekend.

I worked with Gus Bivona at the Hollywood Palladium for years, and with Matty Melnick, Manny Harmon, and a wonderful jazz trumpet player, Lex Golden. Sometimes they would introduce me as Yeoman Rand from *Star Trek*. Lex fired me sometime in the 1970s because I got loaded during a performance, then fell off the riser and embarrassed the band. I was terribly hurt when I was fired, but it was my own fault, a direct result of my alcoholism.

When I got sober in 1981, I had to get down from the bandstand, I had to get out of the dark and into the light, I had to get away from the alcohol and smoke in those nightclubs and stop performing altogether. There's a saying that no souls are ever saved after 10 p.m.—and if I was going to save my soul from the hell of alcoholism, I had to stop staying out after 10. I had to stop being a lady of the evening and start living in the light of day.

I wouldn't trade my sobriety for anything in the world. But I have to tell you something: sobriety is not fun. Alcoholism is a malignancy of the soul, an emotional cancer, and the malignancy has to be cut out. That's the most painful thing—cutting out this diseased part of yourself and letting it heal. The pain doesn't really begin until you get sober. You think you had pain before, but after you get sober, you have to look back at everything you've done, the people you've hurt, the trail of wreckage in your wake—and that's when you recognize what a wretch you really are.

I have 10 times more pain now than when I was drinking, because the truth hurts. Alcohol is an anesthetic against the pain of the truth. When you are sober, you can see the truth and feel the pain—and it's excruciating. That's why it's so hard to stay sober. The more layers of the onion you peel away, the closer you get to the core truth of who you really are. The closer to the truth you get, the more unbearable the pain becomes. Sobriety is not for wimps.

A year after I got sober, I decided I needed to help my mother understand my alcoholism and all the hurtful behavior it had caused over the years. I had told her several times that I was an alcoholic, but she never seemed to grasp what I was saying to her. I took her to a Twelve Step support group for family members of alcoholics. I thought the meeting could help her understand what alcoholism is all about.

One of the things they ask you in these meetings is, "Who is your qualifier?" In other words, "Who is the alcoholic individual causing so much pain in your life?" Your qualifier might be a husband, a wife, a parent, a child. In my mother's case, her qualifier was me.

This picture is a favorite of mine because it was taken by my friend, Leonard Nimoy, in 1980.

When they looked at her and said, "Who is your qualifier?" she said, "I don't even know what I'm doing here! I don't even know any alcoholics! I wouldn't have anything to do with an alcoholic!" The denial was so thick, you couldn't have dented it with a photon torpedo! Here was my mother, who for years had been president of the Women's Christian Temperance Union, who had raised me in an alcohol-free home, who had baptized me and given me a white ribbon in the name of Jesus every year of my childhood and adolescence to symbolize my (supposed) abstinence from alcohol, she simply could not imagine that her daughter was an alcoholic—even though I had been telling her I was for a year! I didn't know how to get through to her.

Step 8 of the Twelve Steps says that we have "made a list of all persons we had harmed, and became willing to make amends to them all." I had a lot of people to make amends to. As part of my recovery, I wrote a personal inventory—78 pages detailing all the pain I had experienced and all the pain I had caused others, all the places I turned left when I should have turned right. I realized I had been an incorrigible child and very tough to raise.

I made amends to my mother a year and a half into my sobriety. I went down on my knees in front of her, and I didn't get up until I had finished listing my sins against her. I asked her forgiveness for all the pain I had caused her over the years, for being such a difficult child to raise, for marrying without even telling her about it, for my drunkenness and sexaholism, for borrowing $5,000 to put on the pyramid game and not paying it back. I offered to make payments to her, but she forgave the debt.

The next question that confronted me was how do I make amends to my father? How can you make amends to someone who is dead? How could I ever make amends for wimping out and smoking dope when I should have been in his hospital room, telling him I love him, telling him goodbye?

Early in my sobriety, I was in a recovery group meeting, talking about how I had never said goodbye to my father. As I was talking, I had a stabbing realization of how horribly self-centered I was, choosing to smoke a joint instead of going up to be with my Dad in his last moments on earth. As that realization hit me, I just came unglued, right then and there. I cried and I cried—I couldn't stop. "The worst of it," I told the group, "is that there's nothing I can do to make it up to him! He's gone and I'll never be able to tell him I'm sorry or tell him goodbye!"

"No, you're wrong!" they told me. "You can write a love letter to your father! Tell him how you feel, how sorry you are, how much you love him! Then take it to his grave and read it to him!"

So that's exactly what I did. I went to Forest Lawn, where he is buried, and I threw myself down on his grave. I was wracked with guilt, shame and pain. I took out my written inventory and for an hour and a half I read to him and told him all the horrible things I had done to hurt him. "Daddy," I said, "please forgive me. I realize now how much I hurt you. You see, I'm a alcoholic. You adopted a child who was sick—I was a defective child with the gene of alcoholism. You didn't know what you were getting when you adopted me, but I know you loved me and you put up with a lot from me. I did all these things without understanding how sick I was."

I listed hurt after hurt, injury after injury, all the things I could think of that I had done over the years to hurt him. Finally, when all my grief was spent, I got up and went home.

A few days later, I opened my mail and found a check for $3,000 from my father's brother. My uncle Clinton Whitney was dying of an incurable disease, so he was getting his house in order and liquidating his estate. The letter read,

> Dear Grace,
> I want you to think of this money as a gift from your father. It comes from my own estate, but I'm giving it to you in the name of your father, Gordon Whitney. I know he loved you dearly, and he was always proud of you.
> Please divide this money as follows: Give $1,000 to your son, Scott; give $1,000 to your son, Jonathan; and keep $1,000 for yourself.
> With love,
> Clinton Whitney

My uncle sent that letter on the very day I was at Forest Lawn, making amends to my father. It was as if my father had sent the check himself to tell me, "Grace, I heard everything you said, and all is forgiven—and just to make you happy and to show you I love you, here's a little bonus! Enjoy!"

That was a wonderful gift from my earthly father—and from my *heavenly* Father, too! I didn't know it then, but an even more amazing and miraculous surprise was just around the corner.

Amazing Grace!

. . . .

I experienced my first vision in Israel.

All my adult life, ever since I converted to Judaism, I had wanted to go to Israel. In 1983, my younger son, Jonathan, was studying at Hebrew University in Jerusalem, and he was planning to have his bar-mitzvah in Israel. At 24, he was older than the usual age for this Jewish rite—but that was my fault. When he was 13, I had divorced Jonathan's Jewish father and was married to a non-Jewish man. So I actually deprived him of a bar-mitzvah when he came of age.

When Jonathan told me he was going to have his bar-mitzvah at the Wailing Wall and he wanted me to be there, I was overjoyed. I thought, *What better time to visit Israel than now?* One problem: I really couldn't afford the trip. The price of the ticket was about $1,100, which was about all I had in my bank account. I asked Beverly, my sponsor, if I should spend the money or not, and she said, "Pray about it. The answer will come." So I prayed, and I sensed that God was prodding me to go. So I went.

The flight to Israel took 37 hours, including time in the air and time waiting in airports. I was awake the whole time, so I arrived in Israel feeling exhausted but thrilled to see Jonathan again. He was my tour guide to the land of Abraham, Isaac and Jacob, and I could scarcely believe I was really walking on that holy, historic ground. I was happier than I had been in years, and very receptive to the sights and sounds and fragrances all around me.

Jonathan and I laughed and talked as we roamed over the hills outside the walled city of old Jerusalem. He had his camera with him, and he snapped a lot of pictures. We were right under the Eastern Gate, which is called the Beautiful Gate in the book of Acts, and is now often called the Golden Gate. I didn't realize the significance of that gate then, but I've since learned that Jews, Christians and Muslims all view the Eastern Gate as the place where God's judgment of mankind will take place, the place where Messiah is to enter the city of Jerusalem.

Jonathan and I laughed and laughed as we made our way down into the Kidron Valley, east of the city, and up the other side, toward the Mount of Olives, studded with ancient churches and elaborate tombs. There were sheep up on the hills as we walked, and Jonathan called to them—"Ba-a-a-a-ah! ba-a-a-a-ah!" And the sheep turned and looked down the hill at him with their quizzical sheep-eyes, calling back to him, "Ba-a-a-a-ah? Ba-a-a-a-ah?" Those sheep thought that this was the most curious sight they had ever seen—a boy who thought he was a sheep!

We came to a place with a wall and a gate, and beyond the gate was a grove of old, gnarled olive trees. I had no idea what the place was until I saw a sign that read GARDEN OF GETHSEMANE. I vaguely remembered from my Sunday school days that this place had something to do with the story of Jesus. But I didn't really under-

That's me in front of the Wailing Wall (above) and with my son, Jonathan, on our 1983 trip to Israel. People place prayers written on folded pieces of paper in the cracks of the Wailing Wall. A friend gave me a prayer blessing her parents and I carried it all the way to Israel in my pocket.

stand the historical significance of this ground where Jesus prayed the night before he was crucified.

While I approached the gate, Jonathan went into the church a short distance away to take some pictures. I put my hands on the iron bars of the gate and looked through, into the Garden of Gethsemane. Suddenly, I felt weak, as if I was about to faint. I had to hold onto the bars to remain standing.

Then I saw Jesus.

He was beyond the iron bars, praying in the garden. His appearance was neither as solid and three-dimensional as reality, nor as unreal and insubstantial as a dream. It was more like an *inner reality*, something that seemed completely real, but real *within me*—not objectively, externally real.

I thought, *But I'm Jewish!*

As if he could read my mind, he turned and looked at me. "So am I," he said.

I didn't say anything to Jonathan about what I had just seen and heard. I kept it to myself. I had never had an experience like that before, and I didn't know what to make of it.

Days later, when it was time for me to return to the States, I was at the airport, getting ready to board the plane, when I realized I hadn't bought a single souvenir of my trip to Israel. I went into a gift shop to look around, and while I was in the shop, I heard the boarding call. Then I saw this darling white lamb on a shelf, and I thought, *That's it!* So I purchased the little stuffed lamb and took it on the plane with me.

Arriving home in California, I picked up my mail—and I could hardly believe what I found: A totally unexpected residual check in the amount of $1,150. It was the entire amount of my plane ticket, plus a little extra. God had paid for my trip to Israel!

A few days later, I went to speak at a meeting in Bakersfield, a couple hours north of L.A. John, a friend of mine in the program, drove me up to the meeting and back home again. During the drive home, I told John about the vision of Jesus at the Garden of Gethsemane. He looked at me with his face alight and said, "Whitney! Don't you know what your vision means?"

I said, "No. I can't figure it out."

"Jesus is *calling* you, Whitney!"

"He is?"

"Of course he is!"

"But why?"

"Because he wants you to follow him."

"But why did Jesus tell me he's Jewish, like me?" I asked. "Jesus isn't Jewish. He's Christian."

"You're wrong, Whitney. Jesus was a good Jewish boy. The people who came after Jesus are Christians, but Jesus himself was a Jewish original. Don't you know what's happening to you? You're getting ready to be born again!"

I looked at him like he was crazy. "Born again? Me?"

"Of course, you. When you had the vision in Israel, wasn't Jesus looking right at you? He's calling you."

I was horrified. "Oh, no! Don't you understand, John? I can't be born again! I can't even say his name! I'm Jewish!"

"Well, then," said my friend, "call him by his Jewish name, Y'shua."

"Y'shua?"

"That's right. Call him Y'shua ha Mashiach."

"Oh, I love that!" I said. "Y'shua ha Mashiach! That name has guts! That name has chutzpah!"

"Good. Now, here's what you do," John continued. "Go home, turn on the Christian TV channel, and watch it every day. And let me tell you something: When you start watching, you are going to be repelled, you're going to be angry, you're going to be sickened by what you see. Don't worry about it. Just keep watching."

So I went home and began watching TV. I had gone back with my second husband, Jack, by that time, and he couldn't even be in the room with me while I had the TV on. "Grace," he said, "you have flipped out! You don't drink and use anymore, and now you're watching this religious crap twenty-four hours a day! What's gotten into you?"

But I just shhhh'd him and kept watching.

My friend John was right: I was repulsed, I groaned, I swore at my TV set! But I kept thinking about my vision in Israel, and of what John had said to me: *Don't worry about it. Just keep watching.*

After a few days of this, I was watching TV and a Bible teacher came on the screen. He was in Israel, walking across the Kidron Valley, toward the Mount of Olives, right where I had been with Jonathan just a few weeks earlier. He stopped in front of the gate of the Garden of Gethsemane. I thought, *That's my gate! That's where I had my vision!*

And he said, "This is the very garden where Y'shua came to pray, the night before he was crucified for you." I was amazed. He had actually called him Y'shua— the Jewish name for Jesus. He really had my attention when he said that!

"As he prayed in this garden," the Bible teacher continued, "his soul was overwhelmed with sorrow, so that he fell to the ground. And he prayed, 'Abba!' That means 'Daddy!' He begged his beloved Father, his heavenly Daddy, to take this terrible cup of torture and death away from him. But he also said, 'Not what I will, but what you will.' Y'shua was obedient to the death of the cross. After what he has done for you, are you willing to follow him? Are you willing to say yes to him?"

And at that moment, I realized that I was ready to say yes to Y'shua ha Mashiach. He had led me all the way to Israel, and had met me there, just a few minutes' walk from the very place where they had nailed him to the cross. After all he had done for me, how could I say no?

I knelt in front of the TV set, and I put my hands on the TV screen. I wanted to get as close as I could to that garden gate where Y'shua himself had first appeared to me. And I said, "Yes, Lord! Take control of my life! Do whatever you want with me!"

I was instantly filled with the most incredible sense of peace I had ever experienced. I had never felt like that on gin or drugs. This was different. This was real.

I'll never understand why God wanted me enough to seek me out—because I sure didn't want him. He chased me down. He cornered me. He held me until I stopped struggling against him. And then he embraced me as his own little child.

In my heart, I felt him say to me, "Welcome home."

My euphoric state lasted 12 hours.

The next morning, I went to the talent agency where I worked as a receptionist. I told the people at work, "Guess what? I just got born again last night!" When I said that, everybody looked at me like I was crazy.

I called my girlfriend on the phone and said, "Listen, the most wonderful thing happened! I got born again last night!"

"You what?!" she screamed. "Grace Lee Whitney, what's the matter with you? How could you fall for that phony line of religious bull?"

Every time I opened my mouth about the change in my life, I got it right in the teeth! That didn't make me any less vocal, but it made me wonder: Why am I getting this from so many people? You'd think people would be happy for me that I had finally found meaning and happiness in my life! Instead, practically everyone I told acted as if I had done a terrible thing.

During the first three years of my sobriety, one of the places where I attended recovery group meetings was the Overcomers Outreach group at the Church on the Way in Van Nuys. I was also baptized at that church by Pastor Jack Hayford.

After the baptismal service, I got in my car and noticed the little stuffed lamb I had bought in Israel. I don't even know why I brought it with me in the car, but there it was. The moment I saw it, I recalled something the minister had said during the ceremony: "Behold, the Lamb of God, who takes away the sin of the world." And I thought, *Oh, my! The lamb of God. He was waiting for me all the time.* To this day, whenever I look at that lamb, it is as if Y'shua is saying to me, "Take me along. Wherever you go, I'm with you."

Looking back, I can see all the ways God kept prodding me, nudging me toward sobriety and toward himself. It was never anything I did. It was always God. I never walked toward him. I always ran the other way. He pulled me, and I resisted—but he never gave up on me.

My coming to God was like getting on a train. I boarded the train, and then sat there. I didn't do anything—the train did all the work. The train was so much bigger and more powerful than I was. It carried me all the way. I didn't have to get out and push. I didn't have to go running down the tracks. I just sat back and let the train pull me to my destination.

I got aboard the train of my sobriety, and God pulled me toward my destiny with him.

Not long after my vision in Israel, my mother went into the hospital. I was two and a half years sober at the time, and I knew she was dying. I went to visit her at the hospital, and she was delirious. As I stood at her bedside, she began talking to me as if I was a little girl. The really strange thing was that I actually began to feel I was her little girl again. Inside, I seemed to shrink down to a small child. I was looking at her through a child's eyes, and I was carried back to the day when I sat on her lap in the rocking chair and she told me I was adopted.

In my mind, I seemed to hear my voice—the voice of a little girl—say, "You mean—you're not my mother?"

Here's the woman who saved my life—Irene Yvonne Chase. I spent years of torment, wondering why my birth mother rejected me. It didn't occur to me that she could have aborted me, just as I aborted two of my babies. Today, I'm grateful to her because she loved me enough to give me life and a two-parent home.

"No," I heard my mother say, "I'm not."

"Well, where is my mother?"

"I don't know where she lives now. She gave you up because you didn't have a father, and she couldn't take care of you."

"Well, where is my father?"

"Honey," I heard my mother's voice in my mind, "we don't know."

Then, standing beside my mother's hospital bed, I asked aloud, "Well, if you're not my mother, then who am I?"

My mother, lying on her deathbed, did not answer.

I shared this incident at the next meeting I went to. As I shared, I realized that from the time I was 7 years old, when my mother first told me I was adopted, until that very moment in 1983, I had never truly known who I was. I didn't know where I came from. I didn't know where I belonged. I felt totally alone.

I started to cry. The people in the meeting tried to reach out to me. They wanted to be my family, and they were. But there was something missing inside me at that moment that even the group could not supply.

I went home that night and went to sleep in the darkness and pain.

The next morning, I got up, got in my car, and started out for the office. The pain grew worse by the moment as I drove across Laurel Canyon. It was the pain of knowing I had been abandoned by my own mother. My eyes filled with tears, blurring the road in front of me. The pain became so intense, it practically doubled me up, like a physical stabbing in my abdomen. I pulled off to the side of the road and stopped the car. "If she's not my mother," I screamed out loud, "then who am I, God? Who am I?!"

And then I heard the voice. It was the voice of a power greater than myself, and it seemed to come from outside of me. I recognized it—the very same voice I had heard at the Garden of Gethsemane. "I am your father and your mother," the voice said gently, "and I will never leave you or abandon you."

I heard those words as clearly as if Y'shua himself had been sitting beside me in the car. The moment I heard his voice, I felt a sense of peace wash over me. I instantly knew who I was.

I was God's own child.

The ninth step of the Twelve Steps says that we "made direct amends to such people wherever possible, except when to do so would injure them or others." I had made amends to my adoptive parents, but I began to feel I really needed to make amends to my birth mother because of all the years of resentment I felt toward her because she had given me away. But how could I make amends to her? I didn't know where she was. I didn't even know if she was alive or dead.

I was staying in my mother's house while she was in the hospital. As usual, I was sitting on the floor in front of the TV, watching the Christian channel. A minister came on and talked about a program that provided homes for unwed mothers, and he interviewed some of these young mothers on the air. They were planning to give their babies up for adoption.

I couldn't believe what I was hearing. This minister was talking about adoption as if it was a *good* thing! I was absolutely riveted, because I had spent a lifetime resenting the fact that my birth mother had given me up for adoption.

So I listened as a young lady named Marianna told her story. "I'm seventeen years old," she said, "and I'm going to have a baby in a few weeks, but I know I can't give her the kind of home she needs. I love my child very much, and I want her to have a stable home, with two parents and a good start in life. Because I love her so much, I've decided to give my baby up for adoption."

As I listened to Marianna tell her story, tears rolled down my cheeks. In my mind, I could see my birth mother there, saying the things Marianna was saying, telling me that she wanted to give her little girl a good, stable, two-parent family. She wasn't rejecting me. She was giving me up because she loved me and she wanted me to have a good life. And when I saw my birth mother in that light, I finally got on the other side of all those years of pain. I finally forgave her and I thanked her and I blessed her—wherever she was.

As I listened to Marianna talk about the loving choice she was making, I remembered the many self-centered, self-willed choices I had made. I remembered the "coathanger" abortion I had when I was 15, the night I went to the Sarah Vaughn concert and stood in the back of the theater with blood running down my legs and filling my shoes, the night the first baby I ever conceived came out of my body like shreds of raw liver. And I remembered another abortion I had in L.A.— an illegal (pre-Roe v. Wade) abortion performed by a sleazy doctor without a nurse or anesthesiologist in the room. (Later, when I learned that this doctor was notorious for molesting the women on the table while they were under anesthesia, I was sick to my stomach for days.)

As I compared the choices I had made with the choice Marianna was making, I realized I had more amends to make. I had killed two innocent babies. I was their mother, and I had aborted them.

I knew what I had to do. I wrote out a check for $800 to the home for unwed mothers—$400 for each baby I had aborted. About two weeks later, I received two bronze baby shoes on wooden bases, plus two certificates, thanking me for the gift. I took the certificates with me to visit my recovery group sponsor, who was in the hospital with terminal cancer. "This is a terrific thing God has done for you," she said. "He allowed you to see that your birth mother really loved you when she gave you up for adoption. And he allowed you to make amends for your two abortions."

Of course, she didn't mean that any amount of money could buy God's forgiveness or replace a human life. Rather, she thought it was amazing that God had graciously allowed me to do something positive and meaningful for others in gratitude for his forgiveness of my selfishness and sin.

Two years later, in 1985—with the help of a fan who had some expertise in locating lost people—I finally found out where my mother had been all those years I was growing up. Unfortunately, I was 10 years too late. That was very painful. I was angry with God for letting my birth mother die before I could find her. Perhaps, in some way that I can't understand, it was a blessing. I don't know.

She lived in Grand Rapids all those years I was growing up in Detroit. I contacted the family, but as it turned out, no one in my birth family wanted to see me except one cousin—and she was wonderful! She flew out to L.A. with pictures and family stories to tell me. It was exciting having that single strand of connection to my birth family. My birth cousin and I still write each other to this day. The rest of the family refused to acknowledge an illegitimate child in the family, so I just let it lay. Today, in my mind and in my heart, that chapter is closed.

Working on the *Star Trek* movies after getting sober and saved was a wonderful experience. It was especially exciting, getting to work with my old friend Leonard Nimoy again. We shot *Star Trek III: The Search for Spock* in late summer and early fall of 1983. Leonard's beloved Vulcan character, Mr. Spock, had died near the end of *Star Trek II: The Wrath of Khan*. In *Star Trek III*, Spock makes his comeback! It is fitting, in a way, that Leonard, a Jewish actor, should play a character who is resurrected from the dead. You know, you can't keep a good Jewish boy down!

Star Trek III marked the first time I had ever worked with Leonard as director. I had a cameo role in the movie—not Janice Rand, but the red-haired Woman at the Window who registers shock and dismay when the *Enterprise* pulls into spacedock, blasted and pitted from the battle in *Star Trek II: The Wrath of Khan*. My job was to represent the reaction of everyone in the spacedock, as well as everyone in the audience, at the sight of our beloved Starship *Enterprise* limping into port.

Leonard got me the part. I had pretty well burned my reputation as an actress by the end of my drinking. But Leonard saw the change in me after I got sober, and he wanted to get me back into the *Star Trek* world. He went to Ralph Winter, one of the producers, and said he'd like to use me in the movie. Winter said he'd like to meet me before saying yes.

There was a big party for people involved with the new *Star Trek* movie at a restaurant on Wilshire Blvd. All the stars and creative people were there. Leonard wanted me to make a good impression, so he told me to pull out all the stops. I had red-rinsed hair at the time, and I wore a turquoise-and-hot-pink Mandarin dress with very high heels. If I do say so myself, I was a knockout! I walked into the restaurant and Leonard and Ralph Winter were standing together. Winter looked at me and his eyes lit up, then he looked at Leonard and smiled. Leonard winked at me—and I knew I had the job.

Though most of the film was shot at Paramount in Hollywood, this particular scene, which involved a lot of special effects processing, was shot at the George Lucas studio, Industrial Light and Magic (ILM), in Marin County. Because there were no lines, it was important that I do a lot of inner work and bring the feelings out in my eyes. The camera was right in my face during most of the shooting.

I had a hard time doing the scene because I was not used to seeing Leonard up on the boom, directing. He was sitting there in his slacks, sports shirt and glasses, giving orders like any director would. But to me, it just seemed ludicrous, as if Mr. Spock had bobbed his ears, gone Hollywood, and was trying to pass himself off as a movie director! He'd say, "Action!" and I was supposed to emote on cue. Instead, I broke up laughing!

While we were at ILM, a number of us were given a tour of the studio. We were introduced to George Lucas, and we met a lot of the artists, animators and model-builders. Most of them seem so young, practically teenagers, yet they were all incredibly talented. They showed us their drawings and paintings and miniatures of starships, Klingons, aliens—a whole bizarre wonderland of movie magic.

Then we were taken into a huge room where the large-scale "miniature" of the *Enterprise* was mounted on a pedestal as if it were soaring through space. The model was enormous—the saucer section alone was at least six or eight feet across. There were about 50 of us in the room, and we spread out around the wall, then someone turned out the lights and we were plunged into pitch-blackness. In a few seconds our eyes began to adjust to the darkness. Suddenly, a switch was thrown and the *Enterprise* lit up like a Christmas tree. All the portholes and running lights began to glow, flash and blink. It was an eerie, unearthly experience. I felt as if I was floating in outer space, and the Starship *Enterprise* was out in front of me—not a model, but a full-size starship hanging in space, carrying some 400 crewmembers around the galaxy.

It was an astounding, disorienting illusion—talk about distinguishing fantasy from reality! It was so beautiful, it literally brought tears to my eyes. The experience of seeing the starship I had served aboard almost 25 years earlier, looking so real I felt I could swim out to it and enter an airlock, was worth the whole experience of making the movie.

That same year, 1983, I started working as a receptionist for the talent management agency Le Mond/Zetter. Bob Le Mond and Lois Zetter managed some of the biggest stars in the business, including John Travolta and Patrick Swayze. (To this day, when I talk about *Next Generation* star Patrick Stewart, I often slip and call him Patrick Swayze.) I got the job because of the lush red hair I had at the time.

Le Mond/Zetter's office was the most incredible place you ever saw in your life—so incredible, in fact, that it was once featured on the cover of *Architectural Digest*. A real babbling brook ran through the middle of the office, over stones and pebbles—you could hear the music of the water running all day long. The white marble walls were draped with big, bold turquoise hangings, and light streamed into the office through cubical glass.

When you stepped into this absolutely stunning, dramatically furnished office, the first thing you saw was me. The day I was hired, Lois Zetter told me, "When people walk in, they're going to see your blue eyes and your red hair sitting in this gorgeous office, and honey, they just won't believe their eyes!"

"You sound just like Gene Roddenberry," I told her. "When Gene hired me for *Star Trek*, he said, 'Honey, you rang all the bells in the "Police Story" pilot, and when they see you in *Star Trek*, you're gonna ring 'em even more!'"

One of our top clients was Jon-Erik Hexum, star of the CBS series "Cover-Up." I answered the phone when the call came in with the tragic news that he had shot and killed himself on the set. He apparently got bored during setups between scenes. Clowning around with a .44 Magnum prop gun which was loaded with blanks, he put it to his temple and pulled the trigger. To this day, no one knows if he thought the gun was unloaded, or if he didn't understand how dangerous blank cartridges can be. The blast from the blank cartridge punched a piece of his skull, about the size of a half dollar, into his brain. Everyone in our office was devastated by the news. Hexum was not only our biggest star, but he was also a warm, funny, likable guy.

Another client was Adrian Zmed, who played a rookie police officer alongside Bill Shatner on the TV series "T.J. Hooker." Adrian would come into the office now and then, and say hello—a nice, friendly guy. Then one day he came in and dropped to his knees right in front of my desk. I stared at him and said, "What on earth are you doing?"

He said, "I didn't realize who you are! I just saw a poster of you with William Shatner on *Star Trek*! You're Janice Rand! I want your autograph! I'm a big fan!"

What a *nice* young man!

❖ ❖ ❖

Leonard Nimoy brought me back into the *Trek* universe for *Star Trek IV: The Voyage Home*, which we filmed in early 1986. This was the "save the whales" movie—one of the best of the *Trek* films. The story: Earth is visited by a huge alien probe that seeks to communicate with the whales in Earth's oceans. Problem: By the 23rd century, all whales have been hunted to extinction. James Kirk and his crew must journey back in time to 1986 and retrieve a pair of live whales (named George and Gracie) to take back to the future and save the world. Along the way, they enlist the help of a marine biologist, Dr. Gillian Taylor (Catherine Hicks), to help them capture the whales and save the future.

While the story sounds dire and intense, *Star Trek IV* actually captures the lighthearted mood of the original series. It's a fun movie, filled with startling surprises and high adventure. Though the "save the whales" theme is the core of the story, the real fun comes from the movie's alien's-eye-view of American society in the mid-1980s, as the *Enterprise* crewmembers grope their way through our bewildering culture and counterculture. Along the way, Mr. Spock learns to swear like a sailor; Scottie tries to communicate with an Apple Macintosh computer by talking into the mouse; and Uhuru and Chekov wander the streets of San Francisco, asking strangers where they can find the "nuclear wessels." The bantering interplay among the characters of this movie is by far the best among all the *Trek* films. *Star Trek IV* is also notable for the many cameo appearances by characters from the original series—Ambassador Sarek and his wife Amanda (Spock's parents, played by Mark Lenard and Jane Wyatt), Dr. Christine Chapel (Majel Barrett Roddenberry), and of course, Chief Petty Officer Janice Rand.

Originally, the movie was supposed to feature comedian Eddie Murphy as a UFO nut who helps Kirk and Spock because he's the only one crazy enough to believe in starships and time travel. Murphy is a big *Trek* fan, and was eager to do the role, but the deal fell through because he had other movie commitments at the time *Star Trek IV* was to shoot. So the part of the UFO nut was totally rewritten and recast. Instead of a wildly comedic Eddie Murphy vehicle, the part became a romantic interest for Captain Kirk, the beautiful, sensitive and quirky marine biologist Gillian Taylor.

Catherine Hicks brought just the right touch to the role of Gillian—sexy, competent, yet vulnerable. You could sense that air of vulnerability in Catherine both on and off the screen. Though a screen veteran (she started in the soap opera "Ryan's Hope," and went on to major roles in *Garbo Talks*, *Peggy Sue Got Married*, *Sable* and the title role in *Marilyn: The Untold Story*), Catherine had an honest, earnest ingenue quality. She was always looking for ways to improve her performance, and she would often ask other actors for ideas and insight about how to play a certain scene.

I saw the innocent, ingenuous side of Catherine Hicks when she came to me, script in hand, about a problem. "See these lines?" she said, pointing to a scene in the script that was to be shot later that day. "I can't say those words!" I looked at the lines she indicated, and sure enough, they did contain expletives that went far beyond the usual PG-rated profanity in the film. "I noticed that you and Leonard Nimoy are really close friends," she went on. "Do you think you could ask him for me—" She was really intimidated by dear, sweet Leonard!

"Let's go talk to him," I said. So we went over to Leonard and showed him the script. "Leonard," I said, "Catherine's not comfortable saying these lines."

He look at the lines, took out his pen, crossed out the objectionable expletives, and wrote in some milder words. It was that easy. Catherine was very pleased.

Majel Barrett Roddenberry and I had many scenes together in the film, and we worked very hard on the dialogue. There was a lot of technobabble in it that was very hard to memorize, and much of it finally had to be put on cue cards. I was disappointed when the film came out, because the bulk of the footage we shot ended up being cut before the movie was released.

One of the silliest memories I have of making that movie is the day they called us all together and told us to keep our underwear locked up in the dressing rooms. The frenzy over *Star Trek* memorabilia had gotten so ridiculous that someone was sneaking into the dressing rooms and stealing the stars' underwear to sell to the fans!

Star Trek VI: The Undiscovered Country is a powerful film, perhaps the best of all the *Star Trek* films. We shot the film in April and May of 1991. The story idea was Leonard Nimoy's. He explained it very simply as "the Wall coming down in outer space." The story of the fall of the Klingon empire closely parallels the fall of the Berlin Wall and the collapse of the Iron Curtain.

The movie begins with echoes of Chernobyl: A disastrous accident shatters the Klingon moon Praxis, sending shock waves out into space. Those shock waves sweep over the Starship *Excelsior*, commanded by Captain Sulu. I serve on the bridge of the *Excelsior* as Captain Sulu's communications officer (in this film, I receive another promotion, this time to *Commander* Rand!). The *Excelsior* offers assistance to the Klingons, but those offers are curtly snubbed. It soon becomes apparent that the radiation from the blast will render the Klingon homeworld uninhabitable within 50 years.

Some within Starfleet (such as Captain Kirk, whose son was brutally murdered by the Klingons) see this event as a chance to vanquish the Klingon threat for good; others, including Spock, see it as an opportunity for lasting peace. Based on the rationale that only Nixon could go to China, the hardened cold warrior, James T. Kirk, is selected to serve as the reluctant ambassador for peace. When the Federation-Klingon peace talks are sabotaged and high Klingon officials are murdered, Captain Kirk and Dr. McCoy get the blame—and end up being sentenced to life at hard labor in the dreaded dilithium mines on the Klingon prison planet, Rura Penthe.

The trial of Kirk and McCoy is broadcast live throughout the galaxy by subspace radio. At the moment they are sentenced, there are reaction shots of crewmembers aboard the *Enterprise* and the *Excelsior*. The director, Nicholas Meyer, wanted to get a close-up reaction shot of Janice Rand for that crucial, dramatic scene. As the crew

From Star Trek VI: The Undiscovered Country. *This was both a joyful reunion and a sad passage, for we knew it was the last time all of us from the original series would be working together. Here, I am Commander Janice Rand on the bridge of the Starship* Excelsior.

was setting up the shot, Nick called me over by the video monitors which are used to give the director an overview of all the camera angles on the set.

"Grace," he said, "did you and Kirk have a thing together on the original series?"

I wasn't sure what he was getting at. "In the show or for real?" I asked.

He grinned. "Both."

I returned the grin, remembering the electricity I had always felt on the old Desilu set when I was around Bill Shatner. "Well…yes."

"Would Janice Rand be upset if anything happened to Captain Kirk?"

He had to ask? "*Bigtime* she would!" I replied.

Nick nodded toward the set. "Can you cry on camera?"

"I don't know," I said. "I used to be able to cry at the drop of a hat. But it's been awhile…"

"Well, Grace, if you can cry on camera, I'll give you a close-up."

My face lit up. "For a close-up honey, I'll do anything!"

Nick wanted an understated cry—no bawling or boo-hooing, nothing that would distort my face. There were not even to be any lines. I would just quietly break down in response to what was happening to Captain Kirk.

There was just one problem: I didn't *know* what was happening to Captain Kirk. The studio had never sent me a complete script. They had only sent me what are called "sides," the pages with my lines and scenes, no surrounding material. So I didn't even know the storyline of the movie. I didn't know what happened before or after my lines—which of course means, I didn't always know what Rand's motivation was in a given scene or what she was reacting to.

So as Nick was explaining what he wanted me to do, I was looking at him kind of dumb. "I want you to think about what happens to Kirk," he said, "and just let the emotions come."

"What happens to Kirk?" I asked.

Nick frowned at me. "Didn't you read your script?"

"They never sent me one."

His eyebrows went up and his jaw dropped. "What!" he exploded. "They never sent you one? Those cheapskates! ... Script! Script!"

And a script boy came running over.

"Get Miss Whitney a script *right now*!"

The guy scurried off and got me a script.

Meanwhile, however, the shot was all set up so I didn't have time to sit and read the script. "Don't worry, Grace," Nick said. "You just get up there, and I'll talk you through the scene."

So I took my place on the set, and the camera rolled. Nicholas Meyer began talking to me about what was going on with Kirk. As he talked about Kirk and McCoy being sentenced to a life of cold misery and torture on the gulag planet, I slowly broke down. My eyes filled up, and the tears began to roll down my cheeks. We got the shot in one take.

The next day, Leonard saw the scene in the dailies, and he came over to me and said that he got a catch in his throat when he saw that scene. That meant so much to me. I was so thrilled that I could still pull it off.

I really enjoyed working on *Star Trek VI*. There were many people on the set who were in recovery like me, and we would go to meetings, then go to the set together. One of the camera operators was a woman who was 17 years clean and sober. We would say the Serenity Prayer* together before each shot. Working on that movie was a real blessing in my life.

On October 24, 1991—just a few months after we had finished shooting *Star Trek VI*—the entire *Trek* world was shocked to learn of the death of Gene Roddenberry. He died just two days after a private screening of the final cut of *Star Trek VI*. He was at his doctor's office, with Majel at his side, when a blood clot stopped his heart. On December 6, 1991, when *Star Trek VI* opened in theaters across the country, the first words on the screen were, "For Gene Roddenberry."

---

*The words of the Serenity Prayer:

"God, grant me the serenity
To accept the things I cannot change,
The courage to change the things I can,
And the wisdom to know the difference."

The Great Bird of the Galaxy

For years, I resented Gene Roddenberry. I blamed him for his part in pressing the EJECT button on Yeoman Rand and Grace Lee Whitney.

Time passed. Gene took me back into *Star Trek*. He told me he was sorry, and that he had made a terrible mistake in writing me out of the series. I forgave him and I began to understand him. When he died, I grieved miserably for him.

My change of heart toward Gene Roddenberry began as I got sober and started to discover how much alike we were. Gene and I are two sides of the same coin.

My life took a major turn when I met Gene and worked for him on three shows— "The Lieutenant," the "Police Story" pilot and *Star Trek*. Over the years, Gene's presence has cast a long shadow over my life, and I continue to feel his influence today, years after he passed away. I remember many philosophical conversations I had with Gene in the spring and summer of 1966, as *Star Trek* was gearing up for production. In addition to talking about the show and my character, Janice Rand, we talked about politics, social issues, equality between the sexes and our mutual atheist convictions (I was a Jewish atheist at the time—I loved the traditions of Judaism but had no faith in the God of Abraham, Isaac and Jacob).

The most in-depth and expansive interview Gene ever gave was his 1991 interview with Yvonne Fern, conducted in the final weeks of his life. Yvonne has become a good friend to me in the past few years. She is married to Herbert F. Solow, the former Desilu studio exec who was the first to recognize the value of Gene's *Star Trek* concept, and who developed the series with Gene and sold it to NBC. Herb and Yvonne are wonderful people, and have always been very kind to me. In Yvonne's book, *Gene Roddenberry: The Last Conversation*, Gene talks candidly about his upbringing and the shaping of his views on God and religion. After reading that interview, plus another 1991 interview by David Alexander, published in *The Humanist*, and after reflecting on my own conversations with Gene Roddenberry, I think I've come to understand him fairly well.

He was born in El Paso, Texas, in 1921, and his family moved to L.A. when he was just a baby. Gene's mother was a devoutly religious Southern Baptist, while his father never went to church, and actively discouraged young Gene from taking the preachers' sermons too seriously. It is statistically quite common when parents are divided on religion for their children to grow up agnostic or atheist as Gene did. By his early teens he viewed everything he saw in church with a jaundiced eye—just as I did at that age. In the *Humanist* interview, he recalls:

In my early teens, I decided to listen to the sermon. I guess I was around 14 and emerging as a personality. I had never really paid much attention to the sermon before. I was more interested in the deacon's daughter and what we might be doing between services.

I listened to the sermon, and I remember complete astonishment because what they were talking about were things that were just crazy. It was communion time, where you eat this wafer and are supposed to be eating the body of Christ and drinking his blood. My first impression was, "This is a bunch of cannibals they've put me down among!" For some time, I puzzled over this and puzzled over why they were saying these things, because the connection between what they were saying and reality was very tenuous. How the hell did Jesus become something to be eaten?

I guess from that time it was clear to me that religion was largely nonsense—largely magical, superstitious things. In my own teen life, I just couldn't see any point in adopting something based on magic, which was obviously phony and superstitious.[1]

Though Gene Roddenberry dealt with symbolism and metaphors on a daily basis as a writer, he took the symbolism of Holy Communion to a literal extreme. The situation he described as "a bunch of cannibals" is really the beautiful story of Jesus, hours before the crucifixion, breaking bread and passing the cup, inviting his 12 closest friends to share his life and sustain themselves on his essence.

But I really know how Gene felt, because I was so much like him—a case of arrested spiritual development, with my own view of God stuck at age 14. There is a certain 14-year-old arrogance in looking at anything you don't understand and saying, "I don't get it, so it must be a load of crap." But that's how I looked at God—and I see my own adolescent arrogance in Gene's words.

I think it's significant that Gene rejected God during his adolescence. It's a time when boys are working out their gender identity, and identifying with the significant male role models in their lives. It's a time when boys compare themselves to their fathers and try to measure up. They try to earn Dad's approval by imitating him. I suspect that Gene rejected his mother's faith in order to identify with his dad, and to win his dad's approval, as this excerpt from the *Humanist* interview shows:

Roddenberry:...A great deal of my early training was due to my father who, mysteriously, never showed up in church. ... He did not think the church was particularly the guidance that he would have pushed me to have. He felt that it was good for me to go to church but be damned careful of what the preachers say. ...

My mother ... took us to church every Sunday, but my father didn't go. He just avoided church. He would mumble things like, "If you had some of the experiences I've had with these people and how phony they are...." There was a preacher now and then that he liked as a human being, but he didn't care much for most of them. ...

The Humanist: Your dad seemed to have escaped a lot of the normally accepted social conventions and beliefs he was exposed to. Obviously, your father was the major influence in your life.

Roddenberry: Much more than I realized. As these interviews have proceeded, I have realized how much influence my father had.

Gene's rejection of his mother's faith reminds me so much of my own rejection of faith at the same point in my life. Gene has talked about how, as a 5-year-old, he ceased to believe in Santa Claus. It reminds me of my disillusionment when I learned that my parents weren't my parents, Santa Claus was a lie—and I concluded that God must be a lie, too. In the *Humanist* interview, Gene says of his religious upbringing:

> I don't remember ever being serious about any of those things. When I sang in the choir, we made up cowboy words to choir songs. The rest of the choir would be singing "Holy, Holy Jesus," and we would be singing something entirely different. At five years old, I was serious about Santa Claus, but at five and a half I had learned it was nonsense. Writers often write these as weighty moments, but in my experience they're not. Santa Claus doesn't exist. Yes, I think back now that there were all sorts of reasons he could not exist and maybe have a little sadness that he is gone, but then I think the same thing about Jesus and the church.[3]

Like Gene, I spent most of my life disregarding and avoiding God. I treated the very concept of God with "contempt prior to investigation." So I identify with Gene. My early faith and his were snuffed out in childhood. Even though his mother raised him in the church, Gene felt very early in life that the Christian faith was "foolish," "full of inconsistencies," and "background noise that you ignore," just as I did. By Gene's own admission, he never seriously bothered to go back and investigate the faith he abandoned in childhood.

And I was no different. I never sought God; he sought me. He led me to Israel, he confronted me in a vision, he overwhelmed me with his presence at the Garden of Gethsemane. I can't take any credit for what God did in my life. Left to my own devices, my own will, I was just like Gene. I didn't want God in my life any more than Gene did.

Gene Roddenberry's avowed atheism didn't keep him from using religious symbolism and themes as grist for his television writing. He talks about writing an episode of "Have Gun, Will Travel," in which a preacher, trying to save a man from the gallows, cuts himself with a hacksaw blade, then makes a symbolic comment regarding blood and salvation. "It's not that I actually believed in blood and salvation being connected," he said, "but that was the way the audience believed. ...Perhaps I was consciously dishonest. Yes, I was, but I knew that a certain amount of dishonesty about such things covered you."[4]

This picture of Gene Roddenberry and me was taken at a convention in the mid-1980s, when I was happily sober.

In the *Star Trek* episode "Bread and Circuses" which he wrote with Gene Coon, the crew of the *Enterprise* encounters a world where parallel evolution has produced a culture identical to the old Roman empire on Earth, but with 20th century technology and television. This Roman world even has a persecuted underground Christian church. In the end, Uhura points out that these underground believers, who are viciously hunted and martyred by the empire, worship the Son of God, and Captain Kirk says, "Caesar and Christ, they had them both."

In his original series proposal to NBC, dated March 11, 1964, Gene outlined a number of story ideas, including one idea that was the basis for "Bread and Circuses." His original outline of the plot shows that Gene had actually planned to go much further in portraying the kind of pro-religious message he himself disdained:

> THE COMING. Alien people in an alien society, but something disturbingly familiar about the quiet dignity of one who is being condemned to crucifixion.[5]

Usually, however, the message of *Star Trek* was that the world of the 23rd century had outgrown its need for God-myths, just as Gene thought that he himself had outgrown such myths at age 14. In Gene's pilot script, "The Cage," the alien keepers force Captain Christopher Pike to undergo mental torture, making him believe he is burning in hell. When the torture is over, the keepers tell Pike that they extracted the hell image from his memories of "a fable you once heard in childhood." In other episodes, such as "The Apple," "Who Mourns for Adonais?," and "The Way to Eden," the attack upon religious faith is more subtle and symbolic. In each case, religious beliefs are shown to be unhealthy and destructive to the believers—and those beliefs ultimately crumble under the cold light of rationality and science.

Obviously, *Star Trek* was a show that frequently dealt with religious issues, even though the creator of the show was not a religious man—at least not religious in any conventional sense. I had many conversations with Gene before and during *Star Trek* regarding the philosophy and meaning of the show. One statement he made to me over lunch one day stands out clearly in my mind: "All literature and all art is really about the existence of God or the nonexistence of God. That's all there is." I never forgot that statement, and I believe it is true on so many levels, including levels that Gene himself probably never consciously realized.

I think science fiction in general, and *Star Trek* in particular, are expressions of a universal human yearning for a bright future out among the stars—a longing for Heaven. So, when we hear Captain Kirk say these words at the beginning of every episode, they stir a religious awe within us:

> Space …the final frontier.
> These are the voyages of the Starship *Enterprise*.
> Its five year mission:
> To explore strange new worlds…
> To seek out new life and new civilizations…
> To boldly go where no man has gone before.

"To seek out *new life*"—to make contact, to reach out and establish communion with other beings. That's a profoundly religious yearning. That phrase also echoes the words used in the Bible to describe eternal life: "Go," said the angel in Acts 5:20, "and tell the people the full message of this *new life*." Or as the apostle Paul said, "just as Christ was raised from the dead … we too may live a *new life*." Each of us, in our own way, is on a mission to seek out *new life*.

And notice this phrase: "To boldly go where no man has gone before"—to transcend this familiar world and move out into the unknown destiny that awaits us all on the other side of death. Whether we see ourselves as warping to the stars aboard a starship or voyaging into deep spiritual space by transcending death, we instinctively sense that a final frontier awaits us. Somehow, we all sense it: Our future is out there, among the stars.

I'm not saying Gene Roddenberry consciously set out to touch our religious core when he wrote those words. In fact, they were actually composed rather hurriedly on the afternoon of August 10, 1966, just minutes before Bill Shatner read them in the Desilu dubbing studio. But I don't think there's any question that those words powerfully express a universal human longing to transcend this present life, and to reach beyond, for a brighter future, an eternal quality of life, a *new life*. We long for a new civilization, like the heavenly kingdom in the book of Revelation. Perhaps, on some subconscious level, Gene tapped into his own hidden longings in those opening lines of *Star Trek*.

I can't say that Gene and writer John Meredyth Lucas consciously recognized the spiritual theme of the episode "The Changeling" when it was filmed in 1967. But it's there all the same. It's the story of Nomad, a wandering robot probe that comes aboard the *Enterprise*. Its programming garbled by some interstellar accident, Nomad comes seeking its creator. And isn't that a metaphor describing our own journey through the galaxy? Aren't most of us really wandering nomads and pilgrims in search of the answer to the puzzling question, "Who made me, and for what purpose? Why am I here and where is my life leading? Where can I find my creator?" Those were the fundamental questions of my own life's quest.

The same theme recurs again in *Star Trek: The Motion Picture* (which, significantly, was originally titled "In Thy Image"). In that film, V'Ger, the lost Voyager probe, returns to the solar system in search of its creator. V'Ger sends a probe to the *Enterprise*—and the probe is in the form of the lost Lieutenant Ilia. The purpose of the Ilia-Probe is to communicate with "the carbon units infesting the *Enterprise*"—carbon units, of course, being people. In that scene, this exchange takes place:

> KIRK
> Why does V'Ger travel to the third
> planet of the solar system?
>
> ILIA-PROBE
> To find the Creator.
>
> KIRK
> The Creator? What does
> V'Ger want with the Creator?
>
> ILIA-PROBE
> To join with him.
>
> SPOCK
> To join with the Creator? How?
>
> ILIA-PROBE
> V'Ger and the Creator will become one.
>
> SPOCK
> Who is the Creator?
>
> ILIA-PROBE
> The Creator is that which created V'Ger.

KIRK
Who is V'Ger?

ILIA-PROBE
V'Ger is that which seeks the Creator.

In another film Gene wrote and produced, *The Questor Tapes*, he presents the story of Questor, an android in search of its creator. I find it easy to identify with V'Ger and Questor, because I know what it's like to be an orphan adrift in the universe, wondering if I have a father or mother, wondering if my life is the result of a creative choice or random chance, wondering if I will ever find my way home. V'Ger's search and Questor's search for the creator was my lifelong search as well.

Gene had long ago concluded that "God myths" were for the uneducated, the immature, the unenlightened. Yet, I suspect that deep within his heart, in the depths of the insecure little boy that still lives inside every grown-up, self-sufficient man, he probably wished that there was a God who would love him and be his friend through life—and who would receive him at the end of life. As Gene himself said, he felt a little sadness that Santa Claus is gone, and he felt the same about Jesus—but his rational mind wouldn't let him believe, just as my self-will-run-riot wouldn't let me believe throughout most of my life.

Though Gene often called himself an atheist, he was actually rather coy on the subject. He believed in the perfectibility of humanity, and a divine spark within all of us. He sometimes seemed to suggest that humanity itself might someday become God, and he identified the God-spark in humanity with creative inspiration. In *Gene Roddenberry: The Last Conversation*, this exchange is recorded:

[Yvonne:] "You're pretty well known for not believing in God. Do you claim him now?"
[Gene:] "Oh, well, people are often pretty well known for things which are not true."
"Well, is it?"
"No, it's not. I believe in a kind of god. It's just not other people's god. I reject religion. I accept the notion of God."
"...You're begging the question, distancing it. 'The notion of God' is not the same thing as God."
"No, but they are equally abstract. I don't humanify God."
"No. You just deify humanity."
He laughs. "Okay, look, whatever it is, we can't know it. But it very well may be there."
"Gene..."
"That answer doesn't satisfy you."

"Does it satisfy you?"

He frowns for a moment. "No, no, it doesn't. Let me think about it. ...God, to me, is intrinsic to humanity. To the whole cause of humanity. To the imaginative principle. To what we create, and think. He—or I should say 'it'—is a source, yes, but more an involvement with the unknown. God is like the leap outside oneself—something that has no discernible source, but is a source. ... I have a faith in something that I can't know, but I don't know what that is. It's not the traditional Judeo-Christian God. It's that thing about humanity that makes them write poetry, paint great pictures—"

"Create *Star Trek*."

"Oh, yes, that was a leap of faith. Creating *Star Trek* was a very spiritual experience, in that definition."[6]

Gene redefines God as the creative spark, "that thing about humanity that makes them write poetry, paint great pictures," and create *Star Trek*—and that is the fundamental difference between Gene's humanistic philosophy and the Judeo-Christian faith. The Bible says, "Then God said, 'Let us make man in our image, in our likeness.'"[7] And the New Testament tells us that God's intention for us is that our character would be "conformed to the likeness" of Y'shua's perfect character.[8] It seems that Gene went the other direction, attempting to redefine God according to the likeness of Gene Roddenberry.

Even if it is true, as such creations as Nomad, V'Ger, and Questor suggest, that some hidden part of Gene wished and longed for God, he seemed unable to get past the notion of biblical faith as a refuge for the ignorant and uneducated. Gene was profoundly annoyed by evangelicals and fundamentalists:

> There will always be fundamentalism and the religious right, but I think there has been too much of it. I keep hoping that it is temporary foolishness. Some of it will always be around because there will always be people who are so mean-spirited and such limited thinkers ... that nothing else in their limited concept can explain what the existence of a god can. There's been a lot of it lately—Youth for Christ and that sort of thing. I'm hoping that it is just a bump in time.
>
> Of course, the only thing that will keep such things from continuing and growing is education.[9]

In "Gene Roddenberry: The Last Conversation," Yvonne Fern catches Gene in a contradiction between his profession of tolerance and his distaste for Christianity:

> [Gene:] "We don't look down on others, as inferior, in the *Star Trek* world. ...We've evolved beyond that—"
>
> [Yvonne:] "Wait. Wait. You're going to have to explain that. This view of tolerance needs to be explored a little more. You're liberal and

tolerant about racial equality, abortion, homosexuality, women's rights, sex, all the popular issues—but when you meet up with, say, a Baptist, for example, you will unhesitatingly condemn him to oblivion. You choose your points of tolerance very carefully. It seems to me that when you say you've evolved beyond something, that's just another way of saying that whatever you are beyond, or think you are, is by definition inferior, that your views are superior. ...I've heard what you had to say about religion, about born-agains and evangelicals in particular. It doesn't sound very tolerant to me."

[Gene:] "Doesn't it? I'm sorry. I never meant to give that impression. If I did, then I will correct it. I condemn charlatans. I condemn false prophets. I condemn the effort to take away the power of rational decision, to drain people of their free will—and a hell of a lot of money in the bargain.* ...There are degrees of idiocy. Some are less culpable than others. But I reject them all, because for most people—not for you, perhaps not for other intelligent people—but for most of these poor devils, it's nothing more than a substitute brain. And a very malfunctioning one. I don't dismiss the people who believe in this or that. I dismiss the structure and, more than that, the very idea of the system of the organized church."

[Yvonne:] "Then you deprive me of my right to daydream my way through a form of idiocy that I particularly like. You sound as evangelical as your opponents."

[Gene:] "That's a terrible statement to make."

[Yvonne:] "Give me a reason for retracting it. If you had the power, would you rid the world of churches?"

[Gene:] "Of course not. I would hope that they would go away of their own volition."[10]

Gene condemns fundamentalists and the religious right as "mean-spirited and such limited thinkers." I have to tell you that I love Christians because they are among

---

*There are, of course, charlatans in every field of endeavor—religious charlatans, political charlatans, medical quacks, and probably even a few charlatans in the television industry. The existence of charlatans in any given field doesn't mean the entire field is bad. As for condemning "the effort to take away the power of rational decision, to drain people of their free will—and a hell of a lot of money in the bargain," there are some (but not me) who claim that *Star Trek* has done exactly the same thing. A classic example: Bill Shatner's famous satire on *Trek* conventions on "Saturday Night Live," when he tells a crowd of Trekkies to "Get a life!"

There truly are a number of *Trek* fans who live in the fantasy world of *Star Trek* because they can't relate to the real world—and there is no question that the *Star Trek* franchise has drained "a hell of a lot of money" from *Trek* fans (sales of *Trek* memorabilia alone, from Vulcan ears to toy phasers, is estimated at over $2.5 billion a year). Personally I feel that both *Trek* fans and the religious faithful usually get their money's worth.

The Star Trek *original series cast members celebrate with Gene as he receives his star on the Hollywood Walk of Fame, September 4, 1986. Gene is the first writer/producer to receive this honor. From left to right: Me, Walter Koenig, DeForest Kelly, Majel Barrett Roddenberry, Leonard Nimoy, Gene Roddenberry, Nichelle Nichols, Jimmy Doohan, George Takei, and Roger C. Carmel. (Roger died only two months after this picture was taken.)*

the best friends and staunchest supporters the state of Israel has. They stand for the preservation of the family, of freedom, of morality—and they are absolutely opposed to antisemitism. So, as a Jew, I love those people. To me, Christianity is the flower of Judaism.

Gene condemns charlatans and false prophets. Well, so did Jesus. He battled extremism, oppression and prejudice. He went head-to-head against people who were *really* "meanspirited and limited thinkers"—and he was nailed to a cross for his trouble. I wish the adult Gene Roddenberry had taken a fresh look at this Jesus that a 14-year-old Gene Roddenberry once rejected.

I think Gene might have been surprised by what he found.

According to Gene, his male organ had a lot to do with shaping his religious views. Here's an exchange from the *Humanist* interview:

> *Roddenberry:* And then the God you consider in your teenage years is the guy who knows you masturbate. This has tormented so many people.

The Humanist: God as the ultimate voyeur.

Roddenberry: So my thinking about religion sort of stultified at that time and I just decided not to pay any attention to it.[11]

Remember, this is the same guy who said he never paid much attention to sermons in church because he was "more interested in the deacon's daughter and what we might be doing between services."

Gene couldn't accept a God who doesn't let you point your sex drive in any direction you damn well please. He couldn't accept a God who holds us to a standards of morality and sexual purity. He couldn't accept a God who would make him sit through a boring sermon instead of doing what he *really* wanted to do with the deacon's daughter in the church basement. And, of course, I understand exactly where Gene was coming from—because I have been there, done that.

Gene never made any attempt to conceal his obsession with sex—with "dipping his wick," as he put it. Near the end of his life, he talked candidly with Yvonne Fern about his views on sex:

> [Gene:] "There may be times when I feel like 'dipping my wick' and I do so. When it's right. When it feels good. People may say, 'Oh that Gene Roddenberry. He's no good. He's an unfaithful husband.' I say unfaithful to what?"
>
> [Yvonne:] "Majel, surely."
>
> [Gene:] "No. Not at all. People aren't concerned in their deepest selves about Majel. They're concerned about themselves, their rules and so on. They mean I am unfaithful to the ideal, their ideal, of marriage. They don't want to consider another ideal. They may be afraid. They may condemn me for breaking a vow they think I made. Whereas in fact, I didn't make it. I could never adhere to an agreement that deprived me of myself. Majel and I have our own agreement. I would be false, a false person, if I did make any other kind of agreement. And I would be a false person if my wife didn't know who I am, what I do."
>
> [Yvonne:] "And is this 'wick dipping' ever an intimate act?"
>
> [Gene:] "You mean, outside my marriage? No. I have varying degrees of friendship with people. I am involved in more kinds of love than I could possibly relate. But no, I can't say that I feel intimate, in the manner we are speaking of, with anyone with whom I enjoy that particular pleasure."[12]

Here again, Gene and I were like two sides of the same coin. In fact, I'm sure that, at the end of my drinking, I was more sex-obsessed and out-of-control than Gene. So I don't judge him. I identify with him. Like Gene, I once thumbed my nose at God and morality.

Sexual immorality has cut a vicious swath through our society, destroying individual lives and entire families. In my own case, the obsession with alcohol and sex brought me to the absolute brink of death before God was able to reach down, take hold of me, and lift me up.

Gene believed that his rejection of the Judeo-Christian God was a scientifically informed choice. In recent years, however, science has been steadily demolishing the atheist worldview.

Let's get one thing straight: while I have cruised the galaxy aboard the Starship *Enterprise*, I certainly don't claim to know the first thing about cosmology or quantum physics. But top astronomers and physicists are telling us today that the scientific evidence forces us to conclude that the universe didn't just happen by chance. In other words, "In the beginning, God..." Here's a sampling of views:

Stephen Hawking, the wheelchair-bound equal of Einstein who once appeared as himself on an episode of *Star Trek: The Next Generation*: "The odds against a universe like ours emerging out of something like the Big Bang are enormous. I think there are clearly religious implications whenever you start to discuss the origins of the universe. There must be religious overtones."[13]

Physicist Paul Davies, author of *God and the New Physics*: "If the universe is simply an accident, the odds against it containing any appreciable order are ludicrously small. ...There surely had to be a *selector* or *designer*. ...In my opinion, science offers a surer path to God than religion."[14]

Leonard Shlain, author of *Art and Physics*, says that the Big Bang, according to today's physicists, was "a hyper-expanding fireball containing light, space, time, energy, and matter. [The physicists'] simulation bears an uncanny similarity to the biblical story of Genesis. The creation of *light* was God's first act. Then He divided night from day *(time)*. Then He separated the firmament from the waters and land *(space)*. He then made the 'things' in the world *(matter)* and finally set them in motion *(energy)*. The computer-generated beginnings of the universe mirror the Bible's cosmology."[15]

Roger Penrose is Rouse Ball Professor of Mathematics at Oxford University. In his book *The Emperor's New Mind* he writes: "The Creator's aim [in designing the delicately balanced forces of the universe] must have been...to an accuracy of

$$\text{one part in } 10^{10^{123}}$$

This is an extraordinary figure. One could not possibly even *write the number down* in full, in the ordinary denary notation: it would be '1' followed by 10^{123} successive '0's! Even if we were to write a '0' on each separate proton and on each separate neutron in the entire universe—and we could throw in all the other particles as well for good measure—we should fall far short of writing down the figure needed."[16] In other words, the odds against our precisely balanced, highly ordered universe coming into existence by mere chance are so astronomical as to be virtually impossible.

So Gene's rejection of the God hypothesis pierces me with sadness. The scientific evidence points toward faith in God, not toward the atheism and humanism of

Gene Roddenberry. On some hidden level, perhaps an unconscious level, I think Gene was groping through life, searching for answers.

The last few times I saw Gene in 1991, I became very alarmed for him. I was sure he was dying, but he didn't seem to be aware of it. I suspected he had a condition we alcoholics know as "jake leg," a neuritis and gout in the legs that is very common among heavy drinkers. I had gone to Paramount for a *Star Trek* event, and I saw Gene coming down the hall. He was limping on his left foot and dragging his right leg along the floor, like Chester on "Gunsmoke." He looked very unwell, and I was shocked at how deteriorated he appeared. I said, "Oh, Gene, you've got to stop drinking! You've got jake leg!"

He said, "I've got what?"

I said, "You've got jake leg. It's from drinking, Gene, it's from drinking!"

He laughed and waved off my concern. "Oh, you're crazy!" he replied.

Not long after that, he was in a wheelchair. A few months later, he was gone.

Gene Roddenberry was a darling guy, a lovable guy. He was charming, witty, a delightful conversationalist. He was brilliant. He was an idealist. He was flawed. He was human. Much of what people think they know about Gene Roddenberry is a myth. Some have deified him, calling him "God-denberry." Others revere him as a saint. Gene Roddenberry was no saint. In most respects, Gene was a perfectly ordinary bundle of human contradictions—hopes and fears, virtues and vices, ideals and illusions, a good side and a dark side.

He was part of my story.

Over the years, I've experienced a whole kaleidoscope of emotions toward Gene Roddenberry, from anger to gratitude, and everything in between. Most of all, I have identified with Gene in so many ways (like I said, two sides of the same coin). And when someone at Paramount called to tell me that Gene had died, I experienced the most awful sense of loss and grief.

Gene's funeral was held at Forest Lawn Cemetery, in the Hall of Liberty. It was the kind of memorial service Gene would have planned for himself—no minister, no prayers, no religious words, not even a coffin. A large picture of Gene was set on an easel, and a film was shown of his life and career. The service opened with Nichelle Nichols singing two songs—Lennon and McCartney's "Yesterday" and a beautiful song she had written for him, simply called "Gene." Majel had invited the fans to be there, and many showed up—a handful even wore Starfleet uniforms. The invited guests sat in the main hall, while the fans were seated in an upper gallery.

Eulogies were said by several of Gene's friends—Nichelle, Whoopi Goldberg, Ray Bradbury, Christopher Knopf, E. Jack Neuman and Patrick Stewart. I sat with a number of old friends—Leonard Nimoy with his wife, Susan, DeForest Kelly, Jimmy Doohan, George Takei and Walter Koenig. More than once during the eulogies, Gene was affectionately referred to as "the Great Bird of the Galaxy," a whimsical title that Bob Justman had given him during those intense, hectic days of the classic *Star Trek* series. Over the years, it became Gene's badge as the creator and highest potentate over the *Star Trek* universe.

After the eulogies, two bagpipers played "Amazing Grace"—a selection that puzzled me. The theme of that famous hymn is God's amazing grace to sinners:

> Amazing grace! how sweet the sound.
> That saved a wretch like me!
> I once was lost, but now am found.
> Was blind but now I see.
>
> 'Twas grace that taught my heart to fear.
> And grace my fears relieved:
> How precious did that grace appear
> The hour I first believed!

That hymn is my anthem. It's the story of this book, the story of my life. People sometimes call me "Amazing Grace," but I'm not amazing—I'm a lost, blind wretch, saved by the amazing grace of God. The reason the piping of that song at Gene's funeral seems so odd is that Gene hated that song. When "Amazing Grace" was bagpiped during Spock's funeral near the end of *Star Trek II: The Wrath of Khan*, Gene objected strenuously, and was overruled by Harve Bennett and Nick Meyer. It really seemed out of place at Gene's funeral—and I doubt he would have approved.

When the service was over, we walked out of the hall and into the bright sunlight, under an incredibly blue sky. There were hundreds of *Trek* fans standing somberly outside. Together, we all waited for the thunder to roll over that quiet, monument-studded lawn. Soon, we heard it: the crescendoing roar of jet engines. A formation of four military jets screamed across the sky. As the planes came directly over us, they performed the "missing man formation"—one jet broke away and veered almost vertically skyward, toward the final frontier, toward:

> the undiscover'd country from whose bourn
> no traveller returns, puzzles the will
> and makes us rather bear those ills we have
> than fly to others that we know not of…
> (*Hamlet*, Act III, Scene 1)

The Journey Continues

. . . .

I'm a woman on a mission. Sobriety is my starship. Eternity is my final frontier. My mission, for as many years as God gives me: to explore this strange world we live in, to live out my new life as a sober, saved human being, and to boldly go wherever I can, carrying the message to anyone who will listen. I've carried this message downtown and uptown. I've tried to afflict the comfortable and comfort the afflicted. I've carried it into women's prisons and to *Star Trek* conventions. In fact, I hope to carry this message all the way to the Klingon Empire! And I know just what I'll say to the first Klingon I meet:

bIqabbe' jupwI'. bIropqu'neH. 'ach DaSaHqu'lu'bej. qaSaHqu' jIH. vogh qaDev 'e' yIchaw'. pa' DaQorghlu'taH 'ej Dalajlu'taH. qepDaq HItlhej jupwI'. paQDI'norghmaj Daparchugh bIQuchHa'qa'laH.*

Translation:

> My Klingon friend, you're not bad. You have a disease. God cares
> for you, and I care for you. Let me take you to a place where you will be
> loved and accepted. Come to a meeting with me, friend, and if you
> don't like what we have, we will gladly refund your misery.

Okay, so my Klingon accent needs a little work. Still, I'll bet you there are a lot of Klingons in need of both the Twelve Steps and the message that God loves them! I'll just bet that a sober, saved Klingon would be as lovable as a tribble!

The *Star Trek* universe is a fun place in which to explore serious issues—even spiritual issues. Did you know that many fans look at the *Star Trek* episodes and movies as spiritual parables? Fans come together at the conventions and have fascinating, lively discussion about the implications for the human soul in stories such as "What Are Little Girls Made Of?" in which a man transfers his soul into an android body, or "Return to Tomorrow," in which the souls of Kirk and Spock are transferred from their bodies to alien receptacles, just like taking a floppy disk out of one com-

---

*My thanks to Lawrence M. Schoen, Ph.D., director of the Klingon Language Institute (P.O. Box 634, Flourtown, PA 19031-0634), for providing the Klingon translation above. Founded in 1992, KLI has over 1000 members in 30 countries, and is devoted to fostering greater understanding of the Klingon language. KLI publishes a quarterly journal, *HolQeD*, and a Klingon literary magazine *jatmey (Scattered Tounges)*. Among the ambitious projects by KLI are Klingon editions of the Bible and the works of William Shakespeare.

puter and plugging it into another. *Trek* fans love to engage in good-natured arguments over the religious implications of the *Next Generation* episode "Who Watches the Watchers?" in which a rational alien society comes to view Captain Picard as a god.

I really enjoy *Star Trek* conventions. I love being with the fans. I owe my life to you, the fans. You were there for me, showering me with love and applause when I was aching so much inside. You were my waystation on the road back to sobriety. You told me I was loved and wanted at a time when I was ready to give up on myself. You allowed me to be *me*, Grace Lee Whitney, not just a character on a TV show. You put up with my flaws and faults and all the crazy stages I went through on my way to serenity and peace. Your love sustained me through the years, more than you'll ever know. I will never forget that. From the depths of my heart, I thank you.

I love going to conventions and being with the fans as a sober, saved member of the *Star Trek* universe. I come into a convention and find hundreds of people who are serious about life, about ideas, about the future, about building a better world, about issues of the soul and spirit. I get up on the stage, and I share not only my *Star Trek* anecdotes, but also my recovery story and my salvation story. I often hold chapel services at conventions, and many *Star Trek* fans come to share, to pray, to have fellowship with other believing fans.

I also encounter many fans who are empty and lonely inside, or looking for a way out of a life of addiction and despair. I've had many conversations with fans who want to change the course of their lives, and who have found hope and strength in the story of my life. And I carry this message not only to the fans, but to anyone who will listen.

In early November 1986, I was working at a *Trek* convention at the Bonaventure Hotel in downtown L.A. Sitting in the autograph line next to me was actor Roger C. Carmel. Roger appeared as the lovable rogue Harcourt Fenton "Harry" Mudd in two *Star Trek* episodes, "Mudd's Women" and "I, Mudd." When I saw Roger, my heart went out to him. He seemed in many ways to be where I was in the last few weeks before I became sober. He had that air of desperation about him. His health was obviously failing. He had gained so much weight he needed two chairs to sit in.

Over the two days we were together at the convention, I had a number of talks with Roger and I told him what my life had been like, what happened when I got sober, and what it was like now. I told him about my drinking, my drug addiction, my food addiction, all the different obsessions that used to rule my life. As I talked to him, he opened up about some of the problems that were controlling his life. He told me he was depressed, he couldn't get high anymore, food didn't satisfy anymore, nothing worked for him. I suggested some Twelve Step programs that could help him.

When I told him my story of how sick I had been and how close to death I came, he couldn't believe it. As I sat there so composed, not drinking or using or overeating, he found it hard to comprehend that I had once been the person I described to him.

I could see a glimmer of hope in his eyes. I knew he was considering the possibility of reaching out for help. I gave him my number and told him to call me if he wanted to go to a meeting. He said he'd think about it.

A week later, I heard the news that Roger had died of complications due to substance abuse and obesity. I cried for him when I heard it. He was such a nice, gentle man, and it was such a needless waste.

Sometimes this message of sobriety can completely change a life. Other times, the message goes unheeded. But I have to carry this message to as many as will listen. I can't save anyone. Saving people is God's job, not mine. But if by telling my story, I can help one or two to find their way down from that ledge, then it will be worth it.

In 1991, a friend called me with horrifying news: My friend Carrie was in the hospital, fighting for her life. Carrie was one of a number of young women I sponsored in my recovery program, and she had been making great strides, getting clean and sober and turning her life around. She had gotten a new job, and her boss had sent her on an errand in his red Porsche convertible. As she was driving, a gang of young men deliberately rear-ended the Porsche. She got out to check the damage— and the men leaped out of their car, abducted her, and drove away in the Porsche.

The men took her to an apartment where at least 10 men took turns raping her again and again. After four days of this, they took her to South Central L.A., shot her twice in the head, and dumped her on the street. She miraculously survived and crawled to a liquor store, where the clerk called 911. At the hospital, the surgeons were able to remove one of the bullets, but the other remains in her head to this day. She was incoherent when I spoke to her at the hospital a few days after the surgery, and it was only later that I was able to piece her story together.

For days, I churned with destructive emotions. I imagined what Carrie went through—how she must have felt, the pain she must have endured for four unending days of terror—and I was filled with anger and hatred toward the men who had done this to her. I wished the most horrible tortures upon them. I was so full of the sin of murder, I would have gladly put a shiv in their hearts with my own hands. The emotional pain was so intense, it literally doubled me up. I experienced a paranoid fear that what happened to Carrie might happen to me. I was even afraid to drive my own convertible with the top down.

One day at work, my manager—who was also in a recovery program—stopped at my desk to talk to me. "Whitney," she said, very calmly and soothingly, "I can see that this business with Carrie is tearing you apart. You're so full of anger and fear, you can't concentrate on your work. I'm concerned that if you go on like this, you're going to go back to drinking."

"I know," I replied, "but what can I do? How am I supposed to feel when my friend is terrorized, raped and shot in the head?"

She didn't try to answer my question. Instead, she took a piece of paper from my desk and wrote one sentence on it, then handed the paper to me. The paper read:

If you cannot forgive the sin, you must forgive the sinner.

I didn't fully understand what that meant, but I felt a faint glimmer of relief inside. The glimmer faded by the end of the day.

That night, I went home to North Hollywood with a terrible rage pounding inside me once more. I stood in the kitchen and looked out the window toward the pool and patio in the backyard. Just two weeks before Carrie was assaulted, I had hosted a swim party for some girls in the recovery program, and Carrie had been out there in my pool, splashing, laughing, and so happy. Now she was clinging to life.

Those words came back to me: *If you cannot forgive the sin, you must forgive the sinner.* I couldn't understand how I was supposed to do that.

I walked out to my patio by the pool. The sun was just going down. It was a beautiful, warm California evening, but I was wrapped up in my pain. There on my patio I prayed. "All right, God," I said to the heavens. "I don't know how to do this, but I surrender all my hate and resentment to you. God, you know that I'm full of rage and fear, and you know I don't even mean what I'm saying, but I can't go on hating like this. So God, I'm going to forgive those men for what they did to my friend. I forgive them in the name of Jesus, and I wish them love, joy, salvation and redemption. All the things I have received from you, I wish for them, and I'm sorry I have resented them this long."

At that moment, the pain and hatred disappeared. It has never returned.

I've added that statement to my "toolkit" of sayings and principles: *If you cannot forgive the sin, you must forgive the sinner.* It's a powerful, practical tool for dealing with life on life's terms. There is a Twelve Step recovery program that calls forgiveness "Step 8 1/2." In Step 8, we make a list of those we have harmed. In Step 9 we make direct amends to those we have harmed. But in between those steps is the step of forgiveness. Today, when there is a difficult person in my life I need to forgive, I pray this prayer of forgiveness:

> God, this is a sick person
> How can I be helpful to him?
> God, save me from being angry.
> Thy will be done.

Forgiveness does not mean there should be no consequences for sin or criminal acts. Though I forgave the sinners who assaulted Carrie, I didn't erase their sin. I knew that they still had to be held accountable for what they had done. I was pleased to hear that, two weeks after Carrie's assault, the perpetrators were captured. Apparently these guys were not overloaded in the IQ department—the police nabbed two of them driving around in that bright-red Porsche convertible. They were tried, convicted and sent to prison.

And Carrie? She made a marvelous recovery. To meet her today, you'd never know the ordeal she went through. She even did a television appearance with me on "The Maury Povich Show" in 1993. God was very good to Carrie—and to me!

When the Marilyn Monroe postage stamp was unveiled at the Del Coronado in San Diego, 1995, Some Like It Hot *star Tony Curtis was joined by the surviving members of Sweet Sue's All-Girl Band. Pictured, L to R, are Penny McGuiggan, Me, Tony Curtis, Mary Foley Cleveland, Marian Collier Neuman, and Sandra Warner Gendel.*

I had an amazing experience at the big Creation Convention at the Pasadena Civic Center in 1991—the 25-year reunion of the *Star Trek* cast. I was in the Green Room with the convention organizer, Adam Malin, and he was preparing to videotape an interview with me, just as he did with the other cast members. Moments before the interview was to begin, one of the security people came into the room, carrying a huge bouquet of two dozen roses. Handing the flowers to me, he said, "The man who asked me to bring these to you said they're from a 'secret admirer.'"

Well, I was intrigued! The videocam started rolling and I sat there with my beautiful roses and Adam started the interview. Afterwards, I walked out on stage to give a talk to the fans, still cradling those gorgeous roses and breathing in their perfume.

Following my talk, I went out on the convention floor to sign autographs for the fans. My friend Kat Campbell was at the table with me, helping out. As I was talking with the fans in line, a man approached me with a small suitcase in his hands. He was a tall, nice-looking man in his early fifties, and he was soft spoken—almost shy. "I know you're busy," he said, "so I won't take up much of your time, but I want you to know that it was I who sent you the roses. I'd also like you to have this." He set the suitcase on the table. "This is my gift of love to you. I've spent the last thirty years writing the letters and saving the mementoes in this case. And I want you to know that I'm ninety days sober today."

There were so many fans in the autograph line that I really didn't have time to talk with him—and besides, I was so surprised, I was practically speechless. I stammered, "Thank you," and he smiled—then turned and melted into the crowd. The entire exchange couldn't have lasted longer than 30 seconds. As soon as he was gone, I went back to signing autographs. I was so busy, I didn't have much chance to think about it until later.

After the day's events were over, a friend of mine, Paul, drove me to my hotel and helped me lug my belongings back to my room. He set the mysterious suitcase on the bed. I opened it—and was astonished at what I found. It was filled with pages and pages of poetry and letters, all addressed to me. There were also gifts—bracelets, lockets, and newspaper and magazine clippings from my entire career.

As I read through the letters, I learned that this man had fallen in love with me many years earlier, ever since he had seen me on the stage in *Top Banana*. He had followed my career in the movies, in TV, in *Star Trek*, and he had bought me gifts and written me letters and poems throughout those years. Finally, he got the courage to bring it all to me and present it to me as a gift.

To this day, I have no idea who that man was. There was no address or phone number on the letters—only the man's first name, John. I never heard from him again. But I wish him all the best in his life and his sobriety—and I want him to know, if he ever reads this, how touched I was by his gesture, his letters and his gifts.

I had another vision in early 1993.

I had been at my son Jonathan's house, baby-sitting my granddaughter. During the afternoon, while she was napping, a strange feeling came over me—painful, disorienting and unpleasant. The sensation slowly passed after a while—but I noticed I had difficulty seeing out of my right eye.

Later, Jonathan and his wife came home and invited me to stay for dinner. After dinner, as I was getting ready to leave, I said to Jonathan, "This afternoon, the strangest feeling came over me. At first, I thought it was a migraine. But for the last few hours, I haven't been able to see out of my right eye."

Jonathan looked at me with a very serious expression. "When did this happen?"

"About two o'clock this afternoon." By this time it was after 6 o'clock. That's the way I am—sometimes things happen to me and I'm not even aware of it until hours later. That's called "the alcoholic blind spot." Like many alcoholics, I don't know if a situation is a good thing or bad thing for quite a while. I can only see in hindsight.

Jonathan wisely insisted I go to the hospital for evaluation. At the hospital, the doctors quickly concluded that I had experienced a minor stroke, and they set me up for an angiogram—a diagnostic procedure in which radioactive dye is injected into the coronary arteries so that blockages can be imaged on a monitor. Apparently, a piece of arterial plaque had broken off from my right carotid artery and had gone into my right eye, resulting in partial blindness. The angiogram would determine whether they would have to go in and clean out the artery.

The doctor offered me Valium to take the edge off the procedure. "How many Valium do you want to give me?" I asked.

"One," he said.

"With me," I replied, "one is never enough, so I might as well go cold turkey." Though I was frightened of the procedure, I decided to trust God to get me through it.

They strapped me on a table in a very cold room, so that I could scarcely move a muscle. They even placed a strap across my forehead so that my head was immobile. Practically the only thing I could move was my eyes, and all I could see was this huge machine towering over me, with cameras aimed at me from various angles. With all of that high-tech diagnostic equipment, the room reminded me of Dr. McCoy's sick bay. It was very *Star Treky*. As the doctors were preparing me, I began laughing. The doctors wanted to know what was so funny.

"I've been here before," I said. "Do you know who I am? I'm Janice Rand from the Starship *Enterprise*. Tell Bones McCoy I want him in here on the double!"

The doctors chuckled. They were very loose and easygoing, and they joked back with me. "You're going to feel warm when the x-ray dye enters your blood-stream," said one of the doctors.

"Oh, I didn't know it was going to be like this!" I said. "Forget Dr. McCoy! Call Dr. Kevorkian!"

The doctors chuckled again, and I tried to settle back and relax.

"Here it comes," said one of the doctors. I didn't have time to wonder what "it" was. There was a loud *pop* as he inserted a plastic tube into the main artery on the inside of my thigh, and I felt the sharp pain of the puncture. Without any anesthetic, I heard and felt the insertion of that tube with painful clarity. Instantly, I felt hot as the dye flowed into my body and spread through my circulatory system. I felt panicky, and the only thought on my mind was, *I want out of here right now!*

I said, "Ooh, that's hot!"

Then I saw Y'shua.

He looked the same as when I met him at the Garden of Gethsemane. His hands were outstretched, and I could see the nailprints in his hands. "Now you know how I felt," he said.

Just like my Gethsemane vision, this vision felt very real to me—but it was an inner reality. I was awake and conscious of everything the doctors were doing to me—but Y'shua was present with me. When he honored me with his presence, I instantly surrendered to his peace and serenity. I relaxed and let the doctors do their work.

Soon I became aware of the doctors talking to each other about my case, and whether or not they should do the procedure to clean out my arteries. They finally decided not to. They were concerned that, in the process of removing plaque from the artery walls, they might dislodge a piece that would go to my brain. When the doctors discussed it with me, they said that I was too vital and active, traveling around the country to *Star Trek* conventions and carrying this message of sobriety. They thought it better not to risk doing something that might leave me in a wheelchair for life. "We're going to send you home," they said, "and turn you over to your Higher Power."

My eye is much better now—I can pass a driver's license test, no problem—although to this day there is a black line across the middle of my vision in the right eye. But the more important aftermath of that experience is the quiet assurance no matter what happens to me, I am never alone.

In 1994, the movie *Star Trek: Generations* was released—a film which bridges the two *Star Trek* generations, the original series and *Star Trek: The Next Generation.* I wasn't in that film, but when it was released, I received many calls from newspapers and radio stations, saying, "We want to know how you feel about the death of Captain Kirk."

Well, until I got the first call, I didn't know Jim Kirk had died! But after the first few calls, I came up with this answer: "Yeoman Janice Rand has always been in love with Captain Kirk—so when I heard he died, I was brokenhearted. But remember, Captain Kirk is played by Bill Shatner, who is Jewish. And Mr. Spock is played by Leonard Nimoy, who is also Jewish. Mr. Spock died in *Star Trek II* and was resurrected in *Star Trek III.* And if you know your Bible, then you know that when a good Jewish boy dies, that's not the end of the story. So don't count Captain Kirk out—if he's half the man I think he is, he'll be back!"

The fans in Portland, Oregon, invited me up there for the Portland opening of *Star Trek: Generations.* It was a packed itinerary—I had dinner with the fans, signed a lot of autographs, spoke to the group, and told my story. Then we were off to the theater to see the movie. I had been up all day, traveling by plane, speaking, and so forth—and I was exhausted! We settled into our seats. The movie started, and it was very good. But there is one stretch in the film where Captain Kirk and Captain Picard encounter each other, and there is a long stretch of dialogue, and the pace of the movie slows way down and, well—

I fell asleep!

I guess I was snoring—and the Portland fans never let me forget it. They needled me mercilessly! I woke up at the part where the saucer section of the *Enterprise* comes down through the atmosphere of the planet and crash-lands in the forest. It's pretty hard to sleep through that!

I thought the death scene of Captain Kirk was brilliantly done. It was the end of an era—the end of my era, in fact. Everyone came out of the theater in tears—everyone except me. It was Grace Lee Whitney in that theater, not Janice Rand. These days, Grace Lee Whitney knows the difference between fantasy and reality. It was a very good movie—but it was *only* a movie.

As for the passing of Captain Kirk—well, the screenwriter giveth and the screenwriter taketh away.

In 1996, I returned to series television to help celebrate the 30th anniversary of *Star Trek,* with an episode of *Star Trek: Voyager.* The episode was appropriately entitled

Here I am reunited with wonderful George Takei as Captain Sulu, along with Kate Mulgrew as Captain Janeway, and Tim Russ as Tuvok in the Star Trek: Voyager *episode entitled "Flashback."*

"Flashback," written by Brannon Braga and directed by David Livingston. In the story, the Starship *Voyager* approaches a nebula that triggers the recovery of a repressed memory in the mind of the Vulcan officer Tuvok (Tim Russ). According to the ship's doctor, the memory must be brought completely into Tuvok's conscious mind or else his brain will be irreparably harmed. In order to accomplish this, Tuvok must mind-meld with Captain Janeway (Kate Mulgrew)—and in the process he experiences a flashback to his first mission aboard a Federation starship—the USS *Excelsior*, commanded by Captain Sulu (George Takei).

That's where Sulu and Yeoman Rand come in. This episode closes the circle with the movie *Star Trek VI: The Undiscovered Country*, in which George and I were on the bridge of the Starship *Excelsior*. Yep, it's George and Gracie, together again! The story combines crisp characterization and warm nostalgia, and helps fill in a few of the gaps in the *Star Trek* saga, adding a nice pastiche to the storyline of *Star Trek VI*. The episode was telecast 30 years to the day after "The Man Trap" first introduced the world to *Star Trek*.

Everyone on that show was absolutely wonderful to George and me. They treated us like *Star Trek* icons, like old pros—even though I had some trouble remembering my lines. I don't know if it was a case of nerves or if Janice Rand was just having a "senior moment" (a little respect, please: that's *Commander* Janice Rand now)—but I wasn't exactly "One-Take Whitney" in this episode. Perhaps it's because I was intimidated by the presence of such a gifted actress as Kate Mulgrew. She has a photographic mind and a strong personal presence. One glance at the script, and she has the scene down pat.

There were scenes in which Janeway (Kate) was in the shot with me as an observer of Tuvok's memories, by means of the Vulcan mind-meld. She was supposed to be invisible to me, so I was not supposed to react to her presence. But I couldn't help it. There she was—Captain Janeway, this wonderfully professional starship captain whom I had watched so many times on my own living room TV! I couldn't remember my lines with her standing there watching me, so I finally said, "Kate, you're intimidating me!"

She said, "Well, then, I'll just have to leave the set because we must get this shot."

"No, no," I said, "I'll do it." So we got it right in the very next take.

I had a strong sense of déja vu while we were shooting that show. We shot much of it on the very same *Excelsior* set we had used in *Star Trek VI*. It had taken the studio workmen a full month to refurbish and redress it to its original condition.

Director David Livingston was a stickler for accuracy and detail. He wanted to completely reproduce the look and feel of the matching scenes in *Star Trek VI*. So he had monitors placed on the set which played the *Exelsior* scenes from *Star Trek VI*. Livingston and the crew were careful that all the sets, props, costumes, hairstyles, dialogue, and every other detail were a perfect match to corresponding scenes in the movie. The result was an episode that very carefully reproduces the tense, dramatic feel that Nick Meyer created in the motion picture.

It was wonderful to work once more with George Takei as Captain Sulu. He was as kind and gracious as always, helping me with my lines, and encouraging me throughout the production. In the role, George was masterful, bold and dashing—and there was talk at Paramount and within fandom of a new *Star Trek* series starring George as the captain of the *Excelsior*, and with supporting roles for me and Nichelle Nichols. The new series hasn't materialized yet—but who knows?

My life has been an adventure—a thrilling, sometimes harrowing trek through my childhood pain, through the entertainment world, through the *Star Trek* universe, into the depths of all sorts of addictions and self-destructive behavior, to the brink of hell—and back again. I wouldn't want to relive it, but I wouldn't trade my life for anyone else's. It's been an incredible mix of highs and lows—an interstellar roller-coaster ride!

My life has been a search for something I didn't even know I wanted. I was searching for love, for my birth parent, for a place to belong, for an understanding of who I am and why I'm here. I searched for validation and contentment in so many wrong places—in men, in my career, in alcohol and drugs, in sex. I didn't understand

*This is my lovely
Granddaughter, Danyele*

that, all along, I was really searching for my heavenly Birth Parent. Only when I found God did I finally realize what I had been seeking so long.

The Truth is a Person. And knowing the Truth will set you free.

I don't want to leave anyone with the impression that sobriety equals salvation, or that salvation equals sobriety. They are two separate things. You can have salvation and not be sober. And you can be sober and not have salvation. As someone once said, "You cannot repent of an illness and you cannot treat a sin."

I know that some people are critical of the disease model of alcoholism. They think, "Oh, that's just a way of shifting personal responsibility off the alcoholic. Calling alcoholism a disease just says to alcoholics, 'It's not your fault. You're a victim. You can't help it that you drink.'" No! Alcoholism is a *self-induced* illness. Understanding that alcoholism is a disease simply helps the alcoholic understand *why* he drinks. But the Twelve Steps tell the alcoholic he is *100 percent responsible* for his own recovery.

A Twelve Step group is not a pity party, nor a gathering place for people who whine about being victims of society or poor toilet training. The Twelve Steps *demand* that the alcoholic take responsibility for the hurt and destruction he has caused others—and to make amends for it. In order to recover, the alcoholic must make a searching and fearless moral inventory of his life; must admit his character defects and sins to God, to himself, and to another human being; must make a list of all persons he has harmed and make amends to as many of them as possible; must commit to an ongoing personal inventory and to a discipline of prayer and meditation; and must actively carry the message of his spiritual awakening to others. If that's not personal responsibility, what is?

All my life, I've had a hole in my gut, with the wind blowing through. I was in pain. I craved validation. That's the disease—the dis-hyphen-ease—of alcoholism. So I began to drink, and the alcohol made the pain and the empty feeling go away. When the alcohol hit the back of my throat, then splashed down in the bottom of my stomach, and that warm feeling began spreading through my body—only then did I feel comfortable in my own skin. I wanted that feeling to continue, so I drank more. I used more. For a brief time, I was able to feel okay—but the emptiness and the pain always came back. Nothing worked for long.

Once I found God, I was finally able to understand what that hole in the gut is: It's a God-shaped hole. It's the place inside you where God is supposed to go. We were created with that hole in us. We were meant to fill it with God, with that one great power that is greater than ourselves. My problem was that I tried to fill it with anything and everything *but* God! I only came to God through the process of elimination.

But it's not enough simply to realize that there is a power greater than your-self. Many people know and love Jesus, but they are still alcoholics and addicts. You can be saved without being sober. I know I'll die saved, but I want to die sober, too—not drunk. So I'm not content to merely have a relationship with God. I have to work the Steps on a daily basis.

I'm working the Steps in writing this book. This book is one of the ways I live out Step No. 12: carrying the message. I'm sharing my experience, strength and hope with you. I'm telling you what it was like, what happened, and what it's like now. You can't lead anyone out of the desert unless you've been to the desert yourself. You can't lead anyone out of the gutter unless you've spent some time there. You can donate money to build a shelter or a rescue mission, but to really *reach* someone and *change* a life, you must have that shared experience, that common language.

I think that's why God saved me, and why he saves a certain remnant of alcoholics and addicts and doesn't let them die in their addictions. A lot of his precious children are out wandering in the desert, they're dying in the gutters, and it's breaking his heart. So he let Grace Lee Whitney go to hell and back so that she could point the way out of the desert, so she could help lift a few souls out of the gutter. That's why I'm alive today. That's why this book exists.

You see, I'm a wretch. Apart from God, Grace Lee Whitney is a miserable wretch who hasn't enough sense to stay out of the gutter. And that's okay. Be-cause, as it turns out, that's exactly the kind of person God was looking for. God uses the foolish to confound the wise. He uses miserable wretches like me to tell his good news to all the other miserable wretches—the news that there is hope, there is love, there is a way out of hell, there is a way *home*.

Several times a week, some friends and I go to Twelve Step meetings in jails and prisons, and we meet women who have sunk as low as I have. They are in the desert. They are in the gutter. They don't know how to get out—but we know. We've been there. We can point the way.

So thank God for miserable wretches like us! I'm a wretch, you're a wretch, we're all in this miserable wretchedness together—isn't it wonderful!

As you've been reading through this book, you might have thought, *That poor woman. Look at all the horrible things she went through. Look at all the awful things she did!* And

I suppose if I wanted to, I could moan about how unfair it was that I was sexually assaulted, and that I missed out on two and a half years of *Star Trek*. I could complain about a lot of things that happened to me, from the time I was born right up to the present day. But that's not how I feel. I'm not bitter about a single thing that has happened in my life. How could I be bitter after all the miraculously *wonderful* things God has done in my life?

I look at all the money, fame and glamour of Hollywood, I think of all the things that were and all the things that might have been—and I echo the words of that hard-headed Jewish rabble-rouser, the apostle Paul: "Everything I used to treasure and value, I now consider a complete write-off for the sake of Y'shua. In fact, I consider everything meaningless and worthless compared with how awesome it is to personally know Y'shua ha Mashiach, my Lord and Master, for whose sake I have lost all those things. To me, all those other so-called 'goodies' are nothing but rubbish, dreck, a pile of crap. All that matters to me now is that I know Y'shua ha Mashiach, and that he completely possesses me!" (Philippians 3:8, the Grace Lee Whitney translation).

It has been quite a tour of the galaxy—and it's not over yet! The longest trek goes on and on, toward the ultimate frontier, exploring strange new worlds, living out a new life as a child of the heavenly kingdom.

So join me in my trek. Boldly go with me.

Our future is out there, among the stars. The entire universe—all of time and all of space—has been given to us by our heavenly Birth Parent. Look, he reaches out to embrace us and welcome us. He invites us to explore infinity with him.

So don't wait. Come on. Live forever!

The journey continues...

The adventure begins...

Now!

Notes
. . . .

Chapter 4: Space, the Final Frontier...
1. Herbert F. Solow and Robert H. Justman, *Inside Star Trek: The Real Story* (New York: Pocket Books, 1996), pp. 75; 155-156.

Chapter 5: These Are the Voyages...
1. William Shatner and Chris Kreski, *Star Trek Memories* (New York: HarperCollins, 1993), p. 283.

Chapter 6: My Cookies and Milk Days
1. Harlan Ellison, *The City on the Edge of Forever: The Original Teleplay That Became the Classic Star Trek Episode* (Clarkston, GA: White Wolf Publishing, 1996), p. 37.

2. Ibid, pp. 140-144.

Chapter 7: A Woman in Free-Fall
1. Psalm 16:11, author's paraphrase.

Chapter 8: Sobriety Is Not For Wimps
1. Deuteronomy 18:10-11 NIV.

Chapter 10: The Great Bird of the Galaxy
1. David Alexander, "Gene Roddenberry: Writer, Producer, Philosopher, Humanist," *The Humanist*, March/April 1991, Vol. 51, No. 2, p. 6.

2. Ibid, pp. 8-10.

3. Ibid, p. 6.

4. Ibid, p. 7.

5. Herbert F. Solow and Robert H. Justman, *Inside Star Trek: The Real Story* (New York: Pocket Books, 1996), p. 125.

6. Yvonne Fern, *Gene Roddenberry: The Last Conversation* (Berkeley: University of California Press, 1994), pp. 54-56.

7. Genesis 1:26 NIV. Note the plural pronoun "us" in that verse. This scripture verse was, in fact, a great awakening for me. When I first discovered this passage after I became a follower of Y'shua, I suddenly realized that the Christian concept of a triune God—Father, Son, and Holy Spirit—is not inconsistent with Jewish scriptures.

8. Romans 8:29 NIV.

9. David Alexander, pp. 16-17.

10. Yvonne Fern, pp. 108-109, 111.

11. David Alexander, p. 6.

12. Yvonne Fern, pp. 101-102.

13. Stephen Hawking, quoted by John Boslough in *Stephen Hawking's Universe* (New York: William Morrow & Co., 1985), p. 121.

14. Paul Davies, *God and the New Physics* (New York: Simon & Schuster, 1983), pp. 167-168, p. ix, emphasis in the original.

15. Leonard Shlain, *Art and Physics* (New York: William Morrow & Co., 1991), p. 252.

16. Roger Penrose, *The Emperor's New Mind* (New York: Oxford University Press, 1989), p. 326, emphasis in the original.

About the Authors

. . . .

Grace Lee Whitney

In a career that spans Broadway (*Top Banana*), movies (*Some Like It Hot*), and countless television shows, Grace Lee Whitney has worked with some of the top names in the entertainment business. Her 13 episodes of *Star Trek* (including such classic episodes as "Miri" and "Charlie X") have secured her a place in *Star Trek* history—as her popularity with the fans attests. Today, when not enjoying the peace and serenity of her home near Yosemite National Park, she is out sharing the message of hope and sobriety at *Star Trek* conventions, in prisons and jails, and on talk shows. She is equally at home carrying this message to the down-and-outers in prison or on Skid Row as to the up-and-outers in Beverly Hills or Brentwood.

Jim Denney

A West Coast freelance writer, Jim Denney has written more than 40 books with a number of different authors, including Supermodel Kim Alexis, Orlando Magic V.P. Pat Williams, and Super Bowl Champions Reggie White and Bob Griese. Now in his forties, he has been a *Star Trek* fan since he was 13.

9 781884 956034